From Antiquities to Heritage

Time and the World: Interdisciplinary Studies in Cultural Transformations

Series editor: Helge Jordheim, University of Oslo, Norway

Published in association with the interdisciplinary research program Cultural Transformations in the Age of Globalization (KULTRANS) at the University of Oslo.

Time is moving faster; the world is getting smaller. Behind these popular slogans are actual cultural processes, on global and local scales, that require investigation. *Time and the World* draws on research in a wide range of fields, such as cultural history, anthropology, sociology, literary studies, sociolinguistics and law and sets out to discuss different cultures as sites of transformation in a global context. The series offers interdisciplinary analyses of cultural aspects of globalization in various historical and geographical contexts, across time and space.

Editorial board: Andrew Barry, University of Oxford; Richard Bauman, Indiana University; Costas Douzinas, Birkbeck, University of London; Thomas Hylland Eriksen, University of Oslo; Lynn Hunt, University of California Los Angeles; Fazal Rizvi, University of Melbourne; Hartmut Rosa, Jena University; Inger Johanne Sand, University of Oslo; Stefan Willer, Center for Literary and Cultural Research Berlin; Clifford Siskin, New York University

Volume 1
From Antiquities to Heritage: Transformations of Cultural Memory
Anne Eriksen

Volume 2
Writing Democracy: The Norwegian Constitution 1814–2014
Edited by Karen Gammelgaard and Eirik Holmøyvik

Forthcoming series titles:
Border Aesthetics
Edited by Stephen F. Wolfe and Johan Schimanski

Understanding Transformations in the Context of Globalization
Edited by Vidar Grøtta, Rana Issa, Helge Jordheim and Audun Solli

From Antiquities to Heritage

Transformations of Cultural Memory

Anne Eriksen

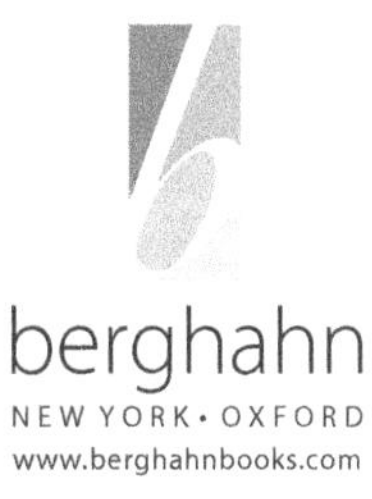

berghahn
NEW YORK · OXFORD
www.berghahnbooks.com

Published in 2014 by

Berghahn Books

www.berghahnbooks.com

The author received support for this project from The Research Council of Norway.

Library of Congress Cataloging-in-Publication Data

Eriksen, Anne.
    From antiquities to heritage : transformations of cultural memory / Anne Eriksen.
        pages cm. — (Time and the world : interdisciplinary studies in cultural
    transformations ; Volume 1)
    Includes bibliographical references and index.
    ISBN 978-1-78238-298-0 (hardback) — ISBN 978-1-78533-205-0 (paperback) —
    ISBN 978-1-78238-299-7 (ebook)
  1. Cultural property—Protection—Philosophy. 2. Historic preservation—Philosophy.
3. Antiquities—Collection and preservation—Philosophy. 4. Cultural property—
Protection—Norway. 5. Historic preservation—Norway. 6. Antiquities—Norway—
Collection and preservation. I. Title.
    CC135.E834 2014
    363.6'9—dc23

                                                                              2013029908

British Library Cataloguing in Publication Data

A catalogue record for this book is available from the British Library

ISBN: 978-1-78238-298-0 hardback
ISBN: 978-1-78533-205-0 paperback
ISBN: 978-1-78238-299-7 ebook

Contents

Acknowledgements

This book is the end product of research interests that have developed over two decades. My initial fascination – during the 1990s – with the role of collective memory in processes of nation building has deepened theoretically and widened empirically over the years. On the one hand, my original interest in nineteenth-century use of historical monuments, popular traditions and oral literature in the construction of national cultures has gradually expanded into investigations of contemporary heritage work as well as of early modern antiquarianism. On the other hand, this growing empirical scope made me see that the 'use of the past in the present' not merely varies according to historical period or political contexts, but that even the idea of history itself and the experience of temporality are historically conditioned factors. The idea behind this book is that the changing ways of speaking about and assigning value to material remains from the past can give important clues to a history of different historical regimes.

Many people have contributed to the development of this project. The idea for the book took shape within the frames of the interdisciplinary research program Cultural Transformations in the Age of Globalization (Kultrans) at the University of Oslo, and I would like to thank its academic director, Professor Helge Jordheim, for encouragement and inspiration. I would also like to thank Professors Richard Bauman and Lynn Hunt for their insightful comments and inspiring suggestions during the initial phase of my work with the manuscript. My work has also benefitted from the grant given me by the Norwegian Research Council.

A number of my colleagues have lived with this book project over the years and have been willing to listen to me and discuss it with me when I felt the need. I would particularly like to thank my colleagues Brita Brenna, Eivind Engebretsen, Jon Viðar Sigurðsson, Ellen Krefting, Kyrre Kverndokk and Anne Birgitte Rønning for fruitful discussions, insightful comments, valuable knowledge – and great patience. Finally, I would like to thank John C. Anthony for his assistance with the language and Tomas Åndheim for his meticulous work with the manuscript in its final stages.

Anne Eriksen
Oslo, May 2013

Introduction

In 1742, Vicar N.J. Bjerregaard started digging into a barrow in his parish of Lardal in Vestfold, in southeastern Norway, hoping to find 'relics from the heathen past'. But despite the best efforts of the peasants he had hired for the work, the vicar was disappointed. The mound contained nothing but some fragile ceramic pots, a piece of rope with a brass handle and a bit of woollen cloth. So much for the glorious past of the noble forefathers (43 queries from the Government Office 1743, ms 181, Lardal, query no 41). Knowing their life and deeds well from the works of Snorre Sturlason and other saga writers, the vicar had entertained quite other expectations for the barrow's contents.

In 2009, the Norwegian Year of Cultural Heritage was celebrated, with 'cultural heritage in everyday life' as its special theme. Among the examples of cultural heritage described on the project's website we find family photographs, the smell of a special kind of industrial pollution in a provincial town, old and new clothes, landscapes, audiotaped memories and inventories of household utensils and home decorations. The project declares itself and its very inclusive profile to be 'all-embracing, both socially and time-wise, and comprising both tangible and intangible cultural heritage. By adopting this theme we are hoping to involve a wide range of the population, including volunteers and professionals on the local, regional and national level' (The Norwegian Year of Cultural Heritage 2009).

There are considerable differences between Bjerregaard's obvious disappointment over the clay pots and other inconspicuous artefacts dug out of the mound and the joy of collecting, preserving and displaying household utensils, love letters and vernacular buildings demonstrated by the people responsible for the Year of Cultural Heritage. Present day heritage workers are enthusiastic about objects from everyday life, while Bjerregaard rejected what he found as merely prosaic household chattels. The terminology used to describe the artefacts has also changed. Bjerregaard looked for what he called relics or antiquities, and the pots did not, in his view, qualify as such. Today, the predominant term is heritage, which comes very close to being an all-inclusive concept, as long as somebody is willing to take on the role of the heir, i.e., to accept the inheritance.

These differences and the processes of change that have brought them about will be the theme of this book. What is to be explored is not the history of specific artefacts, but rather the ways artefacts from the past have been spoken of, evaluated and categorized during the last 250 years and the terms that have been used to name and describe them.

In the eighteenth century, antiquaries like Bjerregaard hunted barrows and other sites all over Europe for objects that could be directly related to persons and events from a literary canon of Norse, mediaeval or classical texts, or even to the Bible (e.g., Sweet 2004; Eriksen 2007; B.E. Jensen 2008). Today, we look for heritage and find it virtually everywhere. One of the aims of this book is to investigate how this concept has come into general use and ended up supplanting or subordinating all other terms that have formerly been in use within the same field: antiquities, vestiges and relics, historical monuments, historical or archaeological artefacts. The Norwegian Year of Cultural Heritage closely follows an international trend, not only in its choice of name, but also in picking everyday life as a topic and in signalling the all-inclusiveness of its approach. What kinds of change do these shifts in terminology and perspective reflect? This book will argue that they do not simply stem from an interest in new kinds of (old) objects, but also express changing ideas about why and in what ways the past is important to the present: ideas about the structural relationship between past and present are changing. In more general terms, such changes can be seen as expressions of different regimes of historicity, an expression coined by the French historian François Hartog. Each regime of historicity is the outcome of a different way of experiencing the temporal aspect of the human condition, hence acquiring its own expressions in culture as well as in historiography (Hartog 2003).

Research Questions and Perspectives

Both 'antiquities' and 'cultural heritage' are terms referring to man-made objects (mainly) from the past. They also convey the idea that these artefacts are in some way valuable. Age and value are entangled, but the relationship between the two will vary in rather complex ways. The pots and other items found by Bjerregaard probably were ancient, but that does not seem to have affected him. To him, it was more fundamental that they were not rare. Pots of this kind were found in barrows from time to time, and they also resembled household utensils used by peasants in his own time. What Bjerregaard *really* wanted to find were artefacts of the kind mentioned in the literary sources: weapons, jewellery and other ornamental pieces signalling the wealth and power of their owners or in other ways carrying symbolic meaning. Today, on the other hand, pots of the kind that Bjerregaard rejected are highly cherished museum pieces, defined as parts of the national cultural heritage. National and international law protect them and other artefacts of their kind not only from theft, but also from otherwise becoming commodities on the commercial market. Museum pieces are valued for their age, for their scarcity and in some cases for their artistic qualities. They are also treasured for the knowledge that archaeologists, historians and other researchers are able to gain from them and for their symbolic significance as parts of national or even global history. The kitchen utensils and other everyday life objects that received attention during the heritage year, on the other hand, were not very old, nor particularly rare (at least not compared with the archaeological material), but even they share the quality of belonging to a world of days gone by, of fleeting memories, of transitoriness and change. Their value comes from the memories that are attached to them, from the stories that are told, but also from the social and cultural reality they reflect. The inclusiveness expressed by the heritage year project can, furthermore, be regarded as a value in itself, reflecting a political programme to make heritage more democratic and accessible, less elitist (Niemi 2009).

This book will explore what kinds of artefact have been regarded as antiquities, as historical monuments and finally as heritage during the period from the mid-eighteenth century to the present. But again, this will not be an inventory of artefacts or collections of artefacts, nor a history of the museums and other institutions built for their preservation and care. The focus is not on the objects themselves and their history during this period, but rather on the categories of objects and on their constitution. How are the categories made, and how are actual objects recognized as belonging to them? How do the networks of meaning implied by these categories or genres change over a period of time? Why is the ancient pot from the mound valueless to Bjerregaard when he is looking for antiquities, while a far newer pot from grandmother's kitchen could be cherished by heritage hunters in 2009 – who at the same time might shun pots like Bjerregaard's for being overdetermined national monuments now on display in museums? The answers to these complex and paradoxical questions are not to be found in the pots, but in the values ascribed to them and in the words and notions used to express those values.

Establishing categories means sorting objects and negotiating which objects belong and which do not: a process of including and excluding. It implies developing terms and concepts and designating them to specific objects. This process always takes place in the present, even when the criterion for designation and inclusion is some kind of age-based value. Recognizing objects as belonging to a category called antiquities, heritage or the like means separating them from the vast number of other objects implicitly characterized by their novelty or contemporaneity. Apart from the simple cumulative dimension – a number of things are older today than they were, for example, in the eighteenth century – the principle of this is relational. Antiquity, history and heritage do not represent absolute qualities but are words that describe different kinds of relations between the past and the present. These relations, in themselves always things of the present, will recognize and single out quite different objects for their 'pastness' against correspondingly varying contemporary backgrounds. What vary are not merely what is 'old' and what is 'new' (or contemporary) in different historic periods but also the relationships that are established and that structure the experience of temporality. Over a period of time the same object – i.e., an old clay pot – may be termed a heathen relic, an antiquity, a historical object or a piece of cultural heritage. The pot remains the same, even if it becomes slightly older, but the changing terminology does something to the way it (and the past it represents) is ascribed meaning in the present. Naming certain artefacts from the past as heritage rather than as antiquities *may* serve to single out other kinds of artefacts than before, but it quite *certainly* reflects other ways of thinking about the meaning and value of such artefacts in the present. The change of terminology indicates that our way of thinking about the past has changed. What do these changes actually imply?

The taxonomy of treasured objects from the past will change over time, the system being under constant negotiation. Normally, some objects will represent obvious fits into the existing categories, while others will challenge them, threatening the borders and the definitions of categories and classes and frequently ending by changing the system. How does this happen? When did pots of the kind that Bjerregaard rejected enter the museums? What processes made grandmother's kitchen pots follow suit, 250 later, under the name of 'cultural heritage of everyday life'? What had happened in between? What kinds of objects are *not* valued as heritage in contemporary society – and why?

Even if the age-based values function as a tool for sorting out and cherishing certain objects compared with others, this does not mean cutting them off from their context in the present. Such an isolation would render the objects meaningless rather than valuable. As we shall see (Chapter 2 in this volume), the connection between antiquities and literature was fundamental to eighteenth-century antiquaries. To Bjerregaard, what mattered was to find artefacts that could be related directly to the heroes and chieftains of Norse and mediaeval literature, whose courage, valour and deeds were equalled only by those of the classical canon. In this case, antiquities referred to a universe of timeless heroism. During the nineteenth century, historic monuments and historical objects came above all to be related to a search for national particulars and to processes of nation building (Chapters 5 and 6 in this volume). In our own time, identity, belonging and 'roots' seem to be the main issues when speaking about heritage. Hence, the significance of the cherished objects is as deeply based on the concerns of every epoch as on any value relating to age alone. This was why Bjerregaard rejected the pots and other inconspicuous items from the barrow: the literary sources had little to say about crumbling clay and smouldering cloth. It was not at all heroic. The home decorations and household utensils inventoried by the Heritage Year, on the other hand, are highly relevant to identity projects. Such material communicates messages about belonging, family bonds and shared family values in a close and easily recognizable setting. In neither of these cases is age alone decisive. Rather, the value of the objects is linked to their existence in the *present*. What is fundamental is that they in some way or another embody a link from the past to the present.

To grasp the full meaning of the changing terminology – from antiquities to heritage – it is then necessary to explore the relationship between these terms and the age-based values they represent on the one hand and the variety of shifting concerns, meanings and interests on the other. Which issues have been relevant and dominant, and how are they entangled with the age-based values? In what ways does the changing terminology reflect such contemporary concerns rather than describe the old objects it refers to? This implies that rather than taking eighteenth-century antiquarianism as a simple indication that 'they were interested in heritage too!' the language used in different periods will be taken to indicate time-specific ways of relating to the past and producing knowledge about it. Correspondingly, the emergence of ideas about 'world heritage' and its preservation from the 1970s onwards will not be seen as the development of a more mature and responsible attitude towards cultural goods of universal value, establishing itself after centuries of ignorance and neglect. Even this terminology, and the set of ideas it communicates, is first and foremost the answer to concerns and challenges specific to our own era. One of the concerns of this book will be to investigate the contemporary issues and interests that the terminology of each period relates to. Does the word 'antiquities' really inscribe cherished objects into the same fields of values and evaluation as does 'heritage'? Is it merely the number and range of objects that have grown, or does the designation of the same objects using different terms imply significantly different ways of relating to them?

The focus on terminology rather than on the objects themselves signals a discursive approach. From what has been said so far, it follows that discourse serves to generate and organize knowledge in specific social contexts. Hence, discourse is understood as a social practice closely connected to other practices pertaining to the same artefacts. Bjerregaard, or rather the peasants he hired for the work, was digging. The Heritage Year people, on the other hand, were largely occupied with inventorying and publishing on the Internet. In between, we find collectors, curators, preservationists, archaeologists, amateur and professional historians, researchers, journalists, visitors to heritage sites, museum guests, and so on, all carrying out a number different practices relevant to the role or profession they are undertaking. In different ways, all these activities represent modes of relating to the artefacts, handling them (directly or indirectly) and evaluating them. The discursive practices represent the advantage of being among the more explicit in several of these aspects. It is they who define the artefacts *as* antiquities, *as* monuments, *as* heritage. They may also to a large degree be said to determine other activities. Bjerregaard would not have hired peasants to open the barrow had he not already entertained the idea that it contained what he called 'antiquities' and that digging was a relevant method for getting hold of them. No less would the Heritage Year people try to chart the smell of industrial pollution or bother to publish other people's family memories if the concept of 'everyday life heritage' was not already established. Hence, discourse is seen as a social practice of major significance.

The terms used to designate the objects themselves will stand at the centre of the investigations: which terms are used and how does terminology change historically? The aim is to use the terminological shifts to trace other developments, concerning the experience of temporality and the changing relations between past, present and future. For this reason, the terms must be contextualized and other words and concepts also brought into the investigation. Terms and phrases expressing change and rupture, tradition and continuities, processes and development will be explored. How are such experiences expressed, which are the predominant? What kind of language is used and which metaphors are chosen? Moreover, what kind of practices are described and discussed, and what do these practices actually imply? What does it mean to dig a barrow or preserve a building? The idea here is not to describe developments in archaeological or preservational methodology, but to examine the way practices related to cherished objects from the past are spoken and written about, to trace ideas and understandings of why and in what ways the past is important to the present. Attention will also be paid to agents and forces: what agents and forces create historic change, whether understood as decay or progress, and how do they function? Finally, the patterns of discourse will be analysed to shed light on which contemporary issues the objects of the past and their value are related to.

Analytically, a discursive approach has the advantage of making it possible to distinguish between the distinctly contemporary concept of heritage and heritage discourse on the one hand, and a more general interest in material remains from the past – the kind of objects that *today* are called heritage – on the other, without identifying the one with the other. This gives a means for circumventing the somewhat futile discussions on 'how old is heritage really?' (For an overview see for example, Harvey 2001). More importantly, the distinction between the contemporary terminology and the general phenomenon enables us to have more nuanced views of how this field has been designated, evaluated and transformed during nearly two and a half centuries.

Between Heritage Studies and Antiquarianism

This book situates itself within two relatively separate fields of research and attempts to bridge them: on the one hand, the heritage studies field, and on the other, the history of antiquarianism. The aim is above all to extend the field of heritage studies by giving it a deeper historical perspective and discussing its theoretical foundations. Studies in this field tend to fix the beginning of interest in what was to become heritage to the period of the French Revolution and, more generally, to the opening of formerly royal collections in Europe to a larger public (Smith 2006: 16ff). The late eighteenth century saw a new interest in the monuments saved from revolutionary vandalism by the work of such men as Abbé Grégoire, Alexandre Lenoir and Quatremère de Quincy and in the cultural goods made available to the general public through the new museums like the British Museum (1754), the Fridericianum in Kassel (1779) and the Louvre (1791) (Pommier 1991; McClellan 1994; Bennett 1995; Sloan 2003). The French looting of Italy in the 1790s and the British Lord Elgin's transport of the Parthenon marbles to London just after 1800, on the other hand, fuelled the first European debates over the moving of artwork – bought or stolen – from one country to another (St. Clair 1998; Eriksen 2001). During the nineteenth century, the work of men like Ruskin, Viollet-le-Duc and others not only contributed to the development of new ways of handling cultural goods of past times, but also to the conceptualizing and evaluation of them in specific ways (Choay 1999). Ways of thinking and talking about material remains from the past were changing (Babelon and Chastel 1994: 57ff). New kinds of old artefacts were valued, and they were valued by new and other groups of people than before. Public collections grew, and during the nineteenth century, preservation of monuments and the building of the large museums became important national tasks.

Laurajane Smith affirms in her book *Uses of Heritage* that 'as has been well rehearsed in heritage literature, the current concept of heritage emerged in Europe, particularly Britain, France and Germany, within the context of nineteenth century modernity' (Smith 2006: 17; see also discussion in Harvey 2001). At best, this is a conditional truth. On the one hand, nobody, or at least marginally few, actually wrote or spoke about 'heritage' in the nineteenth century. They preferred the term (historic) monument. On the other hand, it *is* true that within the contemporary field of heritage studies, the great nineteenth-century interest in historic monuments, museums and preservation work has been given much attention and is regarded as part of more general processes of modernization, which undoubtedly is correct. Smith herself also points to the fact that nineteenth- (and to some degree eighteenth-) century terminology was different, and she particularly examines the use of the term monument in its European context (Smith 2006: 19). Nevertheless, despite her explicitly discursive approach, Smith shows little sensitivity to linguistic nuances and seems to have chosen to regard all terms in use in different epochs as expressions of the same concern. Smith has set herself the task of examining what she contends is a particular discourse of heritage 'that emerged in late nineteenth-century Europe and has achieved dominance as a "universalizing" discourse in the twenty-first century' (Smith 2006: 17). The linguistic and terminological diversity within this discourse is not addressed.

This book takes a different perspective. Even if the interest in cultural goods from the past did gain considerable momentum from the mid-nineteenth century and hence coincides with a very intense phase of modernization, it was not a new thing. Moreover, this interest did not centre on the term heritage, which implies that it most probably followed another logic than the contemporary heritage discourse. The explorations of this book will take these variations as a cue to trace nuances and differences worthy of consideration, rather than seeing them as historically random expressions of one continuous trend or one identical set of concerns. This implies an understanding that the terms employed are important cultural expressions in themselves. They bear significance not merely as reverberations of social reality, but as active elements in it. In her study on the French Revolution, Lynn Hunt has argued that linguistic expressions, in her case utterances of revolutionary politicians, not merely reflect social reality, but could be active means for change. Her claim is that 'words did not just reflect social and political reality; they were instruments for transforming reality' (L. Hunt 1989: 17). In our case, the various ways of speaking about artefacts from the past are seen as means to change the ways such artefacts have been perceived, understood and valued.

The links between nineteenth-century interest in historic monuments and modernization processes are not to be disputed. The historic interest that beset the Western world during the nineteenth century was complex and profound, and a number of its expressions had a very direct bearing on the understanding of material remains from the past. Not least does this apply to the emergence of the new scholarly disciplines that studied these remains, like modern archaeology and source-based history. Nonetheless, acknowledging the link between modernization and the interest in material remains from the past should not lead us to equate such an interest with modernization or to see it merely as a symptom of modernity (Harvey 2001). The link is relevant to a specific historical period, not to the phenomenon as such, and indeed will obfuscate it if made into a defining or all-explanatory factor. People have taken an interest in material remains from the past in other periods too, but for other reasons. Hence, their evaluations have been structured along other lines of thought.

Also, as the discursive approach invites close readings and attention to the nuances of terminology, references to the processes of modernization have quite a modest explanatory value, easily becoming too general. Nineteenth-century nation building aided by inaugurations of historic monuments and twenty-first-century personal identity construction through ethnic or religious heritage might be quite meaningfully related to 'modernization processes', but it might both be equally relevant to investigate how these projects *differ* from one another and how the differences are expressed. Hence, it will be useful to explore how the different terms in question refer to different issues within modernity and how they relate to different aspects or stages of modernization processes. In this way, the generic terms will be broken down, and it will be relevant to uncover the specificities of meaning within 'heritage', as well as 'modernization'.

One aim of this book, then, is to undo the equation between the contemporary interest in heritage and the nineteenth-century interest in historic monuments and see them as cultural expressions of more specific concerns, relevant to their respective periods. Including the older antiquarian tradition in this picture provides a means for developing the perspective further. It implies seeing the developments of the nineteenth century not as a beginning but rather as one stage in a complex and more comprehensive story of different ways of relating to the past.

The invention of the term antiquities – meaning material or other remains from the past – is usually ascribed to the Roman Marcus Terentius Varro, himself avidly interested in the past of Rome. More relevant in this context are the antiquarian studies that became an integral part of Renaissance humanism. With the study of inscriptions, for example, on monuments and graves, coins and medals, as its main focus, this way of studying the past combined humanist methods for studying texts with an interest in material remains – namely, those that carried words or text on them (Momigliano 1990). These texts frequently had (or were given) legal implications, as they in some way concerned genealogy, privileges and property. Antiquarian studies often had important juridical aspects, and the study of material remains could be accompanied by an interest in ancient systems of custom or law (Momigliano 1990: 54ff). Originally concerned with the Greek and Roman past, the antiquarian interest gradually grew to include the national pasts of the various European countries. Classical texts also served as sources to the heathen pasts of these countries, above all Tacitus's *Germania* was important to antiquaries in northern Europe who were hunting for material remains that might confirm what this text had to say about their own forefathers. In Scandinavia, Norse literature came to be used in similar ways. During the eighteenth century, an interest in the mediaeval pasts of the northern European countries was also slowly emerging, not least on the British Isles (Piggott 1989; Sweet 2004; Eriksen 2007).

Only the eighteenth-century phase of antiquarianism will be treated here. The intention is not to write a complete history of antiquarianism, and the eighteenth century suffices to add important elements to the concerns of this book. Belonging to the period before the breakthrough of historicism, in Foucauldian terms to the classical *épistémé*, eighteenth-century antiquarianism represents other ways of organizing knowledge than our modern approach. Hence, it seems reasonable to believe that the terminology specific to this period genuinely reflects a relevant difference. Antiquarianism has often been seen as an early form of archaeology as well as a contributor to the development of the modern discipline of source based history (Schnapp 1996; Momigliano 1990). However, it might be equally important to note that in this period, antiquarian studies were closely related to natural history and its methodology (Sweet 2004; Pomata and Siraisi 2005: 4). Its traditional connection to jurisprudence has already been pointed out (above). Including eighteenth-century antiquarianism means entering a landscape where knowledge was structured in other ways and where scholarly disciplines formed other patterns and relations than what came to happen later. This does not only situate the interest in 'heritage' within a wider historical frame, it also gives a means to ask other questions about the genealogy of the modern concepts.

The Scope and Content of the Book

The book presents a series of case studies based on Norwegian source material from the mid-eighteenth century to the present. The cases are presented in chronological order. However, the aim is not to establish a complete history, but rather to approach the various discursive practices in question through the close reading that case studies make possible. Jean-Claude Passeron and Jacques Revel point to the difference between an example and a case. An example will always be an example *of* something; it represents a category, a theory or some other overarching idea. This means that even if the example itself is specific, local and concrete, what makes it relevant and illuminating will always be its reference to some generality or ambition of such. Examples can be used to explain, persuade or instruct, and their unique energy comes from the way they make the general specific and let the specific reflect the general (Passeron and Revel 2005: 18; see also Lyons 1989). A case, on the other hand, represents a challenge to generalizations, existing theories, dominant categories or habits of thought. It will often originate from a conflict between established rules and the expected outcome of their application. This conflict will produce considerable ambiguities and ambivalences, and the case thus represents a situation which is 'provisoire, mais intolerable' (Passeron and Revel 2005: 16). In this lies also its productivity. The case is 'an enigma to solve, a question to interpret'. This challenge does not, however, mean that the case denies every norm or transgresses all boundaries. Rather the opposite is true, as Passeron and Revel go on to point out that the case is inseparable from the construction and elaboration of theory or normative frames. It is just because the case represents a challenge to existing theories and dominant norms that its existence – and interpretation – supplies a unique possibility to develop theory and explore norms. This dialectic relationship between the normal (or normative) and the 'case' is fundamental and is also what makes the case an important epistemic tool. The case supplies a site for reflection, interpretation and the development of new insights. Even though it represents a challenge to existing theories or preconceived ideas, the case does not remain in its isolated and atypical position. When the enigma has been solved, insights gained and new theories or ideas developed, the case will be reinserted in history and contribute to improved understanding, not merely of its own particularity, but of its context. Nonetheless, a case will never be the means of generalization. It remains a site for explorations and in-depth probing, and its outcome will be new questions just as much as answers to old ones (Passeron and Revel 2005: 20ff).

Using the perspectives discussed by Passeron and Revel, the cases presented in this book will serve as sites of exploration and discussion of theory, rather than milestones along a line of historical progress. Taken together, the cases will not tell a coherent story of historical change over 250 years but contribute to a broader picture of how material remains from the past have been talked about and looked after in different ways over this period of time. They also will suggest a number of themes and perspectives to elaborate on and open for a nuanced understanding. They are not in themselves atypical of their period or context. Nonetheless, they have not been chosen to generalize or present a historical line. What makes them interesting is rather the possibilities they supply to investigate historical difference, to illuminate variety and complexity in the organization of knowledge and to understand the multiplicity and richness of meanings and ideas.

Even if the empirical material comes from Norway, the discourse that is being analysed is not restricted to this country. 'Empirical material' in this context has a double meaning. The material remains to which the discourse refers are located in present-day Norway, a region that until 1814 was part of the twin-monarchy Denmark-Norway. Furthermore, the sources, i.e., the texts that are to be investigated, are also Norwegian and written in Norwegian or Danish, which was the official language of the twin-monarchy. The discourse, on the other hand, is international, and those who speak are members of international networks. Even if the structures of these networks have changed, as have also the technologies to maintain them, this holds true for the entire period. In the eighteenth century, scholarly works were no longer written in Latin. Nonetheless, Latin still served as the common language of the Republic of Letters. Scholars in Denmark-Norway, as well as in other countries, were still able to communicate in Latin. They were educated in Latin literature and history, some also in Greek. Their frame of reference was the classical world, and, as we shall see, together with the Bible, classical literature also functioned as their main supply of historical source material. In Norway, the status of Latin and Greek in education gradually lost ground during the nineteenth century as educational politics acquired a more modern focus and cultural politics was heavily engaged in nation building. But as ethnologist Orvar Löfgren has pointed out, nation building, with its drive towards what is specific and unique to the individual nation, has its own international grammar: to a certain extent, all nations are unique in approximately the same way; they develop the same repertoire of uniqueness (Löfgren 1993: 217f). Apart from the flags, hymns and so on that Löfgren himself mentions as examples of this, it might be added that to the national uniqueness belongs a certain amount of historic monuments and a discourse about them. This national discourse is shaped by an international grammar, implying that even if the monuments referred to uniquely national events, persons and phenomena, they tended to commemorate the same *kind* of events and also to be designed according to iconographic repertoires and symbolic languages that followed international trends. The contemporary heritage discourse is international for other reasons. Its core and primary proponent is UNESCO, whose work also lay behind the heritage term when it came into frequent use from the 1970s onwards. Today, the vocabulary developed by UNESCO has thoroughly influenced the entire field, far beyond the monuments and sites that are, or strive to be, on UNESCO's own World Heritage List. Nonetheless, as the active partners in the UNESCO system always are the 'state parties', the international or even global aspirations of UNESCO's work will always be anchored in individual states, i.e., in nations.

This book may be read as a collection of essays. The next chapter is a discussion of relevant theory, aiming at relating the field of heritage studies and collective memory to the more general perspectives of historicity. The subsequent chapters are more empirical and supply case studies. Chapters 2 and 3 both deal with eighteenth-century antiquaries. In the first of these we once again meet Vicar Bjerregaard, accompanied by other eighteenth-century antiquaries. The aim is to investigate their approach to what they called antiquities or relics and to understand the major impact of textual sources in these studies. The perspective changes in the subsequent chapter. While most of the antiquaries we meet in Chapter 2 subordinate material relics to the authority of texts, and therefore, like Bjerregaard, often were rather disappointed by the actual findings, the protagonist of Chapter 3 represents a very different approach: in 1771 the antiquary and historian Gerhard Schøning published a major work on the partly derelict mediaeval cathedral in Trondheim. The argument of the chapter is that Schøning represents a type of antiquarian work that can rightly be seen as closely related to natural philosophy, with great emphasis on close observation and very detailed descriptions. In Chapter 4 we move on to ruins. In northern Europe particularly, derelict buildings were long considered as rubble, often used as quarries, and generally did not attract antiquarian attention. The term 'ruins' was not in common use until Diderot made them an object of aesthetic appreciation as symbols of time and *vanitas* with his work from the 1760s. This aesthetic approach can also be seen to represent a transition from the older, textually based and systematic view of antiquities to the perspectives of the nineteenth century with its interest in historical development and national particulars. Chapter 5 takes us to the early nineteenth century and the growing interest in mediaeval monuments, heretofore thought too 'Gothic', i.e., too inharmonious and barbaric to merit interest, but now discovered in northern European countries as witnesses of national cultures independent of classical ideals. In Norway, this mediaeval interest was above all related to the country's ornate wooden churches constructed of standing timber. Museums are the theme of Chapter 6. To modern museum visitors, finding historical objects on display is no surprise. Rather, museums are generally regarded as their 'natural' place. The chapter argues that this understanding of museum collections and museum work emerged in the late nineteenth century. The open-air museum with its collections of old buildings is the Scandinavian contribution to this historization of museum principles. In Chapter 7 we turn to monuments and a discussion of Riegl's ideas about intended and unintended monuments. War memorials have had great impact on the development of public memorial culture during the twentieth century, and the chapter explores the development of such monuments in Norway. Chapter 8 addresses the concept of heritage, with particular emphasis on its origin in the UNESCO system and the institution of the World Heritage List. Finally, Chapter 9 continues the discussion of the implications of the notion of cultural heritage, using the Norwegian Heritage Year 2009 as its case. The chapter ends with a conclusion comparing the historicity regime and experience of temporality that is reflected in three main terms that have been investigated throughout the book: antiquities, historical monuments and cultural heritage.

1

Heritage and Cultural Memory

A distinction between the contemporary concept of heritage and the general phenomenon that humans tend to value certain remains from the past is fundamental to the discussions in this book. The actual expressions that this evaluation of relics from the past acquires are subject to historical change. Heritage, as it emerged in the later parts of the twentieth century, with heritage studies as its corollary, is one such historically specific expression. As has been pointed out, both the theoretical premises and the empirical definition of heritage studies are somewhat vague (see, e.g., Harvey 2001: 319f). This is probably not due only to the composite character of the field of study and the fact that analytical work is often entangled with administrative concerns as well as with tourism and a diversity of commercial activities. An even more important reason is that the tendency to equate the contemporary concept with the more general phenomenon inhibits analysis. Without precise distinction, the word 'heritage' is used both as a generic concept and as a more historically specific term, which may work well on an empirical level, but which blurs theoretical understanding.

Seen in a somewhat wider perspective, the contemporary interest in heritage can be understood as part of the more general concern with the social and cultural aspects of memory, emerging in the 1980s and still flourishing (cf. e.g., Erll and Nünning 2010, Olick, Vinitzky-Seroussi and Levy 2011). Sociologist Paul Connerton has recently related this to the perhaps even more general issue of forgetting and argues that the fundamental reason for the present ubiquitousness of memory is 'that modernity has a particular problem with forgetting' (Connerton 2009:1). Now an extensive field engaging scholars from a number of different disciplines, memory studies have produced a veritable flood of scholarly works. Among the more ambitious attempts at developing the field, also on a theoretical level, are books with evocative, even poetic titles, such as *The Texture of Memory* (Young 1993), *The Future of Nostalgia* (Boym 2001), *Stranded in the Present* (Fritzsche 2004) and *Present Pasts* (Huyssen 2003). Even more extensive is the work of Aleida and Jan Assmann, with the ambition of developing a comprehensive theory of culture and cultural transmission centred on the concept of Cultural Memory (J. Assmann 1995; A. Assmann 2011). Corresponding to established convention, it will be capitalized in the following to distinguish the Assmannian concept from cultural memory as a generic term (cf. Erll 2011).

The amount of productivity alone makes the field of cultural memory difficult to delineate and define clearly. Nonetheless, attempts at doing so tend to focus on some fundamental works. Defining the field, these works at the same time raise some major issues which are still under debate. To describe what has been called the 'memory boom' in cultural theory, historian Anna Green typically presents three main works on the field (Green 2008: 100). While all have been highly influential, they also represent quite different positions. The first text is David Lowenthal's book *The Past is a Foreign Country*, from 1985, which opened a debate on history, heritage and memory. Lowenthal understands heritage as artefacts, landscapes and buildings, as well as commemorations and historical reenactments. He argues that the preoccupation with identification, protection and display of historical artefacts, in other words the work to turn them into heritage, prevents true historical knowledge (Green 2008: 100, Lowenthal 1985). Lowenthal makes no secret of his critical attitude to the heritage 'version' of the past. Raphael Samuel, in the next text referred to by Green, emphatically has rejected Lowenthal's and others' critiques of what he at least saw as popular expressions of historical sensibility (Samuel 1994). Scornful of academic disdain, he admitted that 'living history' – or heritage – was present-minded and that it blurred the boundary between fact and fiction, but he nonetheless argued that it was 'less megalomaniac than the idea of "scientific history"' and more attentive to the small details of everyday life (Samuel 1994: 197f; Green 2008: 101). Green points out that heritage 'incorporated a wide range of sources and perspectives not easily subsumed under one ideology or national narrative, although Samuel acknowledged that, as a whole, heritage could represent a search for a sense of the "indigenous"' (Green 2008: 101). It may be added that Samuel's perspective here shows clear relation to his earlier work on oral history and can be said to reflect the same wish for more democratic ways of doing and presenting history.

The third project included in this core literature of cultural memory is Pierre Nora's large work *Lieux de Mémoire*, published in seven volumes between 1981 and 1992 and engaging a number of authors. In this ambitious attempt at constructing an alternative 'narrative' of French national history, Nora's own concept of *lieux de mémoire*, or sites of memory, stands at the core. Nora argued that sites of memory crystallized collective memory, but also that this happened only when the society had undergone a kind of rupture with its past and when traditional forms of 'organic' memory no longer existed (Green 2008: 102, Nora 1989).

The essays in the work, about such different themes as literary texts, food, ideologies, founding people, religion and secular symbols, are attempts at describing important elements in French national identity without suggesting that this identity is a fixed phenomenon, but rather showing how realms of memory can draw on a wide variety of cultural myths and ideologies. Nonetheless, Green points out that despite the attempt to present national history from new perspectives, the work still 'reflects the traditional focus of the historian, with reliance upon archival sources and the records of the elite' (Green 2008: 102). Compared with Samuel's perspective, seeing history from the margin and from below, Nora's approach to collective memory is 'centrist and top-down', Green contends (Green 2008: 102). It may be added that this impression is further enhanced by the fact that there are very few individual historical agents in Nora's work. The forces shaping collective memory and constructing the *lieux de mémoire* are to a great extent represented by institutions or by people acting on the behalf of institutions. Not only are the ordinary men and women of the nation largely absent, the focus in general is not on individual agency. This is probably due to the wish to avoid the traditional perspective, with the deeds of great men at the centre of political history, but the result is that the *lieux de mémoire* seem to emerge from some kind of magic growth, driven by superhuman forces, rather than by more precisely described agency.

Green ends her presentation of the three key texts by pointing out a paradox. These works, as well as the entire 'memory boom', make clear that 'in the rapidly changing world of the last half of the twentieth century, connections that made memory meaningful as a means of explaining the present had been severed, but at the same time individuals and societies turned to their material heritage to construct their own sense of indigenousness and narrative continuity' (Green 2008: 102). However, while all three authors addressed the issue of memory in contemporary society, the overall picture appeared quite anarchic and fragmented. To what extent, Green asks, do *lieux de mémoire* and heritage reflect 'collective memory' (Green 2008:102f)?

Despite the openness, or even anarchy, of the field, a main target of explorations of cultural and social memory in the last three decades has been the situation in modern societies. In their different ways, the works seek to investigate what has happened to memory after some supposed rupture with 'tradition', 'organic memory' or the like caused by modernity. More specifically, this modernity often is associated with processes of nation building. The memory, memorials, symbols and so on that are investigated are most often related to national cultures and the construction of national identities. This way of constructing and using collective memory has been of great importance, but it has also given the processes of nation building a kind of paradigmatic status in memory studies and made theories developed to understand national memory spill over into the investigation of other and more general cultural memory concerns.

Another aspect concerns the numerous attempts to distinguish heritage and cultural memory from 'history proper', not least in the early works in the field. For the three authors presented by Green, this has been a key question. In these debates, the idea of history itself is rarely examined; history is quite simply equated with modern, source-based scholarship. Even this ties the debate to modernity, as it presupposes the existence of the modern academic discipline of history. What has been discussed is cultural memory and heritage and their *relation* to the history produced by academic work and in scholarly contexts. The terms are most often seen in a hierarchy, with history towering at the top and the more problematic categories of memory and heritage inhabiting the lower rungs. Sentiment, eclecticism, present-mindedness or even blunt ignorance have been among the features pointed out as distinctive to these somewhat suspect categories. As indicated by Green, the hierarchy is more or less openly related to questions of class and power relations. In more recent literature on cultural memory, this obsession with the distinctions between memory and history seem to have faded away, possibly due to an increased self-confidence among students and authors in the field (e.g., Erll and Nünning 2010).

In his investigation of the conceptual history of 'heritage', historian Bernard Eric Jensen focuses on largely the same foundational texts as Green, but he also refers to Ralph Hewison's book *The Heritage Industry. Britain in a Climate of Decline,* from 1987. Hewison saw the interest in heritage as a nostalgic attempt at returning to a glorious national past and described how a growing heritage industry was transforming the entire British society into a gigantic museum (B.E. Jensen 2008: 38; Hewison 1987). Contrasting Samuel explicitly with Hewison, Jensen's presentation gives a clearer picture of the political implications of this debate. Samuel's response to the critics of heritage – from Hewison, Lowenthal and others – appears as a determined defence of a more democratic history. Samuel's reason for choosing memory rather than history as his generic term was a definition of popular history, academic history writing and the heritage industry as different expressions of the same cultural memory work (B.E. Jensen 2008: 38f).

Even if other precursors also may be found, the work of French sociologist Maurice Halbwachs is commonly recognized as a main influence behind the interest in cultural memory. In his work *Les cadres sociaux de la mémoire* from 1925, Halbwachs argued that memory was fundamentally social and, bearing this in mind, coined the term 'collective memory'. Despite the still ongoing debates about whether or how memory can be collective, how shared memories are constructed and transmitted, where the agency lies in the processes, as well as a number of other questions raised by Halbwachs' work (see, e.g., Young 1993; Warring 1996; Erll and Nünning 2010; Olick, Vinitzky-Seroussi and

Levy 2011), he must be credited for having introduced the study of memory as significant to the understanding of culture and society. The influence from Halbwachs is also the reason why the German historian scholars Aleida and Jan Assmann have made memory the key concept in their work on a cultural theory (J. Assmann 1995). The project of Assmann and Assmann aims at developing an entirely new way of theorizing culture, built on the twin concepts of Cultural and Communicative Memory (J. Assmann 1995; A. Assmann 2011; see also B.E. Jensen 2005/2006). The starting point for this work is a realization of the fundamental differences between collective memory that is based on simple everyday interaction, be it by oral transmission or embedded in cultural practices, and that which is institutionalized and transmitted by ritual or media. In their terminology, the first is called communicative memory, while Cultural Memory is reserved for the second. The two forms are presented in sharp contrast to one another (J. Assmann 1995). The communicative dimension has however been given relatively little attention in the subsequent work of Assmann and Assmann. Their contributions to a further development of the theory have been centred on the institutionalized and mediatized aspects and, hence, on the concept of Cultural Memory. The term 'culture' in this concept is not identical with the current anthropological use of the word, but is delimited to culture as 'monument', that is the staged, stylized and institutionalized high culture. Astrid Erll thus has pointed out that '"Cultural Memory" does therefore *not* describe all manifestations of "memory in culture"; rather it represents a subset of this: the societal construction of normative and formative versions of the past' (Erll 2011: 30, italics in original).

The work of Aleida and Jan Assmann is distinguished by a far more profound historical perspective than the works cited above. Hence, their theories on memory as a cultural force are not tethered to modernity and the processes of nation building, but have a far wider scope. As an Egyptologist, Jan Assmann has done highly influential work on the impact of Egyptian religion on the development of Judaism, basing his argument on the ideas of religion as cultural memory. As a professor of English literature, one of the important contributions of Aleida Assmann is her distinction between the two forms of memory as *ars* and *vis* respectively. The first term refers to memory as art or technology, going back to the topology of ancient mnemonics. The second concerns memory as a force and its potentiality to change and transform. Assmann contrasts the two by saying that as *vis*, 'memory is not a protective container but an immanent power, a driving force that follow its own rules' (A. Assmann 2011: 20). Of particular relevance to the discussions in this book is her argument that the understanding of memory as *ars* was eclipsed by the concept of memory as *vis* during the latter part of the eighteenth century, meaning also that 'the spatial paradigm of mnemotechnics gave way to a temporal focus' (A. Assmann 2011: 21). This change can then be used as a basis for a historical typology of memory cultures (cf. Erll 2011: 35) that corresponds well with the development described by Koselleck in his work on the concept of history and the experience of time (below).

Despite the common origin in Halbwachs and a general consensus about the influence of the major works from the 1980s and 1990s, no common understanding exists of the social and cultural aspects of memory. Also, despite the agreement that memory is closely interwoven with such concepts as identity and heritage, no clear theories describe these relationships. Furthermore, as both Green and Jensen point out, there is a high degree of terminological variety. Even if 'collective memory' is often used as a generic term, different scholars prefer to qualify this original Halbwachsian concept by replacing it with terms like 'collected memories', 'mnemonic practices', 'cultural memory', 'imagined communities', 'invented traditions', 'theatres of memory', 'sites of memory', 'social remembering' and 'collective remembrance' (Green 2008: 106, cf. also Erll and Nünning 2010: 2f).

One reason for this plurality, or apparent confusion, is most likely that even if the study of memory now is established as an important issue in the historical and social sciences and has become an international and interdisciplinary field marked by great vitality, it involves scholars and disciplines with rather different interests and concerns. It is not obvious that, say, studies of trauma and studies of history didactics are interested in memory in the same way or that scholars working with political history focus upon the same dimensions of memory as those working with art. Despite recent attempts at presenting memory studies as one field, now in the process of consolidating itself (Erll and Nünning 2010; Olick, Vinitzky-Seroussi and Levy 2011), it is not self-evident, for example, that historical and sociological investigations of memory share the same concerns. The awareness that memory is not merely individual, that it is an important aspect of both culture and society and that changes and transformations in memory can be studied historically has led to significant reorientations in cultural theory and to the development of new conceptual frames. Nonetheless, this does not necessarily imply that the rather broad and general interest in memory – in society at large as well as among scholars – is one and the same thing or that this interest should amount to one, coherent field of study with a strict and concise terminology.

A theoretically well-informed analysis of this complex picture has been carried out by Astrid Erll. She points out that 'cultural memory' always implies figurative meaning, and underscores that 'there are two different uses of tropes in cultural memory studies which should be distinguished: "cultural memory" as metaphor and as metonymy' (Erll 2011: 97). Metonymically, she argues, cultural memory concerns remembering 'as an individual act, when the focus is on the shaping force that sociocultural surroundings exert on organic memory'. Metaphorically, on the other hand, the term 'memory' creates 'linguitic images for the organized archiving of documents, for the establishment of official commemoration days, or for the artistic process of intertextuality' (Erll 2011: 97). Erll's important point is that even if these two forms of collective memory can be separated analytically, they continuously influence one another through their interplay of the individual and collective levels. They do not empirically exist without each other. Her conclusion is that 'the "cultural" memory of individuals and the cultural "memory" of social groups and societies are two possible ways to describe (and study) "memory in culture"'. Neither of the areas thus constituted can be viewed exclusively, because the cognitive and the social level only can be understood through their interaction with another (Erll 2011: 101). According to Erll, cultural memory as an umbrella term thus can be defined as 'the sum total of all processes (biological, medial, social) which are involved in the interplay of past and present within sociocultural contexts' (Erll 2011: 101).

Seeing heritage and heritage studies as part of the more general interest in memory thus represents an important contextualization, but it does not supply a distinct theoretical framework or more clear-cut empirical definitions. The perspective rather makes clear that the interest in heritage is one part of a larger pattern characterized by other ways of relating to the past than those conceptualized by more traditional historical terminology. One common denominator in memory studies in general, and heritage studies in particular, is the attempt to explore and understand these ways of relating to the past, accompanied by a recognition that the concept of 'history' alone is insufficient for doing so. The contemporary focus on heritage, commemorations, memorials and so on thus may be seen as the expression of a specific relationship between past and present, characteristic of our time. Correspondingly, the developments of memory and heritage studies as academic fields are attempts at coming to terms with these ways of living with the past and of understanding the cultural experience of temporality that lies behind it.

Such 'ways of living with the past', or rather the specific ways that cultures organize their experience of temporality, is what François Hartog has termed *régimes d'historicité*, or regimes of historicity. In this book, Hartog's perspective will be applied to the different ways of relating to the past that are expressed in the terms antiquities, monuments, heritage and the like: they will be seen as the cultural expressions of different historicity regimes.

Regimes of Historicity

Developing his concept, Hartog originally described historicity regimes in two ways. In the strict sense it means the ways in which a society relates to its past. In a wider sense, it also means to signify the 'mode of self-awareness of a human community' (Hartog 2003: 19).[1] It was intended as a tool to compare different kinds of histories, he maintains. Later he has also come to see its potential 'to shed light on the modes of relating to time: the ways of experiencing time, here and there, today and yesterday. The ways of being in time' (Hartog 2003: 20).[2] Furthermore, Hartog underscores that the idea of historicity regimes above all is useful to understand the moments of 'crisis of time': Periods when the habitual articulations of past, present and future lose their self-evidence and undergo some kind of change (Hartog 2003: 27).

Hartog refers to the anthropology of Marshall Sahlins as an important inspiration and source when working on the idea that different cultures experience temporality in very different ways and therefore develop different historicity regimes. A perhaps more specific influence comes from Reinhart Koselleck and his understanding of historical time as emerging from the tension between the 'space of experience' and the 'horizon of expectation' (Koselleck 1985: 267ff). It follows from Koselleck's model that with modernity, the gap between these two factors is widened and the tension increased. Past experience – individual or collective – is no longer adequate or even relevant for handling the future. Experiences of the past and expectations for the future are separated, and from these grow a new consciousness of time and temporality, which Koselleck identifies as specifically modern and historical.

More specific consequences of this are illustrated by Koselleck's analysis of the dissolution of the *magistra vitae topos* in history writing, and the emergence in the German context of the word *Geschichte* rather than *Historie* as the term for history. The older word, frequently used in the plural, denoted the narratives of the traditional *magistra vitae topos,* presenting the past as a collection of examples either to be followed or avoided: History was the 'teacher of life' – *magistra vitae.* This logic was based on the presumption that past experience was relevant to handle future situations: they would fundamentally resemble those of the past, in the same way as the nature of human beings – their virtues as well as their vices – would always be of the same kind. The modern term *Geschichte,* on the other hand, used as a collective singular, denotes historical narrative that 'was expected to provide the unity found in the epic derived from the existence of Beginning and End' (Koselleck 1985: 29). In its modern usage, history became the narrative of single events, but also of their long-termed consequences as elements in comprehensive processes of change. In this view, the future was open and progress was seen as an autonomous force. The horizon of expectation no longer overlapped with the space of experience.

According to Koselleck, the new term established itself during the eighteenth century, more precisely in the years between 1760 and 1780 and parallel to the new philosophy of history. Common to a number of historians and philosophers of the time was the recognition of 'the destruction of the exemplary nature of past events and, in its place, the discovery of the uniqueness of historical processes and the possibility of progress' (Koselleck 1985: 32). Koselleck also adds that 'history as unique event or as a universal relation of events was clearly not capable of instructing in the same manner as history in the form of exemplary account' (Koselleck 1985: 28).

Koselleck's discussion relates to his analysis of what he call the 'Sattelzeit', the breakthrough into modernity and the period from approximately 1750 to 1850 or 1870. Hartog's concerns are wider. Starting from Koselleck's idea of a tension between experience and expectation, and the specific understanding of temporality that can emerge from this relationship, Hartog declares that 'it is this tension that the regime of historicity wants to illuminate', and it is this distance that his theories are exploring (Hartog 2003: 28). His own investigations are not restricted to one period. Hartog turns the question of a relationship between experience and expectation into a more general matter of the experience of temporality and the cultural expression that this experience acquires. He directs his attention to 'the categories that organize these experiences and allow them to be spoken of, or even more precisely to the forms or modes of articulation of those universal categories or forms that past, present and future are. How, according to the place, the time, and the society are these categories, simultaneously of thought and action, set to work, and how do they make possible and perceptible the unfolding of an order of time? Which present, and aiming towards which past and which future is the matter, here or there, yesterday or today?' (Hartog 2003: 27).[3] Despite this rather ambitious goal – or perhaps because of it – Hartog has repeatedly insisted that his concepts and theories are not to be understood as a contribution to the philosophy of history, nor as an abstract model, but that they simply constitute a heuristic tool (Hartog 2003: 26; Delacroix, Dosse and Garcia 2009: 140). It gives a means to explore and denominate the tension between experience and expectation in different cultural contexts (Delacroix, Dosse and Garcia 2009: 142). This is also how he uses it himself in the analysis in his *Régimes d'historicité*.

Starting from Pacific 'islands of history' (clearly inspired by Sahlins), Hartog moves on to an investigation of the regime of history expressed in *The Iliad* and then to the temporality of mediaeval Christianity and its eschatological worldview. From this he continues to an analysis of Chateaubriand and the experiences of temporality expressed in his *Mémoire d'Outre-Tombe* (published posthumously from 1848) and other texts. Chateaubriand is made into a kind of protagonist of Hartog's book, representing a bridge between an older historicity regime, marked by the *magistra vitae* logic, and the modern historicist. The latter part of Hartog's work presents the historicist regime of the nineteenth century and then goes on to the works of Nora on *lieux de mémoire* and further to the present obsession with heritage (*patrimoine*).

A fundamental concern is whether heritage and the present interest in memory represent a historically new way of relating to the past, a new regime of historicity (Hartog 2003: 22). Hartog's thesis is that today, due to extreme acceleration, the distance between the space of experience and the horizon of expectation has become so great that a complete rupture has taken place and the production of historical time has come to a halt. From this is born what Hartog calls '[t]he contemporary experience of a perpetual present, fleeting and nearly immobile, seeking despite everything to create its own historical time' (Hartog 2003: 28).[4] This regime, named 'presentism', is characterized by an extreme and immediate historization of the present or the very close past (Hartog 2003: 207). It is seen as the consequence of a 'crisis of time', an answer to the experience of dramatic rupture between past and present. In its isolation from both past and future, the present becomes the sole motor of this regime's continuous creation of heritage. Explaining this seeming contradiction between rupture with the past and extreme interest in it, Hartog points out that heritage never is nourished by a sense of continuity, but on the contrary feeds on fractures and questionings of the order of time. Heritage is a way of living with these fractures, acknowledging them and trying to locate or reduce them (Hartog 2003: 204f). What distinguishes the heritage drive of the presentist regime, then, is 'the speed of its extension, the multiplicity of its manifestations and its strong presentist character, at the same time as the present has acquired an extensiveness that it never before has had … The memorial is preferred to the monument, or the monument is turned into a memorial, the past has more attraction than history; the present more than the past, recollection and emotion dominate over reflection and distant consideration; the valuation of the local is accompanied by the search for a "history of one's own"; and finally this heritage is in itself produced by acceleration: We must hurry before it is too late, before the night falls and yesterday has completely disappeared' (Hartog 2003: 206).[5]

The Cult of Monuments

Hartog underscores that he has not intended to give an overview of all the different historicity regimes that can be traced in human history or that his theories represent any kind of teleology. His study concentrates on those regimes that have been most notable in European culture, not least because they have had the most enduring influence. Furthermore, Hartog concludes that the explorations of the book clearly show that the emergence and formulation of a new historicity regime will always take time and that the regimes hardly ever exist in their pure form (Hartog 2003: 208). This understanding distinguishes

Hartog's regimes clearly from Foucault's model of *épistémés*. Despite the focus on tension, crises, rupture and change, Hartog's theories are without the sharp boundaries and dramatic leaps that characterize the shift between *épistémés*. Hartog's insistence that his theory represents no more than a heuristic tool and should not be read as an attempt at a more complete theory of history also serves to distinguish it from a Foucauldian way of thinking. The theory is used to explore the change and interplay of regimes rather than to highlight the difference between them.

Nonetheless, on the basis of his exploration of select authors and their texts, Hartog does present a chronology of historicity regimes said to have dominated European thought from antiquity to the present. The more recent of them are relevant for the present study. The study of Chateaubriand presents the older *magistra vitae* regime, in full accordance with Koselleck's presentation of this pattern of thought (above): history is an instructive collection of examples from which can be deduced wise, good and fair ways of acting in the future. The reason for this is not so much what modern thought would call historical stability or continuity as a fundamental belief in the identity of the past and the present. For Hartog's argument, the importance of this lies not only in the fact that past experience can be judged adequate for dealing with future situations, but also that this regime of historicity is distinguished by its orientation towards the past. This will be the regime of the eighteenth-century antiquaries, deeply influencing their interpretations of ancient artefacts, shaping their discourse and directing their interest in things of the past.

The dissolution of the old *topos* implies that experience loses its instructive value, but equally important is the way the temporal structure changes. In the new regime – according to Hartog inscribed between the years 1789 and 1989 – the future acquires a new role (Hartog 2003: 116f). History is no longer regarded as a collection of examples, but as a process of development towards an open-ended future. This idea is accompanied by an understanding that events take place not merely *in* time, but *by* it: time itself becomes a historical actor. By the same token, the historical attention shifts from the exemplary and imitable to the unique. With this regime, history was established as a 'science of the past'. Only the scientist, the new history scholar, is able to understand the meaning of past events and to analyse the underlying structures of the historical processes. Hartog points out how an expectation of synthesis and generalization followed the discipline of history during the nineteenth century, together with an inclination towards teleological history writing. The new historians were expected to be able to find patterns and to establish laws that would explain past events and assemble all historical facts. Such an operation could only be executed from the future – the present of the new scholars – towards the past. The past must be seen from the future for its true meaning to be discovered. As the hoped-for synthesis and laws of history were forever postponed, however, the point of decisive understanding was continuously passed on beyond the present of the scholars into an even more open future (Hartog 2003: 117).

The nineteenth century saw the birth of a number of disciplines all informed by the new regime. In addition to history itself, archaeology, ethnology and folklore studies, religious history and modern historical philology entered the scene, sharing the basic assumption of history as a process of change. For the present study, it is also important that museums were established as public institutions in the modern sense, displaying artefacts from a past that most often was presented as a chain of periods or epochs, all with their distinctive character and all separate from one another. Artefacts became representatives of types thought to demonstrate development and progress in a close to organic growth. The protection of monuments and buildings, according to their historic value, was also institutionalized in this period, most often on a national scale, as such monuments were held to bear witness to the historical development of the nation. This was the time of the grand national histories, but also of the 'modern cult of monuments', as described by Austrian art historian Aloïs Riegl in 1903.

Riegl distinguished between different motivations for cherishing remains from the past, whether or not they were originally erected as monuments or later made into such by their modern 'cult'. His terms for these two categories of monument are, respectively, intended and unintended monuments. Riegl described how the different motivations to erect and preserve monuments replaced one another historically, much in accordance with the schemes later presented by Koselleck and Hartog. A hallmark in the nineteenth century (though with its roots in the Renaissance) is what Riegl called the historical value. He based his definition on 'the modern notion [of history] that what has been can never be again, and that everything that has been constitutes an irreplaceable and irremovable link in a chain of development' (Riegl 1903/1982: 21). Hence, the uniqueness of the monument is what is valuable and also the way it represents and refers to events or stages in the long chain of change which is history. While intended monuments, whose history equals that of human culture, are erected to celebrate a specific person or event, unintended monuments are only possible on the basis of a modern understanding of history and a modern experience of temporality. The 'essence of every modern perception of history is the idea of development', Riegl asserts (Riegl 1903/1982: 21), and it soon becomes clear that he also identifies this development with 'progress'. Hence, the modern cult of monuments is more advanced than that of former periods. In this way, Riegl not merely sees the monuments themselves as historical, he also presents the appreciation of monuments as a product of historical development, in a dual way situating his own present as the future of the past. Pointing even further towards the future, he argued that assessment of the monuments' age value would most likely be the next stage of development (Riegl 1903/1982: 31ff).

According to Hartog, the historicist regime has been under threat of dissolution since the 1980s. The 'memory boom' is an expression of this, even if movements like early-twentieth-century futurism had heralded it. Hartog takes Nora's work on the *lieux de mémoires* as his case study, seeing this new way of writing history as the outcome of a dissatisfaction with more traditional national history. Nora's work, and not least the concept he developed, attempts to come to terms with what happened to collective memory during modernization, when the 'organic' memory of the traditional *milieux de mémoire* had dissolved and modern history was taking its place. Nora's answer is that the *lieux de mémoire* developed as a kind of substitute to the older forms of memory in an age of modern history. In his much-cited words, the sites of memory are like 'shells on the shore when the sea of living memory has receded' (Nora 1989: 12). While Nora then explores one rupture in the feeling of history, Hartog sees his work as the expression of another and possibly also as an introduction to the present age of heritage.

The presentist regime, and the dominant position of heritage within it, has already been discussed. Its distinctive feature is a lack of direct communication with both past and future, leading it to circle around the present, to historicize it and to see the past exclusively from the perspective of its usefulness to the present. In an interview from 2009, Hartog adds some questions about the true nature of this regime. Does presentism come from deficiency or from abundance? Is it simply a contemporary hiatus before we return to believe in a more or less glorious future, or does it represent a genuinely new mode of temporal experience caused by the revolution in information technology and globalization (Delacroix, Dosse and Garcia 2009: 145)?

Hartog gives no answer to these questions, and neither will this book attempt to do so. Nonetheless, the concept of historicity regimes and the theories presented by Hartog will supply an analytical framework for the explorations to be undertaken here. The perspectives draw attention to the experience of temporality and to the cultural expressions of this experience in different historic epochs. The way artefacts from the past are spoken about, assessed and valued, the reasons that are expressed for preserving them, all reflect modes of relating to the past and ways of experiencing temporality. Furthermore, the idea of historicity regimes is genuinely comparative. Contrary to what is the case in heritage studies and a number of the dominant theories on collective memory, this perspective does not assume concepts or models from one period to be generally valid and thus does not run the same risk of anachronism. It provides a tool for investigating and comparing the experience of temporality during the entire period from the eighteenth century to the present without imposing one single (and frequently teleological) perspective. What is unfamiliar in the older periods will not have to be relegated to lofty categories like of 'premodern' or 'traditional', which frequently is nothing more than an effectual contrast to the modern. Instead, discourse that is specific to former periods may be investigated in its own right as the expression of other historicity regimes and their ways of producing and organizing knowledge. Even if Hartog is clear that different regimes may exist side by side, or at least overlap considerably, his perspective fully justifies a consideration of each epoch quite literally 'on its own terms'. These terms represent more than random designations of objects which in themselves may remain the same from the eighteenth century until today. They are time-specific expressions of different experiences of temporality, in themselves primary sources for an understanding of shifting notions of historicity.

Bearing this in mind, the notion of antiquities belongs first and foremost to the past-oriented regime of the *magistra vitae topos*. The interest in 'historic monuments' is not merely typical of the nineteenth and early-twentieth centuries, the term also belongs to the future-oriented regime of historicism and the then new historic disciplines. The monuments are unique witnesses of the history mainly regarded as a chain of events producing continuous change. And finally, the idea of heritage and the great interest in memory are equally typical as expressions of the presentist regime of our own age. More important than such a categorization in itself, though, is the exploration of the internal logic of the respective regimes that have produced and upheld these concepts. What kind of logic reigns within each regime? What is the rationality that makes it meaningful to speak of heritage rather than monuments or of monuments rather than antiquities? What value system and what way of organizing knowledge do the different terms articulate? And not least, how and when have the regimes dissolved or been overtaken by new ones? What does it mean when 'monument' no longer is felt to be an adequate term for a Viking-age barrow, for example, which is then renamed 'heritage'? Or, correspondingly, what implications are there in the fact that Norway's Central Office of Historic Monuments changed its name in 1994 to Directorate for Cultural Heritage? Given that the objects the Central Office/Directorate works with are not supposed to change much – it is largely the task of this institution to preserve them – it is probably not material reality that lies behind the new name. Instead, we must look at the rationality the work and words are inscribed in and the experience of temporality the discourse is organizing.

NOTES

1. [L]a modalité de conscience de soi d'une communauté humaine.
2. [P]our mettre en lumière des modes de rapport au temps: des formes de l'expérience du temps, ici et là-bas, aujourd'hui et hier. Des manières d'être au temps.

3. [L]es catégories qui organisent ces expériences et permettent de les dire, plus précisement encore sur les formes ou les modes d'articulation de ces catégories ou formes universelles que sont le passé, le présent et le futur. Comment, selon les lieux, les temps et les sociétés, ces catégories, à la fois de pensée et d'action, sont-elles mises en oeuvre et viennent-elles á rendre possible et perceptible le déploiement d'un ordre du temps? De quel présent, visant quel passé et quel futur, s'agit-il ici ou lá, hier ou aujourd'hui?

4. D'òu peut-être cette expérience contemporaine d'un présent perpétuel, insaissable et quasiment immobile, cherchant malgré tout à produire pour lui-même son propre temps historique.

5. [L]a rapidité de son extension, la multiplicité de ses manifestation et son caractère fortement présentiste, alors même que le présent a pris une extension inédite ... Le mémorial est préféré au monument ou ce dernier revient en mémorial, le passé attire plus que l'histoire; la présence du passé, l'évocation et l'émotion l'emportent sur la prise de distance et la méditation; la valorisation du local va de pair avec la recherche d'une 'histoire à soi': enfin ce patrimoine est lui-même travaillé par l'accélération: il faut faire vite avant qu'il ne soit trop tard, avant que le soir tombe et aujourd'hui n'ait complètement disparu.

2

In Search of Ancient Heroes

When he hired local peasants to open the barrow in the hope that inside it he would find antiquities, the vicar Bjerregaard in Lardal (see Introduction) was not acting on a mere idiosyncratic whim. Hunts for ancient burials were frequent all over Europe in this period and part of what was becoming common antiquarian practice. Though the digging was not without elements of the treasure hunt, this type of antiquarian project has been seen as the beginning of modern field archaeology (Piggott 1989: 62; Schnapp 1996: 275ff). In the context of this book, anticipatory aspects are less important than the fact that by starting his project, Bjerregaard demonstrated his knowledge of relevant methodology and his competence as an antiquary. The digging was inscribed in a specific field of knowledge production with its own practices and ways of speaking about ancient objects.

As an eighteenth-century European antiquary, Bjerregaard is quite typical. In the kingdom of Denmark-Norway, vicars were civil servants and men with university educations, but most of them had rather modest incomes and few private means. As Rosemary Sweet has pointed out, antiquarianism was the domain of the elite: it demanded taste, leisure and education. The work supplied a field for demonstration of taste and style and a specific kind of cultural competence (Sweet 2004: 31f). On the other hand, it was far less expensive and time-consuming than, for example, going on a grand tour or building up an art collection. Antiquarian work normally focused on the local past, and many of the artefacts in question were cheap – even free – in acquisition. This made antiquarianism a pursuit easily available to country gentlemen who nourished intellectual interests and wanted to build up collections, but had modest economic means: civil servants and the lower nobility (J.M. Jensen 2008; Sweet 2004). This chapter will explore some aspects of eighteenth-century antiquarianism as it was practised in Norway. Departing from the idea that the work represents another historicity regime than later periods, one main concern will be to investigate what kind of knowledge the antiquaries sought to gain. What were their questions, what objects did they consider relevant and what kinds of argument do their discussions present? What answers were considered relevant? How do ancient objects relate to one another and to the time of the antiquaries themselves? And what experience of temporality is distinctive to antiquarian production of knowledge?

In his now classical account of antiquarianism as a tradition of knowledge separate from that of history, Arnaldo Momigliano identifies the absence of chronology as one of its distinctive features. Leaving chronology to history, antiquarianism 'was systematic and covered the whole subject section by section: it was descriptive in a systematic form, not explanatory in a chronological order' (Momigliano 1990: 61). Moreover, while historians seldom went to the archives, and even more rarely actually quoted the sources they might have used, the work of antiquaries was distinguished by 'an extensive use of material remains' (Momigliano 1990: 66). The aim was to reconstruct ancient life, originally identified with Greek and Roman antiquity. As antiquarianism spread to northern Europe, the interest turned to the different national pasts. In the eighteenth century this had become a major concern. To Scandinavian antiquaries, it meant exploring the world of the old Norse civilization.

Based on the study of artefacts rather than manuscripts, antiquarianism had given an answer to the Pyrrhonism of the seventeenth century. When history came under Pyrrhonistic attack for working with written material that easily could be forged or strongly biased by interest, and the historians themselves were criticized for their service to dynastic or other political causes, antiquaries pointed to 'evidence of undisputed authenticity – coins, statues, buildings, inscriptions', and proclaimed their disinterest in any ongoing political strife (Momigliano 1990: 72). Even if antiquaries were well aware that objects – for instance, coins – could also be forged, they pointed to the fact that for one false coin, there would always be numerous others to compare with. In spite of this, Momigliano points out that antiquaries used far more literary evidence than they cared to admit. Moreover, their invoked impartiality could be questioned, as antiquaries frequently were more involved in religious and dynastic politics than they actually claimed (Momigliano 1990: 73). One reason was that the coins, medals, tombs and inscriptions they worked with frequently referred to issues of genealogy, privileges and (inherited) property and hence could be highly relevant for contemporary concerns, juridical as well as political. Furthermore, a number of antiquaries were deeply interested in custom and law, and their attempts at reconstructing ancient practices could at times have a bearing upon the conditions of the present.

Antiquaries saw their work as complementary to that of the historians and claimed to add dimensions of knowledge about the past that were highly useful to history, but only available by the means of antiquarian methods. Most historians, on the other hand, took quite another view. The image of the antiquary as muddle-headed and little interested in the 'real' history of political life and chronological order, a true enthusiast of potsherds, half-effaced inscriptions and old stones, was established quite early (Sweet 2004: 4ff). Nonetheless, the antiquarian method fuelled the development of the modern, source-based discipline of history in the nineteenth century (Momigliano 1990: 75; Sweet 2004). Momigliano also argues that during the eighteenth century, the two traditions of history and antiquarianism began to merge. A central figure in this was Edward Gibbon, who united the perspectives of philosophical history and antiquarianism in *The History of the Decline and Fall of the Roman Empire* (1776–1788).

Topographies and the Space of Experience

Few Norwegian writers embarked upon projects that were exclusively antiquarian. The preferred genre was the topographic description, treating antiquities as one of several topics. Such texts are the main source of Norwegian eighteenth-century antiquarianism. Even though they often have been presented as an early form of local history (Sandnes 1970), these topographies are clearly more informed by the antiquarian tradition than by that of historiography. Like the antiquarian texts, the topographic descriptions focus on a restricted territory or region. The subjects are presented thematically, not chronologically, and information is normally based on the author's own investigations in the field. Thematically, topographic texts do of course include far more than antiquities, but a general feature is that observations and descriptions of what can actually be *seen* dominate the presentation. In some cases it also appears that the author has been building up a collection, either of natural history items or antiquities and inscriptions. The texts thus have a very material basis, even if, as we shall see, the use of literature plays an important role.

There are several practical reasons for the local horizon of these texts, stemming both from the topographic genre and from the political contexts in which they were written. Nonetheless, the local perspective of the Norwegian topographies, as well as of traditional antiquarian works more generally, also has more theoretical implications. The systematic and nonchronological character of antiquarianism, pointed out by Momigliano and others, relied heavily on spatial explanations. Space and spatiality were important as explanatory elements and did not only provide a means to limit the field of investigations. Spatiality was central to antiquarian epistemology and an important element of its contribution to historical study. At the same time, it was closely related to the other main aspect of antiquarianism, the fundamental interest in materiality. Despite the dominant role of texts in the antiquarian work examined here, it is also obvious that the antiquaries' interest in texts was different from that of the historians. While the writers of history were occupied with the teachings that could be drawn from history, and with describing events and deeds of political and military consequence, the aim of the antiquaries was rather to connect these persons, deeds and events with landscape, sites and artefacts. This makes them approach the texts in ways of their own. Nailing texts to the materiality of both artefacts and landscape, the antiquaries' happily assess that the past can be found in their own close presence. The past might be a place where people do things differently, but it is not a foreign country. It occupies exactly the same space as the present, and the space of experience very literally overlaps with the geographical.

As antiquaries did more generally, even the Norwegian topographers tried to link their study of material remains to the work of the historians. The literary sources that were identified as history, or quite often 'histories', in accordance with Koselleck's observations on the plural form (introduction; Koselleck 1985), played a vital role in this effort. Nonetheless, Bauman and Briggs remark that despite their quite extensive use of textual evidence, antiquaries were not concerned with textuality per se. Rather, 'the primary focus of antiquarian inquiry is on relics of past ways of life, formerly coherent, that had survived in distressed form into the present. Notwithstanding the operation by which antiquities are entextualized for inclusion in the antiquary's collections – a significant part of the very process of constituting them as antiquities – textuality is only incidental to antiquarian inquiry' (Bauman and Briggs 2003: 89). Antiquarian work produced texts and was partly based on text, but the essence of this tradition of knowledge still was materiality in its broken form as *remains*.

Norway, in union with Denmark until 1814, did not establish its own university until 1811. The commission of antiquities (*Oldsagskommisionen*) that was founded in Copenhagen in 1807 was supposed to collect antiquities from the entire realm. In actual practice it served as an incentive to found a separate Norwegian commission and collection from 1810 to prevent exportation. Shortly after, this collection became the basis for the new university. During the eighteenth century, only one scientific society existed in the country. In 1760 the bishop Johann Ernst Gunnerus established *The Royal Norwegian Society of Sciences and Letters* in Trondheim (Andersen et al. 2009; Chapter 3 in this volume). Topographic monographs proliferated from the 1760s onwards and gave more or less comprehensive descriptions of one parish or one county. Some authors have clearly taken a special interest in antiquities, while others are more interested in matters of natural history or economics. The same kind of texts, though normally shorter, appeared in the *Norwegian Topographical Journal* (*Topographisk Journal for Norge*), issued in ten volumes from 1792 to 1808. An inspiration for both the journal and the monographs can be found in a corpus of texts some decades older. In 1743 the Government Office (*Cancelliet*) in Copenhagen issued a list of forty-three questions that should be answered by all civil servants. The idea was to collect material for an extensive description of the entire Norwegian part of the realm. The government wanted to chart natural resources, industries and geographic and economic conditions in this less known and somewhat remote part of the kingdom. The endeavour was in accordance with the state's cameralistic policies and aimed at economic development and agricultural improvements (Djupedal 1955–57; Herstad 2003: 15f). Historical and antiquarian themes were no main concern to the project, but were considered in some questions. Among the respondents, some took special interest in antiquarian topics and supplied more information than was actually requested. The vicar Bjerregaard, describing his search for 'heathen relics', is one of them. To others, the questionnaire was an inspiration to start the work on more extensive topographic texts. The bailiff (*fogd*) Iver Wiel seized the opportunity to send a comprehensive description, already composed, of his district Ringerike and Hallingdalen. In this very thorough work, later published in the *Topographic Journal*, a discussion of antiquities and antiquarian themes is given a prominent place.

What's in a Name?

In his answer to query no. 41 on the 1743 list, Bjerregaard responded that the large number of barrows in Lardal 'makes it reasonable to believe that in heathen times, people of distinction have lived here'. This assumption lay behind the opening of the mounds and was the reason he expected them to contain 'relics' (Røgeberg 2003–05 3: 403). It was also the reason for his disappointment: the nobility of the past had not left behind any artefacts equivalent to their social standing. Others had been luckier, though. Bjerregaard notes that some years earlier, a heavy golden ring had been found and sold for the value of 6 *Riksdaler* (a sum more than sufficient to buy a cow). He then goes on:

> At a farm named Gavelstad, there is a wooden building of very old age, about which the owners think has existed since heathen times. The building, and in particular its doors and windows are crafted with great artistry, and shows this edifice to have been the residence of people of rank.
>
> At a farm called Skudum I have been shown a great number of old parchment letters, issued in the times of King Haakon, Queen Margrethe and King Eric of Pomerania.
>
> During the war that is called the Svale war, Swedish troops arrived in Laurdal, and when they were not honoured and served the way they wanted to be by the vicar's wife, a lieutenant shot and killed the vicar's manservant at the doorstep of the vicarage and brought the vicar himself, Christen Bugge, before the general (Røgeberg 2003–05 3: 403).[1]

The vicar gave the general proud answers to his attempts at inspiring awe, making the infuriated lieutenant ask whether he should shoot or stab the man.

Prohibited to do either, the lieutenant struck the vicar's face. But the general presented him with a red silken cloth to dry his blood, and accompanied the gift by disclosing his aristocratic name as a sign of respect (Røgeberg 2003–05 3: 403).

The anecdote about the vicar is also reported in other sources and has probably been well known locally. It fits into a tradition of narratives emphasizing the pride and independence of people in Norway who refused to subordinate themselves to authorities not of their own choice, be it enemies during war or the representatives of king and government. In the present context, it may be more important to note the structure of Bjerregaard's narrative. The information is presented in chronological order, beginning with the supposedly heathen 'people of rank', going on to the mediaeval kings and their parchments and ending with the war against the Swedes that took place in the years 1563–70. Nonetheless, the leaps are considerable and the time span great. What holds the presentation together is neither causality nor temporality, but rather the fact that the persons and events involved all belong *here*, in Bjerregaard's own Lardal, and, moreover, that some material traces can be related to the past they represent: the ancient building, the barrows, the golden ring, the parchments and the vicarage itself. The space of history is identical with the territory of Bjerregaard's own parish.

Bjerregaard's interest in the old artefacts is closely related to the wish for identification. Who were they? Even if he does not know the names of the people of the most remote past, Bjerregaard determines them to be 'people of rank' and 'distinction'. According to several other authors, the urge to provide identification is even more specific. For the interpretation of mounds and standing stones a general point of departure was Snorre Sturlason's *Chronicle of the Kings of Norway* (*Heimskringla*), where it is said that Odin, whom Snorre treats as a historical person, introduced burnt burials, but that he also declared mounds to be built in honour of all men of consequence. When Frey died at Upsal, he was buried in a mound, and after that, many people took up this new practice (Ynglingesaga, Chapters 8, 11). Snorre's presentation – and the great authority it carried – implied that barrows and standing stones were not in themselves considered very enigmatic. Their explanation was already given; they were memorials erected in the honour of powerful men and great warriors. Conversely, this implied that any site with barrows or standing stones once had been the domain of such persons. The antiquarian challenge was then to chart the constructions and identify the great men: who exactly were these persons? The favoured answer was not merely 'a chieftain', 'a noble person' and even less 'somebody from the ninth century', but a name, a genealogy and preferably also a historic narrative. The narratives were found in Snorre and other Norse and mediaeval literature. Such texts represented a supply of stories not only thought relevant to the interpretation of barrows and ancient artefacts, but also representing an indisputable truth that objects and constructions were compared to. Antiquarian work largely consisted of inventorying the artefacts to connect them to the correct textual information.

A number of mounds traditionally bore names referring to persons. Iver Wiel writes about King Halvdan's mound at Ringerike, Hans Jacob Wille about the so-called Glom's mound in Flatdal in Telemark, Holm about King Spang's mound at Spangereid in Agder and Gerhard Schøning about the mound of Orvar Odd in Sogndal in western Norway (Wiel 1743/1970: 127; Wille 1786: 50; *Top. J.* 1795: 32; Schøning 1771: 482). These names are found in contemporary folklore of the authors' own time, while they also, in some of the cases at least, connect to persons and events known from literary sources. The antiquaries never question the traditional names, but rather try to make the connection between folklore and literature even more explicit.

Hans Strøm, best known as a natural historian, makes a number of antiquarian interpretations of this kind in his topographical description of the region of Sunnmøre, where he was also a vicar. Starting from the barrows and their folklore, he presents etymological interpretations based on names, and in some cases he ends in the sagas. Strøm quotes the peasants who say that the Roald farm on the island of Vigra can trace its name from a king called Roe, buried in what is called the king's mound. Strøm develops his argument: 'if this is so, then Roald or Ro-old must without doubt be the same as Roehald or Roehold, that is King Roe's holding or residence' (Strøm 1762–66: 56).[2] From Rødøy at Ørsta he describes a mound that has been opened, so that the 'coffin' made from five large, flat stones could be seen. 'The local people all agree that it must be the well-known giant Listur Bleike (or, as he is named in the old tongue: Listr hine bleiki), whose story is told in the saga of Eigil Skallagrimsson … that is buried here' (Strøm 1762–66: 224).[3] While Strøm is quite sceptical to popular traditions in his work as a natural historian, he seems quite happy to accept folklore as a basis for antiquarian interpretations.

Based on this logic, the investigation and interpretation of mounds and what might be seen inside them becomes largely a matter of recognition, rediscovery and localization. The answers exist already, in Snorre and other texts. The barrows that could be investigated throughout the country were compared to this material, and in the cases where the mound and the literature were judged to correspond, all relevant questions were considered answered. The issue at stake is always 'which mound' or 'whose mound'? When barrows bore names that could not be found in the literary sources, the name was ascribed fundamental identificatory and hence explanatory value. In Strøm's text, the name Roald appears to be satisfactorily explained by the assertion that it means King Roe's holding – even if no king of this name is reported in the literature. Glom's barrow in Telemark is named after the giant Gloms Sundbø, about whom nothing else is known. Nonetheless, the names are accepted as sufficient explanations. The argument, taken from Snorre's presentation of the ancient custom, indicated that the mounds and stones granted the local presence of powerful men.

Riegl argues that the most ancient form of monuments is what he calls 'intended monuments', i.e., constructions and edifices made explicitly to celebrate or commemorate important events or persons (Chapter 1 in this volume). Among his examples are the columns and triumphal arches of imperial Rome. Riegl points out that such monuments traditionally have been erected in the rather immediate aftermath of the event or life that is being celebrated, and also that they frequently were destroyed or simply fell into oblivion when the responsible ruler or dynasty was no longer in power. Consequently, intended monuments are directed towards the present and the future rather than the past (Riegl 1903/1982). Snorre's description of ancient burial customs supplied the antiquarians with ample reason to regard all standing stones and barrows as this kind of monument. The logic also implied that when the antiquaries themselves used the term 'monument' or 'ancient monument' to describe such barrows, stones and so on, they understood the constructions to have been intended as monuments by those who once erected them. It was the intention of their constructors, not the long time that had passed, that made barrows and stones monuments.

The principle of recognition was also applied to other kinds of objects and contributed to more unintended monuments. From Spangereid in Agder, the judge Holm describes how traces of King Olav Trygvasson still can be observed:

> [S]ome big stones standing erect can still be seen at the place where the king and his men held shooting competitions, and where Eynar Tambeskjelff, well known in history with his bow named Tamb, is said to have shot his arrow half a *fjerding* [i.e. approx. 0.6 km.] (*Top. J.* 1795: 37).[4]

In the same area, Holm also identifies a number of traces of Aslaug Kråka, known from the saga of Ragnar Lodbrok as an orphaned princess who was brought up by a peasant couple that treated her very badly. Her nobility was recognized by King Ragnar, and she ended up becoming his wife. In this case, Holm's argument is based on local names and traditions and also builds on investigations carried out by the historian Tormod Torfæus in the late seventeenth century (*Top. J.* 1795: 35f).

The objects and traces that are interpreted in this case have not originally been intended as monuments, but they are turned into such by the antiquaries' attention and their method of combining objects that still can be seen, with textual (and in some cases oral) testimonies. According to Riegl, this way of making historic monuments out of artefacts or constructions that had never been intended as such represents a more specifically modern attitude to history, commemoration and temporality. It is no longer the objects in themselves or some original intentions that create monument value, but rather the initiative of later generations alone. For such monuments to be made, the span of time between the origin of the artefacts and the present must in itself be experienced as important to the monument makers.

All the objects that are discussed in the antiquarian texts seem to represent one single and temporally undifferentiated past. All objects are ancient, but the remote past that they represent has no temporal structure of its own. Instead, it is organized in two different kinds of space: that of the actual landscape and that created by the literary sources. Oral folklore functions as the bridge between the two, but despite the fact that legends and names have been recounted by living peasants inhabiting the authors' own present, even the popular traditions appear as belonging to the same past as the other elements. In their analysis of antiquities as fundamental to the notion of modernity, Bauman and Briggs argue that antiquities per definition always will be broken, shattered and incomplete: 'indeed, it is their survival into the "modern" era … as "remains" that constitute them as antiquities. That is to say, the antiquity is a hybrid form, mediating between past and present' (Bauman and Briggs 2003: 76). In the early modern period, folklore and oral traditions were also regarded as 'antiquities' sharing this mediating task. This is why Strøm willingly accepts folklore as evidence in antiquarian matters while he sneers at popular ignorance and superstition when it comes to natural history. Folklore is of the same kind as material antiquities: broken remains from the past that have survived into the present. Conversely, it has no value for natural history, which is *not* structured by the break between past and present that is constitutive to antiquities.

The Implications of Space

The work to connect names to sites serves to localize history, embedding the narratives of the literary sources in the local landscape. By implication, this principle also works the other way around, starting with local sites and constructing a narrative. The idea that fields of mounds or cairns are evidence of large battles is very common in topographic texts. Most authors seem to find this self-evident. The possibility that such fields can have developed over a considerable span of time and that their graves are not related to one single event or point of time does not seem to strike them. Iver Wiel and the vicar Chr. Palludan both interpret a field of mounds by the Tandberg farm at Ringerike as the trace of an ancient battlefield: the fallen warriors are buried in the mounds. As additional proof, Wiel informs that children tending sheep have found numerous arrow tips, spurs and pieces of bone in the earth by the mounds (Wiel 1743/1970: 153). Strøm argues in the same fashion. At Haram, in the Sunnmøre district, there is a plain filled with barrows of considerable size. They are placed in rows, and each is surrounded by large stones. 'The spectator will soon think that in ancient times a large battle has taken place here, and that the persons who fell during the struggle have been buried on the battlefield' (Strøm 1762–66: 26). Their idea of history is not one of processes, neither of the study of change and continuity over time. As they see it, the interpretative challenge is rather to find out which battle has taken place on this site and, preferably, also who took part. The same rationality implies that when two mounds lie close to one another, they must be the graves of two warriors or kings fallen in single combat, and the authors search for their names. Because the mounds are memorials, they must be connected to memorable, i.e., historical, events and persons, the argument goes. And as they occupy the same space, they must also represent the same time or, more correctly, the same past events. To this way of thinking, the temporal dimension is not in itself ascribed much explanatory value. Rather, it is the spatial situation that supplies the necessary causal links, and it is space that structures interpretations and produces understanding. The events that the mounds are parts of have taken place *in* time, but are not really produced *by* it (cf. Chapter 1 in this volume).

Snorre's assertion that mounds are built over great men, taken together with an understanding of history as the deeds of such men, forms the basis for the notion that the mounds are built over exactly *those* great men whose deeds are recounted in the 'histories'. While every great man known from history can be expected to have his mound, it should by implication be possible to connect every mound or field of mounds to specific persons or events from the 'histories'. Nonetheless, this proved to be problematic. Strøm (above) had to admit that King Roe of Roald was 'unknown'. It also seems remarkable to these authors that most often no narratives can be found about the huge battles that must have been the source of the large fields of graves. From Veblungsnes in Romsdal, Gerhard Schøning describes 'a large field of small circular cairns, very close to each other. Hence, it appears that at this site, very long ago in heathen times, a large battle must have taken place, about which no legend or history exists any more' (Schøning 1778: 135). From Ringerike, Wiel confronts the same puzzle:

> At the Tandberg farm a king by the name of Tane is said to have lived, and the farm has its name after him. No clue to the time that he lived can be found in the histories; perhaps he was one of the minor kings, of whom memory is effaced (Wiel 1743/1970: 151f).[5]

A king with a mound should also be found in the histories. An intended monument ought by implication to be connected with something or somebody specific to be commemorated. When this is not the case, a different explanation is needed. Musing over the phenomenon of intended monuments (barrows) and unknown persons, the local judge Palludan asserts that even if King Tane of Tandberg and his neighbour at Veien are not mentioned in the histories, the names and position of the mounds indicate that oral folklore about the two kings who fell in one single combat must be true. He also attempts to solve the enigma of the field of mounds between the two farms by referring to Jonas Ramus. This renowned scholar was a former curate of Norderhov parish. In 1719 he published a book on the ancient kings of Norway. Palludan cites Ramus's hypothesis that numerous ancient persons and families must have been forgotten, for 'those that are recorded in his genealogical registers, are not sufficiently numerous to fill the entire span of time' (Røgeberg 2003–05 3: 68).[6] Combining the two problems – anonymous barrows on the one hand and the lack of a sufficient number of people to fill historical time on the other – Palludan then argues that the persons missing from the genealogical registers may be identical to those in the anonymous mounds. Even if their names have been forgotten, the mounds' undisputed role as intended monuments turns them into proof that more people have lived than those who are mentioned in the histories.

Even if antiquarian work did not itself aim at producing a collection of exemplary narratives about great men, antiquarians shared the historians' vision of history (see Chapter 1 in this volume). They did not question the *magistra vitae topos,* but rather sought to supply the historians' narratives with material evidence, confirming what the 'histories' already told. Attention is oriented towards the past, and the production of knowledge is focused on reconstruction. But even if the past is remote, the antiquarian reconstruction is for a large part understood in terms of recovering names, persons and events. The expectation is that the past will not actually prove to contain anything yet unknown. The reason is that even if the ancient way of life is regularly mentioned as less polished and hence different from that of the authors' own time, it has already been described in the 'histories'. Indeed, some core elements are regarded as fairly constant: The fight for power, battles and conquest, heroism and the fame of great men is what history is about, in ancient as well as in all times. There is nothing really new in history – or the 'histories'. It is all there already, contained in the space of experience that in this case is found in literary sources. Traces of events that do not fit in or have not been heard of before create confusion. But these new experiences – or experiences of novelty – do not serve to change the categories and notions already in use. Instead, they are incorporated into existing notions and ideas, even if it must be admitted that the existing 'histories' do not cover all that has been.

Hallingdal and Thrace

The most complex antiquarian argument is presented by Iver Wiel in his description of Ringerike and Hallingdal (1743). While more elaborate and erudite than most of his fellow antiquary topographers, Wiel's argument is still typical of their way of reasoning. Wiel presents a number of antiquarian investigations that he has undertaken himself. He also describes the difficulties of copying runic letters from withered stones and his even greater difficulties reading them. He frequently refrains from any interpretation, humbly leaving this to more erudite men. He also regrets the lack of instructive books to help him, but is still able to refer to the works of the great Danish scholar Ole Worm (1588–1654). One example of Wiel's work will be discussed here to show his method and mode of argument.

In the mountain valley of Hallingdalen, Wiel has seen some large, heavily ornate horns. He takes them to be ancient drinking vessels, a still valid interpretation. One of them is accompanied by a legend. On Christmas Eve, a peasant seeks out a mound and calls forth the fairies believed to inhabit it. A woman appears, offering the peasant a drink. He takes the horn from her, but instead of drinking, he empties it over his shoulder. Some drops fall on his horse and burn its tail, revealing it to be a dangerous compound. A spear is hurled after the man and horse as they gallop away down the slope. The peasant catches the spear between his arm and waist and hears a voice calling: 'Keep it as you have won it'. A curse follows the mysterious words: for nine generations, members of his family will be crippled! Wiel adds that old folk still remember that in this family, somebody always had a physical disability. By now, so much time has passed that the curse has come to an end (Wiel 1743/1970: 179ff).

Wiel has examined the horn closely. It comes from an ox, is brown from age and measures 3/4 *alen* (approximately 45 cm) from one end to the other. The wide end has a gilded brass ring bearing the names of the three magi: Melchior, Balthazar and Kaspar. The centre has a brass plate with a crystal and in the narrow end a tube and a button, both gilded. Wiel also says that the horn has been kept at Halsteingård in Hallingdal for the last two centuries; earlier it was at the Sata farm. Other than this, he makes no attempt at dating it. His argument is about *how* the drinking horn has been produced, not *when* it was done.

The legend offered as explanation is a version of the so-called fairies' horn legend, a migratory narrative now documented in most of northern Europe (Christiansen 1958: ML6045). In some versions, the man who has been buried in the mound proffers the horn, making it quite clear that it is ancient and very literally belongs to 'the ancestors'. In Wiel's version, the mound is populated by fairies, which relates the legend to other stories about costly objects won from them. According to popular tradition, the fairies lived their lives much in the same way as humans, but underground, in mountains, rocks and mounds. Their realm was dark and hidden. Fairies frequently sought contact with humans, for instance through marriage or the exchange of one of their own children for a human.

Such contact was always perilous to humans – the risk was to lose one's own healthy child or to be charmed by a supranatural suitor and carried away to his or her dark abode forever (Solheim 1952). The Norwegian word for being spellbound – *bergtatt* – literally means 'taken into the hill'. In Wiel's legend, the supranatural danger is the drink that burns the horse's tail. Had the man tasted it, he would have come to a bad end. Nonetheless, oral tradition also presents contact with the fairies as tempting. Their women were beautiful, and the fairies were in possession of great wealth – like the costly horn. In this legend, as well as in narratives about the fairies' silver, the point of the story is that humans succeed in winning some of these treasures, but at the same time the cost of their boldness is high.

Wiel does not seem to know other Norwegian versions of the legend. He does not see it as a migratory legend, but as specific to the horn at Halsteins-gård. However, he also points out that the horn resembles the so-called Oldenburg horn, which he knows from Hamelmann's *Oldenburg Chronicle* (1599). Wiel has seen an image of this horn, which is kept at the *Royal Kunstkammer* in Copenhagen. In this case, the story is about the German count Otto (tenth century). Once out hunting, he was offered a drink from a horn by a young woman. She appeared from a mound and said that the drink would bring luck to him and his family. When the count refused, she cast a spell instead. Like the peasant from Hallingdal, the count escaped with the horn (Hamelmann 1599). Wiel does not tell this story, however, but rather seems to assume that it was known to his readers. And his suggestion is that somebody who has seen the Oldenburg horn could

> *ad Imitiationem*, as far as his skills went, have made one like it, and then told the story about finding the Oldenburg horn. This was heard by a superstitious peasant, and he and others slowly made their way into the narrative that is now told among the peasants, so that the words of Horace may be applied to it: *Mutato nomine de te Fabula narratur* [trans.: a story is told about you, but with another name] (Wiel 1743/1970: 182).[7]

The disabilities that followed the peasant's family for nine generations constitute an argument against this theory. However, Wiel points out that disabilities might easily occur in any large family without having a supranatural cause. He also states that horns of this kind were quite common in 'ancient times' and ends by deleting both the story of the legendary origin and his own theory of imitation. He concludes that the horn's sole distinctive features are its age and artistry of design.

The existence of other horns in the same area opens for comparison. One is kept at the Strand farm in the parish of Ål. It is huge, and today – according to Wiel – no oxen with so large horns exists. This proves it to be ancient, even if Wiel thinks that this horn is somewhat younger than the first. He makes no further attempts at dating the horn, but says that it resembles one that is presented by Ole Worm in his work *Monumenta Danica* (1643). The horn from Strand is furnished with ornate brass and stands on feet. An old dagger is kept with the horn, and Wiel postulates a connection between the two. Even if he finds the etymological interpretations presented by Worm somewhat 'extravagant', Wiel agrees that for horns, nothing fits better than to derive the Latin word *cornu* from the Greek *keras*. The reason is that Xenophon relates that the Thracians drank wine from horns after having greeted one another at feasts. This has also been the custom in Hallingdal! The connection is proved both by tradition, by the dagger, which probably has been a pocket weapon 'used at banquets, which seldom took place without murder and manslaughter', and with parallel traditions of Wiel's own time. He says:

> When they arrived at a banquet, they are said first to shake hands, and to take drink from a horn. Then they sat down, and the drinking merrily went on. When all were drunk, they started to quarrel and fight:
>
> *Inqve repentinos convivia versa tumultus*
> *Assimilare freto possis, qvod svæva qvietum*
> *Ventorum rabies motis exasperat undis*
> [*You might compare the banquet, changed into a sudden tumult, to the sea, which, first calm, the boisterous rage of the winds disturbs it by raising its waves*]
>
> Then they drew their daggers, the lights went out, and everyone hit those he could, whence a large loss of both friends and foes frequently followed (Wiel 1743/1970: 115f).[8]

Today, the peasants in Hallingdal use wooden bowls instead of horns and knives instead of daggers. Apart from that, nothing has changed, and no law has succeeded in ending these ungodly ways. Wiel puts his trust in the present crop failure, which will diminish the availability of beer and hopefully make the banquets less violent.

The structure of these comparisons is quite complex. On the one hand, Wiel compares local custom in 'ancient' and present times. The ancient is represented by the somewhat unspecified past that produced the horns, while the 'present' is the life of contemporary peasants. At the same time, Wiel also compares Norwegian customs (past and present) to what Xenophon says about the Thracians. Nonetheless, this is not a case of modern ethnography. The past tense in the passage above is somewhat unspecified, as are also the actors. It is not obvious *when* these customs were in use, neither *who* actually behaved in these ways. The obvious reason is that the words are not Wiel's own. The paragraph is partly a paraphrase, partly a quote. Wiel takes his description from Worm, who builds on Xenophon. The Latin inserted words are from Ovid. Consequently, nothing of what is being said originally concerned peasants in Hallingdal, in the past or present. The passage refers mainly to Xenophon's description of the ritual banquets of the Thracians (in *Anabasis*), while the Ovidian quote is taken from *Metamorphoses.* What is remarkable is that Wiel inserts these quotes and phrases so seamlessly into his own text that all difference in time, place and actors dissolves, most specifically, in relation to the actors. The word 'they' slides unnoticeably between referring to the inhabitants of Hallingdal in ancient times, to the present inhabitants of the same valley and to the Thracians of Xenophon's Greek world. Apart from the use of Latin and some Greek in the quotes, there are no grammatical traces to whom the word 'they' actually applies to. Thracians and the peasants from Hallingdal merge into one.

This does not imply that Wiel suggests any historical connection in a modern sense between ancient Thrace and Hallingdal. He does not claim that the peasants of Hallingdal have learned their ways directly from the Thracians. The similarity is rather of a typological nature. What most explicitly relates the two cases is the reference to Worm's etymological interpretation, deriving the word 'horn' from Latin and Greek. This also gives a clue to the relation between the two elements of comparison on a more general level: it is not symmetrical and it represents more than the juxtaposition of two randomly chosen groups.

Wiel's text is saturated with Latin (and some Greek) phrases and quotes throughout. In some instances they constitute a meta-level, giving Wiel the opportunity to reflect and comment on his own work from the perspective of the indisputable authority of classical authors. In these cases, the function of the quotes is similar to the *magistra vitae topos* in historiography. They refer to timeless truths. When it comes to the discussion of ancient custom, like the use of horns, another dimension is added. The quotes are drawn into the argument itself, supplying comparative material. Nonetheless, the exemplary character of the classical texts still is valid and the juxtaposition of Hallingdal and Thrace is not so much a comparison as a measuring point. Xenophon's description of Thrace represents more than empirical data. Belonging to the corpus of texts by the classical authors, it is a standard and a measure for other cases. The classical texts present universals, in this case concerning 'the banqueting customs of ancient nations'. Such universals may be expected to occur even in quite different geographic contexts, concerning other ancient tribes. Consequently, when new data, for instance from Hallingdal, can be found to correspond to them, these new examples are considered to be explained. This also implies that the true meaning of the traditions from Hallingdal is not so much to be found in their local context as in the typology and patterns that can be deduced from classical texts. These texts, by Xenophon and others, describe the ancients with the greatest possible authority and are thus applicable to all subsequent cases. This is also the reason why Wiel allows his description of the customs of Hallingdal to merge with those from Thrace, letting the specificities of time, place and actor fade away. This does not represent an imprecise rendering of ethnographic data. Wiel has fashioned his presentation to demonstrate how completely the customs of Hallingdal fit the universal pattern of the 'ancient way of life' as it is presented by the best and most authoritative writers of history – the classics.

A Familiar Realm

The antiquaries were investigating a remote past. Despite its exoticism, this past still appears close and familiar in many ways. Bjerregaard judged the objects found in the mound uninteresting, and his assessment was not unique. Opening the large mound at Spangereid, Holm reports that it contained nothing 'apart from the usual clay pots' (*Top. J.* 1795: 32). From northern Møre, Schøning mentions a small mound found to contain nothing but 'some rusty arrows and a small chest decorated with rings, of which I acquired one, but which is quite unremarkable' (Schøning 1778: 28). One reason why these artefacts were uninteresting or unremarkable was that they were broken, rusty and destroyed, but they were also judged to be too similar to utensils and tools that were in regular use by the peasants, who themselves were also some sort of 'antiquities'. While their household utensils resembled the remains found in the mounds, peasant traditions and ways of life, on the other hand, could be seen as the last remains of the more glorious world of the ancients. Conversely, the fact that the fragmentary state of the objects in the barrows was due to their old age, and hence to what we would call history, had no independent value and was not given any explanatory function. Even if antiquarian work was about ancient times and ancient things, it was not about time or temporality.

The past represented by antiquities also appeared known because it could already be found in texts of great authority. It normally was taken for granted that these texts – classical, Norse and mediaeval – were identical with history, or rather 'histories'. As we have seen, findings contrary to this were explained by incorporation into the logic of this textual universe rather than taken as a serious challenge. Finally, the past also appeared close because it was imbedded in the landscape. Even if the authoritative texts and the 'living antiquities' of peasants gave important clues, it was this spatial dimension that most fundamentally made the past comprehensible and tangible.

NOTES

1. Paa en gaard kaldet Gavelstad staar en bygning af træ som er ældgammel og hvorom beboerne har den tanke, at den har staaet siden de hedenske tider. Bygningen, især

hvad vinduer og døre angaar, er konstig forarbeidet og viser, at fornemme folk har der boet i fordum tider.

Paa en gaard kaldet Skudum har ieg faaet at see en mængde pergementsbreve, udgivet i kong Haagens, dronning Margretes og kong Eric af Pomerens tider.

Da den krig ble ført, som bliver kaldet Svalekrigen, kom et partie svendske til Laurdal, og da de i Præstegaarden blev af konen ej saa æred og tracteret, som de vilde, skiød lieutenanten præstens tienestekarl ihiel i studedøren og førte præsten, nemlig Christen Bugge bort til generalen ved den svenske armèe.

2. [E]r dette saa, da bliver Roald eller Ro-old uden Tvivl det samme som Roehald eller Roehold, det er Kong Roes Tilholds Sted og Boepæl.

3. Indbyggerne her i Egne ere alle af den Meening, at den bekiendte Kiæmpe Listur Bleike (eller som han kalles i det gamle Sprog: Listr hine bleiki) om hvilken mældes i Eigil Skallagrims Krønike … ligger paa dette Sted begraven.

4. [D]er findes store Stene endnu oprejst, hvor han og hans Mænd have skudt i kap med hinanden, og hvor den i Historien berømte Eynar Tambeskjelff med sin Bue, som kaldtes Tamb, skal efter Rygtet have skudt en Piil en halv Fjerding langt.

5. Paa Gaarden Tandberg siges en Konge at have boet ved Navn Tane, hvoraf Gaarden skal have faaet sit Navn. Hvad Tid han har levet paa, seer man ikke noget Spor til i Historierne; men maaskee han maa have været en af de smaa Konger, hvis Ihukommelse kan være uddød.

6. [M]ange Personer og Slegter ere forglemte, eftersom de der udi hans Slægtregister ere optegnede, ikke kan forslaae til tidens længde at opfylle.

7. [K]unde ad Initiationem, saavidt hans Lejlighed strakte, have forfærdiget sig et, og saa fortalt Historien om hvorledes samme Oldenburgske Horn blev fundet, hvilket er hørt af en superstitieux Bonde, og af ham og andre i Tiden forandret til den, som nu gaaer iblandt Bønderne, saa at dette Horatii kunde appliceres derpaa: *Mutato nomine de te Fabula narratur.*

8. Naar de kom til Gjæstebud, siges de først at have hilset hinanden med Haandtag, hvorpaa de bleve tildrukne med et Horn, derpaa satte de sig ned, og gik det da lystig til med at drikke. Naar de bleve fulde, begynte de at larme og klamres:

    Inqve repentinos convivia versa tumultus
    Assimilare freto possis, qvod svæva qvietum
    Ventorum rabies motis exasperat undis

Derpaa trak man Dolken, slukkede Lyset, og lod saa træffe hvem træffe kunde, hvorved stort Nederlag ofte skede saavel paa Venner som Uvenner.

3

Antiquarianism and Epistemic Virtue

Among Norwegian eighteenth-century scholars Gerhard Schøning (1722–1780) stands out, in part due to the large number of works he published and in part because of the great authority he is ascribed by his contemporaries. His main fields were history and antiquarianism, though some of his works also concern natural history. Moreover, Schøning worked as a topographer, and in minor works he discussed issues of economics and agricultural improvement, the reasons for bad crops and the question of public store houses for grain. In this chapter, Schøning's work will be employed to discuss the ways he navigated between different traditions of knowledge – what we today would recognize as different disciplines – and how he developed his arguments according to the various ideas of knowledge and scholarly work that these traditions represented. The main interest will be Schøning's antiquarian investigations. How did his understanding of antiquities and the task of the antiquary relate to his work with history on the one hand and to natural history on the other? The argument will be that if we are to understand the antiquarian tradition of this period, exploring its relationship to history is not sufficient. Ideals and methods from the new natural philosophy, not least natural history, must also be taken into account.

In 1751 Schøning was appointed principal (*Rektor*) of the cathedral school in Trondheim. He arrived in the city accompanied by his close friend, the Danish historian and nobleman Peter Frederich Suhm, and the two men started a productive scholarly companionship. In 1760 a scientific society was founded in Trondheim, initiated by the new bishop, Johann Ernst Gunnerus, and supported by Schøning and Suhm. It later acquired the formal name The Royal Norwegian Society of Sciences and Letters. Schøning's work during these years cannot be understood without considering the activities of the society and his collaboration with Suhm. In 1765 Schøning was appointed professor in history and rhetoric at the Sorø Academy in Denmark and left Trondheim. His scholarly profile changed and became more purely historian, though he also undertook extensive antiquarian and topographic journeys through parts of Norway in the years 1773–1775. The aim was to 'seek out and collect what might still be found concerning either the history of Norway or our antiquities and other such matters' (Schøning 1778: introduction).[1]

Schøning's major antiquarian work was finished as early as 1759 and published in 1762 (Daae 1880: 33). The extremely thorough *Beskrivelse over Dom-Kirken i Trondheim* (Description of the Cathedral in Trondheim) is still accepted as an important source on the history of the cathedral. When he died in 1780, manuscripts of two ambitious projects were left unfinished. One was a complete publication of Schøning's topographic and antiquarian journeys (the final volume was not to appear until 1926); the other was his ambitious study of the history of Norway, *Norges Riges Historie*. Two volumes had appeared so far; a third was published in 1781 with an introduction by Suhm. Schøning's original plan had been to write the history of Norway up to his own time. As it now exists, the work ends with the death of King Olav Tryggvason in 995.

Schøning's work appears to be a good example of Momigliano's thesis on history and antiquarianism as two separate lines of knowledge, but it also brings complexity to this picture. The phrase quoted above, where Schøning presents his aim to look for material that is relevant *either* to history *or* to antiquities, can be argued to reflect the idea that this represents two different ways of gaining knowledge about the past. However, this distinction is not easily followed into the text he published from the journeys. Schøning reports to have collected old diplomas and documents of historical interest. He also provides a number of descriptions of old churches (and some other buildings), runic inscriptions, standing stones and fields of ancient graves, but he does not explicitly discuss what kinds of knowledge these different types of material represent. Moreover, his methods – and the way he presents them – have explicit references to other traditions of knowledge, i.e., the new natural history. Schøning's work makes it clear that antiquarian work was more than history in a systematic rather than a narrative form, and that its basis in material evidence had a distinctive and independent epistemological value.

Facts from Stones

Originally the shrine of Norway's patron saint and christening king, St. Olav (d.1033), the cathedral of Trondheim had suffered severe damage and decay since the Reformation and Norway's subordination to Denmark in 1537. In the eighteenth century, large parts of the mediaeval structure lay in ruins. Schøning's explicit aim with his work was to show the ancient glory of the cathedral – and implicitly of the nation. The thorough and meticulous work gained Schøning a still lasting scholarly reputation. Today, the book is used as a historical source, but is also still considered to be a valuable scholarly work. Schøning's study situates itself within well-established frames of European antiquarianism, even if no exact model has been identified. The Scandinavian tradition, exemplified by Olof Rudbeck, Johan Peringskiöld and the Danish Bircherod family, contains no works that are directly comparable, neither in achievement nor method (Ekroll 2004; Eriksen 2007; J.M. Jensen 2008).

What distinguishes Schøning's book is above all the structure. A strong interest in the physical remains of the building dominates the work, and a thorough description of the structures and ornaments fills approximately its first half of the book. Since the Renaissance, antiquarian work had largely been occupied with documents, monuments, inscriptions and other remains that could give genealogical information about princes and nobility. As antiquarianism had an important legal strand, the genealogical investigations and the study of documents and inscriptions were closely related to an interest in the history of privileges, property and goods. The physical buildings or remains of buildings, on the other hand, had received far less attention. Architectural historian Françoise Choay observes that until the nineteenth century, 'conservation' of ancient buildings and physical structures mostly meant producing books of plates. Rarely were buildings repaired or maintained once they had passed out of use, and even highly cherished monuments were used as quarries or rebuilt for new purposes. Ancient buildings were important witnesses to past glory, but to preserve them, images were long held to be sufficient (Choay 1999; see also Sweet 2004: 242 and Chapter 4 in this volume). Erik Dahlberg's enormous work from the early eighteenth century, *Suecia antiqua et hodierna*, containing 353 engravings showing Swedish castles, fortresses and towns, is the best Scandinavian representative of this strand of the antiquarian tradition.

In the presentation of his model of the two traditions of knowledge about the past, Momigliano has pointed out that antiquarianism bore a close relation to natural history and the new natural philosophy (Momigliano 1990: 56f). Rosemary Sweet adds that the relation had a dual aspect. On the one hand, both naturalists and antiquaries were seen by their critics to waste time and resources in petty speculation and an obsession with detail. On the other, there was also an important epistemological and methodological connection between the two strands of scholarship. She summarizes the situation by saying that 'antiquaries and natural historians moved in similar circles, were governed by the same epistemological models, belonged to the same culture of inquiry, and in addition, habitually conducted their work within the same regional framework. The parish or county was the obvious unit within which to record and describe both natural history and antiquities' (Sweet 2004: 12).

Despite these pertinent observations, neither Momigliano nor Sweet has developed the perspective further. William B. Ashworth presents a more elaborate analysis. Investigating the developments of natural history in the period 1550–1650, he points out that 'the antiquarian spirit did have a considerable effect on natural history, because the two fields overlapped considerably. There was, after all, no firm line between the Saxon urn, the stone axhead, the fossilized shark tooth, the unicorn horn, the agate' (Ashworth 2003: 152). Natural historians who were exposed to the antiquarian attitudes to evidence developed new understandings. When artifactual evidence was made standard for determining truth, old humanist traditions became irrelevant, Ashworth claims. His argument points to the importance of considering the epistemological value of materiality in antiquarianism, as well as the methods and ideals that conditioned such a production of knowledge.

The relevance of natural history as a key to understanding Schøning's work on the cathedral is confirmed by his own introduction to the book. The aim is to please, Schøning declares, in particular to please his compatriots and fellow citizens. Nonetheless, to many people, his book will be uninteresting. This does not just apply to those lacking in judgment. The book is not written for foreigners, and to an Arab, not to say a Chinese, it will be without importance. Others will find the book quite useless due to its insignificant topic. Mustering a defence, Schøning asks – rhetorically – whether it is not the case

> that many books have been, and still are being, written about things that at first glance, and to an unskilled eye in particular, must be regarded as most insignificant, about flies, gnats, fleas, insects, mites etc.: which still are read with pleasure, when they are well written, and are not regarded as useless if not by persons who either have read just one book, or are without taste and knowledge of studies and the sciences (Schøning 1762: introduction).[2]

This is a defence of trifles. The insects are examples of the utmost trivialities. However, comparing a cathedral, albeit in ruins, to a gnat might seem a bit far-fetched, even if the aim is to create a dramatic effect. And the gnats are not alone; a whole range of insect species is mentioned. It can be argued that the enumeration not merely concerns the triviality of small and inconspicuous animals, but is a direct reference to the field of natural history.

Natural history never became a major issue with Schøning. His work on the aurora borealis concerns the age of the phenomena. Schøning has searched ancient texts for information that might pertain to the light and thus prove it to be of great age. His writings on agricultural improvement and (eventual) climatic change show the same penchant for employing historical material. Nonetheless, as a co-founder of The Royal Norwegian Society of Sciences and Letters, and a close friend of Gunnerus, he was well acquainted with the field and with the practices and methods that had become requirements for producing natural history knowledge in the eighteenth century. It is to this kind of knowledge and these ways of producing it that he refers in his introduction.

Lorraine Daston, historian of science, has described how the new-style naturalists of the seventeenth century quickly became the target of ridicule, especially due to the disproportional relationship between the object of study and the time, resources and passion involved. As has already been pointed out, this ridicule mirrors the scorn which had long been heaped upon the antiquaries. Their knowledge was deemed useless and the social consequences grave: 'Too much attention paid to the wrong objects spoiled one for polite society, as well as for the sober duties imposed by family, church and state. There was a pedantry of things as well as words, and the naturalists, passionate for microscopes or insects, bored their interlocutors by speaking of nothing else' (Daston 2004: 104). Again insects, due to their size and – apparently – utter insignificance, supplied the ultimate case. But there was also another side to this. Daston points out that the naturalists, thus accused of wasting energy and emotions, hastened to defend their position. By the eighteenth century this defence represented a tradition of its own, not least building on connections to natural theology. The naturalists' concern that the attention they lavished on nature could border on idolatry had its answer:

> Throughout the eighteenth century, natural theology – the worship of God through the study of his works – supplied the motivation and rationale for an expenditure of attention that contemporaries perceived as uncomfortably close to religious reverence. Entomologists were particularly fervent in their declarations that divine providence could be discerned in the design of a fly's wing or the industry of a beehive – in part to defend themselves against charges of triviality, but also in part to redeem even the most lowly objects as repositories of divine artistry and benevolence (Daston 2004: 105).

Entomology thus became the paradigmatic case for justification of the new natural philosophy. Even if Schøning's line of argument has no theological references, the logic is the same. The naturalists' defence of their pursuits supplied him with relevant and highly applicable rhetorical resources. Just like the study of insects, the detailed and resource-consuming study of a ruined edifice will produce insights into far larger and much more important matters, perhaps even more so than the study of conspicuous things. The work is thus not motivated by selfishness or unsuitable interests in the worthless or vain. Quite to the contrary, this utterly demanding work on humble things brings knowledge that is deeply useful, not just to those engaged in it, but also more generally. In Schøning's case, this knowledge is not about God the artisan, but about national grandeur and (now lost) splendour. Arguing for the utility of his work in this way, Schøning does not place it within an antiquarian tradition in particular, and he does not refer to other works of the same kind. On the other hand, neither does he present his own work as something conspicuously new. His line of argument situates the work on the cathedral confidently within a more extensive and well-established field including 'Logic, Metaphysics, Mathematics or Physics', which, according to Schøning, are the useful sciences in contemporary life (Schøning 1762: introduction).

Those who will appreciate the book are those who can recognize the amount of work needed to produce it, Schøning declares, in other words those who know the methodologies involved. Not everybody will understand 'how detailed one must collect and seek, if anything worthy is to be gained and as completely as possible, how carefully one has to watch, not to be deceived or to deceive others, and finally will understand what pains, patience and use of time all this must needs cost' (Schøning 1762: introduction). His description and evaluation of the work correspond well to what Daston has called a 'practice of heroic observation'. More than any professional status, this is what distinguished the new naturalists and was understood as a combination of talent, discipline and method, she maintains. Observation was much more than merely seeing, it was defined as a kind of mental as well as visual dissection (Daston 2004: 109f). To be communicated, the observations then had to be turned into descriptions, which meant rendering the dissected object into language. In this process, something happened: observations 'grew'. The texts, with all their details, became alarmingly lengthy. Also, their texture mirrored the structure of the observations, just as much as the object observed. Each object was shattered into a mosaic of details where even 'the tiniest insect organ loomed monstrously large'. The parts overwhelmed the whole; the small became larger than the big (Daston 2004: 12).

Schøning comments on these problems himself. Some might think the book should have been shorter, he says, and that that would have saved him costs and labour. But he does not agree to the objections and says that he cannot think of anything that might have been excluded if the text should be 'as complete as one of its kind ought to be' (Schøning 1762: introduction). The question is about more than the size or price of the book, it is a matter of method. The main aim has been to achieve 'completeness', which means following certain methodologies. Firstly, one has to make very strict and disciplined choices. The book is not long because Schøning has written down everything that occurred to him. He has selected only that which really concerns the project and just as systematically suppressed and excluded all that does not. Secondly, the relevant material has to be presented in the right order. The text must correctly replicate the spatiality inherent in the observations. Thirdly, reflection must be proper (*behørig*), which seems to mean well-considered, not rash and impulsive. Thus, Schøning can conclude that the very extensive character of his book is not coincidental, but rather the necessary outcome of his choice to follow the ideals of a certain kind of scholarship.

From Mortar to Grammar

Walking is the first step of the methodology. Schøning's declared intention of 'going through' the building must be understood quite literally. The dissection is structured by a movement through the church. Attention to the continual movement is maintained by regular insertions, such as 'coming from the chapter-house we now arrive at the southern nave' (Schøning 1762: 42) or 'from here one ascends by 19 steps of stairs to …' (Schøning 1762: 54). This means that the physical structure of the church is systematically transformed into the physical experiences of a human body: one walks, steps, ascends, descends, arrives, meets and leaves. In this way it becomes very clear that behind the observations there is an observer. Daston and Galison argue that the scientific observation, so highly cherished by Enlightenment naturalists, was more than a mere methodology; they call it a genuine 'technology of the self' (Daston and Galison 2007: 234). Following Foucault, they describe this as 'practices of the mind and body (most often the two in tandem) that mould and maintain a certain kind of self' (Daston and Galison 2007: 198). The observational techniques required keen senses, concentrated attention, patience and exactitude, and as examples they mention 'the frozen pose of the field naturalist, the delicate manipulations of the microscopist, the observatory vigils of the astronomer, the lab-note-book jottings of the chemist' (Daston and Galison 2007: 234). Schøning's disciplined walk may easily be added to the list.

Words describing the visual experience itself are, on the other hand, very scarcely used during this exercise. Instead Schøning tells us what *is* to be found at the various locations in the church. Despite the subjectivity inherent in the method of walking from post to post, continuously taking new standpoints, the observations themselves are presented without a correspondingly subjective perspective. The elements of architecture do not appear as seen *from* somewhere or *by* somebody; they just are there on the spot reached by the walker. The physical presence of the observer is vital to rendering the structure of the church comprehensible, to transforming it from mere material to sense data. But once there, the observer steps back for the observation itself.

The structure gained by walking this way is not just a means of grasping the building architecturally and spatially, but also temporally. On the one hand, the building in its entirety is presented as an organism with a lifespan now past. On the other hand, each part of the church also represents a phase in an organic life cycle, lived through by the observer who moves physically from the youth of the church, represented by the chapter-house, through the 'blooming' fashioning of the choir to its decay and old age, located in the ruined western nave and the facade. In this way, Schøning demonstrates a lively interest in the temporal dimension of history. He is not merely a chronicler of names, dates and deeds, but is also interested in change and development evolving within temporal frames. However, Schøning has no perspective that helps him connect his ideas about organic development to historical temporality. Despite his very thorough knowledge of the cathedral, he does not relate the differences in decoration and building styles to historical processes of development and change. Even if he is very much aware of the differences in the design of sculpture and decoration in the various parts of the church, he does not elaborate on style and draws no distinction between the Gothic and the Romanesque elements. Schøning declares that the entire cathedral is a 'Gothick building, though one of the most regular' (Schøning 1762: 28). The word 'Gothic' does not indicate style in a more specific way. It seems to be used traditionally, meaning barbaric and irregular, in contrast to classical and harmonious, and as a generic term for all mediaeval structures (Choay 1999: 56f). Instead, differences are related to the numerous kings, princes and bishops known from documents and history writing to have contributed to the improvement and embellishment of the cathedral. The crudest parts of the building are identified as the most ancient, but above all the variation is explained with reference to the respective rulers' wealth and power. The most elaborate high Gothic parts (choir and octagon) are thus seen as being built during the reign of the most powerful bishop.

Schøning presents his results in ways that mirror the structure established through the process of observation. A randomly selected passage from the description of the northern nave will serve as a starting point.

> On the northern side, the ambulatory starts with two steps, on which one enters it from the stairs of the tower, and is two feet wide, but 45 long. It has three *ARCADES,* one very tall in the middle, 16 feet wide, and two smaller ones on the sides, which are both 8 feet wide. The same have each had four **pillars**, apart from which there also have been two on each pillar between the *arcades,* and at each corner of the ambulatory two, which altogether makes 20; and their heads have been decorated partly by floral-works, partly by curled leaves, as also have the arches of the *arcades* with a list of the pyramidical excision, among numerous others. Over the *archivolt* of the largest *arcade* there has been, as if lying on the outside of the wall, a wide edge, which seems to bend inwards, and has, as can be seen on the outside, without doubt in the same way, where it ends, had two **heads** or postures (Schøning 1762: 55).[3]

With 142 pages of this kind, Schøning's description is very dense, and his presentation is rich in detail. As Daston pointed out, the attempt to communicate the visual dissection of the object observed also generates texts that appear broken and in some way fragmented. Transformed into text, the normally hierarchical relationship between small and large, few and numerous, part and whole, becomes one of juxtaposition, with the artificial balance of apparent uniformity as its outcome. Describing an arch of sixteen feet does not take twice as many words as describing one of eight feet, and a tall middle arch rises no higher above the lines of the book than the smaller lateral ones. Also, the (destroyed) ornamented moulding inside the church can be instantly compared with the (preserved) exterior one without spending time to go out to look, while twenty identical pillars do not have to be mentioned twenty (identical) times.

When the structure of the cathedral is presented textually, it is transformed and restructured, and the greater the ambition of detail and exactitude, the more profound is the transformation. The more detailed, the more distinct becomes the juxtaposition of large and small, high and low, middle and lateral, the more blurred becomes the rendering of the actual physical structure of the church. Transformed into facts, the stones of the building lose their specific weight, and the spatial relationship between actual blocks is substituted by the relationship between words printed on a page. What binds the structure together is no longer mortar, but grammar. As a result, Schøning's efforts to give a complete and comprehensive description of the church quite paradoxically end in producing a fragmented and incoherent picture. In Schøning's time the building was in bad repair and parts of it were no longer in use. Nonetheless, it was still a main church in the city and a cathedral. These aspects are veiled in Schøning's text. Even if the reasons above are all linguistic, the diligent work contributes strongly to making the cathedral appear as an antiquity in the way described by Bauman and Briggs: broken, shattered and incomplete (Bauman and Briggs 2003:76; and Chapter 2 in this volume).

For this change to take place, the observations, i.e., the sensorial impressions, have been turned into words. Terms, concepts and definitions all represent the carvings of the knife of dissection. Arches and achivolts, pillars, columns and cornices are cut out from the mass of stones and mortar and made separately discernible, clearly distinguished facts. Some of the words in use are Latinized terms from the vocabulary of classical architecture, and a number of them are explained in the text or in notes. In other cases, Schøning had to invent terms. Still in the northern nave of the church, he says that its archivolts are 'decorated with a frieze of the carving that we will call the *piramidical* [*sic*]'. The italicized word is followed by a note: 'Because it consists entirely of small pyramids or square knots, on each side of which is normally carved a triangle, or the smaller pyramids are hollowed' (Schøning 1762: 48 note f).[4] The composite pillars of the choir call for complicated descriptions and the development of specialized concepts. They 'have all been of white marble, and their base an *elliptic,* and in both ends arched, circle, wherefore we shall call these pillars *elliptic circular,* to separate them from the *cylindrical circular,* of which kind all those are, of which we so far have spoken' (Schøning 1762: 75).

The definitions explain the part of the church in question, informing the reader what words like 'cornice' (*karniss*) or 'podium' actually mean or how the elaborate composite pillars actually look. At the same time, precisely by being defined and explained, they make it clear that they themselves are not mere words, but rather tools to be applied in very specific procedures. With their help, the enormous edifice becomes a large but manageable amount of elements, parts and units. Once established, the terms and tools can then be employed to create elaborate descriptions:

> At last we come to the upper or second part of the outermost wall [of the choir], which in its foremost edge, towards the church on both sides, has **two** very tall *elliptic*-circular **pillars**, and their capitals embellished with two rows of flowers. The two windows on the south-eastern side have all together **three** *cylindrical*-circular **pillars**, with double flower-works above them, and their arches one row of the hollowed pyramidical carving between two rounded edges; above which, as well as up under the vaults, is another closed arch, with the same decoration and **two pillars** underneath, whose capitals also are embellished by double hollowed flower-work (Schøning 1762: 88).[5]

Epistemic Virtues

By means of words, the stones of the cathedral become facts. But what kind of facts do the words actually produce? Above all, Schøning is concerned with shapes and numbers. The terminology he develops, for example, in such expressions as 'piramidical carving' or 'elliptic circular' pillars, is first and foremost about forms and shapes. Once the shapes have been defined and given their names, they can be counted. Schøning seems obsessed with numbers. In every section of the book, elements are counted, as shown in this passage from the description of the choir:

> The interior wall of the choir also is an octagon, and has, when seen from the outside, **three windows** in each of its five sides, of which the middle one is higher, while the two others, which are closer to the eastern nave, have only two each, making altogether **nineteen**. [The arches of the windows reach the cornice, ending] with five ARCADES, the one taller than the next, and the one in the middle tallest of all, supported by 12 very tall and slender **pillars**, three and three together under each point of the *arcades,* though the edges or sides closest to the eastern nave each have only four *arcades* with **nine pillars** … (Schøning 1762: 81).[6]

This way of looking at the church presents us with a last connection to the period's new natural philosophy. Schøning conducts his research like any Linnean botanist would. With his definitions and terms, he establishes a taxonomy of the church, fixing its genera and species, even in some cases proposing a binominal nomenclature: 'elliptic circular'. Within these taxonomic frames, he counts the cathedral's arches, pillars, windows, capitals and so on as if he were counting the petals and stamen of a plant. He describes the shapes of its carvings, profiles and friezes. Using this method, his 142 pages reach a conclusion: the cathedral of Trondheim has 3,361 columns and pillars. It also has 316 windows, 40 sculpted figures and 343 smaller ones (though the original number of figurines must have been almost double this, according to Schøning).

Reaching these very precise results must have cost a tremendous amount of work. It has not only needed counting, recounting and adding up, it is also fundamentally based on the extensive taxonomic work of providing definitions and nomenclature. To arrive at these numbers, it is quite simply necessary first to decide what is what. Which elements belong to which category, and what *are* the categories? The numbers can have been no mere trifle to Schøning but are a real and significant result of his investigation.

The rigorously systematic character of Schøning's work makes it clear that antiquarian work was more than history's neighbour, more than one of the two twin traditions that converged into modern source-based history some decades later. Connections to natural history are fundamental. They concern practical and methodological issues of how to carry out an investigation through attentive observation, of 'dissection' and of the production of a text virtually devoid of narrative elements. Also important to a genuine historization of the antiquarian tradition is the way this methodology on a deeper level reflects a certain set of what Daston and Galison call epistemic virtues, basing their argument on Foucault's notion of technologies of the self (cf. above). Daston and Galison say that 'epistemic virtues in science are preached and practiced in order to know the world, not the self'. But 'as long as knowledge posits a knower, and the knower is seen as a potential help or hindrance to the acquisition of knowledge, the self of the knower will be an epistemological issue'. They conclude that 'epistemic virtues are virtues properly so-called: they are norms that are internalized and enforced by appeal to ethical values, as well as to pragmatic efficacy in securing knowledge' (Daston and Galison 2007: 39). The technologies of the self, as well as the actual methodology in use, thus can be understood as means of realizing the epistemic virtues held valid and obliging. This not only implies producing knowledge that also is valid but is just as much about shaping and maintaining a certain kind of scientific self.

In their discussion of objectivity, Daston and Galison argue that epistemic virtues, and the accompanying scientific selves, are historical and changing. New epistemic virtues emerge, and even if the older ones do not automatically disappear, they acquire new meanings in the new context. Daston and Galison show how the ideals of objectivity developed during the latter half of the nineteenth century, supplanting those which they call 'truth-to-nature'. The epistemic virtues of truth-to-nature are described by Daston as being characteristic of the natural philosophy and new natural sciences in the seventeenth and eighteenth centuries, i.e., those also shown to be at work in Schøning's investigation (Daston 2004). Thus, his way of working as well as his way of explaining his project – and of course his results – are not merely due to the use of certain methodologies or even to certain technologies of the self, but must fundamentally be seen as the materialization of these historically specific virtues. Schøning not only fulfilled the purpose of showing the ancient glory of his fatherland and its most important cathedral, but also demonstrated his competence in producing knowledge and shaping a scientific self according to valid ethical claims.

Schøning, the Historian

In his history of Norway (1771–1781), Schøning built on the results from his own earlier publications on history and on his collaboration with Suhm. The work was published during the period of Schøning's antiquarian-topographic journey, and about ten years after the study of the cathedral. Schøning's parallel production as a historian and an antiquary, respectively, opens a unique opportunity to compare the two genres, not merely with respect to contents and structure, but also in terms of the epistemic goals they were used to serve. The two lines of Schøning's work can be read into the Momiglianian model, but will at the same time offer possibilities for a closer investigation of the relationship between these two kinds of erudite work. A major difference is that in Schøning's history of Norway, references to material remains are extremely scarce. It does not appear to have been important to Schøning to locate the historical events in actual landscape, or to seek out material traces of them in the shape of such things as graves or standing stones. The 'game of identification', so eagerly played by the topographic authors (Chapter 2 in this volume), is not played here. Schøning does not try to establish correspondences between historical persons or events and specific material remains in his own time. One reason may be that inventories of antiquities in Norway did not exist, and that prior to his travels Schøning knew only small parts of the country from his own experience (Daae 1880: 47). Nonetheless, the differences between this work and the study of the cathedral are so considerable that other reasons obviously are relevant. Both works are the results of meticulous studies, but they are clearly based on different ideas of scholarly work and of knowledge about the past.

In the introduction to the first volume of *Norges Riges Historie,* Schøning self-confidently presented his work as the first proper history of Norway. The work of his predecessors is nothing but 'collections or store-houses', he declares, from which a proper history can be developed (Schøning 1771–81 1: introduction). Tormod Torfæus, who had published a Latin history of Norway in 1711 and for whom Schøning expressed high esteem in a number of instances throughout his own work, had 'collected, excerpted and translated everything that concerns Norway in our old histories, and particularly in Icelandic documents, but how much is not yet to be done? … He has left to others to arrange everything that he had collected in its right order, to place all things in their right time and their right place; in short to compose the history of Norway' (Schøning 1771–81 1: introduction).[7]

In his biography of Schøning, historian Ludvig Daae points out that the order and arrangement which Schøning called for included strong literary ambitions. Schøning wanted to write – or 'compose' – a pragmatic history, distinguished by rhetorical elegance and fulfilling didactic purposes (Daae 1880: 71f). In his obituary for Schøning, also printed as the introduction to the posthumous third volume of *Norges Riges Historie,* Suhm says that Schøning's great idol as a history writer was Polybius, whom he modelled his style after, a style that is 'clear, orderly, manly and, when the related events permit, beautiful' (Suhm quoted in Schøning 1980: introduction). Historians of the nineteenth century have offered less positive evaluations of Schøning's emulation of his idol. He was criticized for his 'far too strong wish to imitate Polybius; he is too much the pragmatist, judging events according to modern standards' (in Daae 1880: 82).[8] Schøning's 'polybian ambition' situates him within a tradition of pragmatic history. History should be truthful and clear in its presentation of causes and effects. The resulting structure would make the composition harmonious, and the lessons of history would be easy to understand. Both rhetoric and didactic qualities were important elements in this the production of knowledge.

It can thus easily be argued that *Norges Riges Historie* is composed according to the *magistra vitae topos* described by Koselleck, with an emphasis on the political (and in some cases moral) lessons to be drawn. It also puts great weight on correct chronology – a prerequisite for the causal analyses – and has its focus on political history, presenting the lives and deeds of princes and lords. The demand for exactitude of method, so clearly expressed in the investigation of the cathedral, have its parallel in Schøning's historical scholarship. However, the different setting influences the methodological issues. Even if Schøning takes a great interest in sources and their varying reliability when writing history, his methodological concerns are above all about literary style.

He is, for instance, quite vehement that on some occasions, eloquence and elegance in history will have to make way for scholarly exactitude and efforts to meet the challenges posed by a scarcity of reliable sources. Any educated person will understand that the historian has to seek

> as if with a lantern in his hand to collect or choose the material, then use scales to judge its value, then a square to fit it together. The situation presents one to other concerns than a play with words or to sprinkle history with elegant maxims, sayings, and other such flowers. It is true, that a number of passages could

> have given me the occasion for such reflexions, and I do not blame those, who
> embellish their history with them, when they are appropriately placed and
> used with care and moderation (Schøning 1771–81 1: introduction).[9]

For his own part, Schøning declares to have been fully occupied with what he calls 'the difficult illumination of history'.

Maxims and sayings were used to enhance the moral or political message in history, to make explicit the lessons to be learnt. Together with the insertion of speeches and 'quotes' allegedly from the historical agents themselves, these were distinctive and well-known features of the rhetorical tradition in history writing. Schøning's stand against them represented nothing new. It signals his stance in a debate that had been started by the humanists and further developed by the new critical philosophy of the seventeenth century (Grafton 2005). Schøning's reference to scales and squares expresses his wish for an exactitude that was distinctive to mechanics and the new sciences and for their precise tools to be applied to history as well. However, by adding a very explicit defence of the staple devices of rhetorical history (though used with moderation!), Schøning makes clear that he does not want to distance himself too far from this tradition.

Even if political history, chronologically ordered according to the lives of chieftains, kings and lords, dominates in *Norges Riiges Historie*, other themes also receive considerable attention. In his introduction to the second volume, Schøning declares his ambition not merely to write a history of political life and military events, but to present the ancestors 'in their activities, their customs, their house-life, their religion, their sports and their ideas'. As examples he mentions agriculture, commerce, laws and government, as well as magic, religious buildings and beliefs, and funeral customs (Schøning 1771–81 2: introduction). These are issues normally treated in antiquarian, not historical, works. When Schøning finds them relevant, it is because the real value of history is its ability to instruct about human disposition, human errors and human genius – as well as their causes and effects. Schøning urges his readers to study and admire the 'ancestors' and their way of life. Our forefathers distinguished themselves through 'a frugal way of life, bravery, great courage, love of their fatherland, practice of all kinds of sports; and by noble thoughts …' (Schøning 1771–81 2: introduction).[10] Phrases such as these leave no doubt that Schøning considers history to be *magistra vitae*, but it is also evident that the most important lessons to be drawn are not about political life. Neither are they aimed at kings and leaders in particular. The lessons of history rather take their material from the traditional fields of antiquarianism, and concern moral conduct and civil life.

Throughout *Norges Riiges Historie* a number of excursuses are inserted to treat this kind of issue. The starting point is usually an actual event. The frames of general chronology are not broken and the structure remains true to Schøning's declared intention to switch between an 'epochal' and an 'episodical' presentation (Schøning 1771–81 1: introduction). Despite the insertion of the excursuses, the text never acquires the more systematic form distinctive to antiquarian studies. Mainly literary sources are used, and in some cases comparisons are made to the customs of other nations; for instance funeral customs among 'the ancestors' are compared to those of the Tatars. The natural history of Pliny is also evoked to argue that burying the dead in the earth is the most ancient and natural burial method (Schøning 1771–81 2: 378). References to material remains are scarce even here, and when they do occur, they are given in a very general way. Again, this may be due to the lack of more specific knowledge, but even here other elements also seem to play a part. In the comparatively few instances where Schøning does refer to still existing material remains, as in the case of the mounds whose traditional names were held to be the tombs of heroes known from Norse literature, they receive no more than a mention. Mounds and other artefacts are not presented as evidence in themselves, not even potentially, but figure rather as phenomena whose significance is supplied by the literary sources. They are not used to find out more about the funerary customs of the ancestors, but merely treated as confirmation of textual information about burials. Despite Schøning's explicit interest in phenomena beyond those regularly treated in histories based on literary sources (the lives and deeds of kings and heroes), it does not seem that he considers ancient objects as possible sources for anything else than what is already known from the texts. Material remains are not ascribed independent evidential value in history. Literature remains the primary source, and combining small pieces of evidence from a number of texts is the preferred method. Considering Schøning's great reliance on material evidence in his study of the cathedral, the stance may seem surprising.

The reason seems to be that the kind of truth that interested Schøning in this work was historical. As has been pointed out above, that implied composing a harmonious structure of causes and their effects in a correct chronological order. It also meant presenting narratives that could be instructive to the readers and impart clear lessons of history. Despite the switching between the epochal and the episodic form, this idea of the writing of history left no room for the nonnarrative explorations of the evidence of material remains. Information that could be drawn from such evidence did not contribute to the real tasks of a history writer. It was not causal or narrative and was not ascribed exemplary value. Thus, Schøning's inclusion of topics usually treated by antiquaries in his history does not imply that he actually blurred the two traditions of knowledge. The systematic exploration of material evidence remained irrelevant to history.

Other reasons must then be found for Schøning's inclusion of themes that normally were treated by antiquarians in his historical work. While Momigliano and others (Sweet 2004: 29f) have argued that the systematic methods of the antiquaries fuelled the birth of the modern discipline of source-based history and the gradual dissolution of rhetorical history, Mark S. Phillips proposes other perspectives on the development. According to him, what happened during the late eighteenth and early nineteenth century was not that history stopped being rhetorical and pragmatic, but that its rhetoric changed, as did also its audience. Traditionally a part of the education of princes and nobility, history emphasized political life and military deeds and served to enhance the glory and support the political legitimacy of this or that dynasty. During the eighteenth century, however, the reading public grew. It now included men and women from the emerging bourgeoisie, who found that their way of life and their interests were not – as yet – included in history. To keep its old function of *magistra vitae*, this meant that the range of topics treated in historical works had to be extended to include commerce and civil life. Also, as this new audience had a highly developed competence as 'sympathetic readers', history had to be told in new ways. The readers demanded narratives that allowed them to engage in moral and emotional questions and that made it possible to identify with the historic persons. This situation led to great creativity and to experiments with new genres (Phillips 2000). Phillips argues that to understand the development, it is necessary to consider a far wider range of books and genres than those traditionally included in the history of history writing. Memoirs, dairies, literary history and even novels are among his recommendations (Phillips 1996, 2000).

Schøning's wish to include the whole way of life of the 'ancestors' in his history of Norway fits well into this picture. So does his argument that history is more than the military exploits of great warriors. The issues addressed by Schøning in his excursuses concern mainly, but not exclusively, civil life. For a great part, their relevance to Schøning's own time is also strong. Patriotism is an overarching theme, as is also the issue of national character. Schøning is vehement that people in Norway ought to live according to the climate and geography of their own country rather than seek to imitate foreigners – 'as we now for a long time have done' (Schøning 1771–81 2: introduction). Better to emulate the forefathers. More specifically this urge to imitate concerns the practice of sports (particularly skiing), the bringing up of children (no pampering) and the choice of food and drink (a frugal diet without alcohol, tea or coffee) (Schøning 1771–81 1: 20ff).

As a historian, then, Schøning remains true to the classical ideals of harmonious narrative about causes and effects, chronological order and clear lessons to be learnt. Antiquarian competence, though acquired through the study of the cathedral, does not interfere with his historical work. Topics that also are found in antiquarian studies are included, but 'transformed' into history. They are presented as exemplary lessons of history, for a large part pertaining to civil life and in a number of cases with a very clear address to contemporary issues. Information that might have been gained through the study of artefacts and material remains is not included, and the narrative is not fractured by a more systematic treatment of this kind of source material.

The investigations in this and the preceding chapter have explored some of the differences that distinguished the two approaches to the past from each other. They concern method and material as well as epistemology. They also concern scholarly ideals and epistemic virtues. Both history and antiquarianism explore the past, but they do so in ways that affiliate them to different neighbouring disciplines. Pragmatic history makes no secret of its close relation to literature and rhetoric, and the correspondence between antiquarianism and natural history should not be underestimated. Despite the differences, though, both history and antiquarianism were based on the same experience of temporality. To neither tradition was the past 'a foreign country'. It was, rather, a parallel but incomplete universe. The past had taken place in well-known locations, whose geography and structure generally overlapped with the space of experience of the scholars who described it. If the past was enigmatic, this was due mainly to its fragmentary character, not to remoteness or any profound difference. Moreover, antiquaries generally had an idea that they nonetheless knew much of what was lacking – it could be read out of histories and confirmed through the study of inscriptions, coins and documents.

NOTES

1. [A]t opsøge og samle hvad endnu kunde være at finde, enten den Norske Historie eller vore Old-Sager og andre saadanne Ting vedkommende.

2. [O]m ikke mange Skrivter ere skrevne og endnu skrives om Ting, som ved første Øiekast, i sær i ukyndiges Øine, maae ansees for meget ringe, om Fluer, Myg, Lopper, *Insecter,* Mider &c: som dog læses med fornøielse, naar de ere vel skrevne, og som ikke ansees for unøttige uden af Folk, som enten have kun læst een Bog, eller have ingen Smag og Indsigt i Studeringer og Videnskaber.

3. Paa Nordre Side begynder Omgangen med tvende Trin, paa hvilke man fra Taarn-Trappen stiger op i den, og er tvende Fod bred, men 45 lang. Den har trende AR-CADER, en meget høi i midten, 16 Fod bred, og tvende mindre paa begge Sider af den, som ere i Bredden hver 8 Fod. Samme har hver for sig havt fire **Pillarer,** foruden hvilke der endnu paa hver Pille mellem *Arcaderne* have været tvende, og ved hvert Hjørne af Omgangen og tvende, hvilket bliver tilhobe 20; og har deres Hoveder været stafferede deels med Blomster-Verk, deels med krusede Blade, ligesom og *Arcader*nes Buer med en Liste af den piramidiske Udhugning, mellem adskillige andre. Oven omkring den

største *Arcades Archivolte,* har gaaet, ligesom uden den paa Muren, en bred Kant, der ligesom bøier sig ind ad, og har, som uden til sees, uden Tvil paa samme Maade, hvor den endes, havt 2de **Hoveder** eller Postyrer.

4. Fordi den bestaae af lutter smaa Piramider eller firekantede spidse Knuder, paa hvilke hver Kant eller Side igien er gemeenligen udhuggen i en Triangel, eller og de smaa Piramider udhulede.

5. Nu komme vi endelig til den yttre Muurs øverste eller anden Afdeling, som i de foreste Kanter mod Kirken har paa begge sider tvende meget høie elliptisk-runde Pillarer, og deres Hoveder zirede med to Rader Blomster. De tvende Vinduer paa Syd-Østre Side har tilsammen **Tre** *cylindrisk*-runde **Pillarer**, med dobbelt Blomster-Verk over, og deres Buer en Rand af den hule piramidiske Udhugning mellem to runde Lister; over hvilke, saa vel som op under Hvelvningen, gaaer en anden lukt bue, med samme Staffering og **Tvende Pillarer** under, hvis Hoveder og ere zirede med dobbelt hult Blomster-Arbeide.

6. Den indere Chorets Muur er ogsaa en Ottekant, og har, saa vidt deraf udvendig kan sees, i hver af de fem Kanter **tre vinduer**, hvoraf det i Midten er det høieste, men i de tvende andre, som ere det Østre Kors nærmest, og vende derimod, kun tvende i hver, tilsammen **Nitten**. [Over Vinduerne i hver Kant gaaer fra begge Sider af dem en Afsats eller Liste op i en spids til det øverste af Muren under Carntisen af Taget, og giør en spidsig Fronton], med fem ARCADER under, den ene høiere end den anden, og den i Midten høiest, understøttet af 12 meget høie og smale Pillarer, tre og tre sammen under hver Spids af *Arcaderne:* dog har de tvende Kanter eller Sider, som ere det Østre Kors nærmest, kun hver for sig fire *Arcader* med **Ni Pillarer** ...

7. [H]avde af de gamle Skribenter, men af de islandske Documenter især samlet, udtrukket og oversat alt, hvad der løber ind i den norske Historie, men hvor meget blev endnu ikke tilbage i den norske historie at forrette? ... men at bringe, hvad han har samlet i behørig Sammenhæng; at henføre enhver ting til sin rette Tid og sit rette Sted, kort, at forfatte deraf det Norske Riiges Historie, det har han alt sammen overladt til andre at udføre.

8. [E]n altfor kjendelig Higen efter at efterligne Polybius; han vil formeget pragmatisere, bedømmer Forholdene efter en nyere Tids Maalestok.

9. [L]igesom med Lygten i Haanden, for at samle eller vælge Materialier, nu med Vægten, for at prøve deres Værdie, nu med Vinkel-Hagen, for at passe dem tilsammen. Her faaer man andet at tænke og at passe paa, end at spille med Ord, eller at bestrøes Historien med ziirlige Maximer, Sentenser og andre saadanne Blomster. Sandt nok, at mange Steder kunde have givet mig anledning til Reflexioner; jeg laster ei heller dem, som udpynte deres Historie dermed, naar de anvendes paa det rette Sted, eller bruges med Skiønsomhed og Maade.

10. [I] en tarvelig Levemaade, i Tapperhed, i et høit mod, i Kiærlighed til Fædrenelandet, i at lægge Vind paa allehaande Lægems Øvelser, i en ædel Tænkemaade ...

⊱• 4 •⊰

Ruins and Time

With the exception of Schøning, antiquaries in eighteenth-century Norway took little interest in old buildings or remains of buildings. One reason might be that they could not be related to the heroic world of old Norse literature, as no building was older than the Middle Ages. Considering the general ignorance about the exact age of ancient constructions (see, e.g., Chapter 5 in this volume on the age of the stave churches), it is, however, of greater relevance that a lack of interest in built constructions can be regarded a common feature of the antiquarian tradition (Choay 1999; Sweet 2004; Hartog 2003). As was pointed out in Chapter 3, drawings were long held to be sufficient to preserve the memory of a building. This has made Choay develop the term 'iconographic preservation' (Choay 1999: 70). What was important was not the physical structures as such, but to save the *memory* of a building and its history. The actual buildings were used as quarries or demolished so their sites could be put to other use. Only fragments of sculptures or inscriptions were collected, studied and conserved, either for their artistic value or because they were ways to keep alive the memory of persons and genealogies. In her investigation of the antiquarian tradition, Rosemary Sweet argues that 'preservation' of ruins long meant 'ensuring that the intangible memory of those whose lives and devotion it commemorated were saved from oblivion' (Sweet 2004: 242). She further underlines that the buildings or ruins themselves rarely were used as the main sources of knowledge about their own history: 'The materials with which ecclesiastical antiquaries worked were therefore primarily textual ones: the charters granted to monasteries, the endowment of churches, the epitaphs and inscriptions to be found within. The physical structure of the church itself was very much a secondary consideration' (Sweet 2004: 242). Ruins were simply demolished buildings. Their decay could be lamented, but what could be more specifically gained from the buildings were still just fragments of knowledge about such things as genealogy. This also was the really important knowledge, worthy of being saved from oblivion. Apart from this, the physical remains of buildings were not of antiquarian interest.

A Nordic example of this kind of antiquarian work is Magnus Borænius' dissertation on Vreta Abbey in Östergötland in Sweden, defended at the University of Uppsala in 1724. The abbey, established in the early twelfth century, had close relations to royalty, its first abbess being Ingegerd, a sister of King Karl Sverkersson. After the Reformation, the buildings decayed. Modern excavations and restoration of the still quite imposing ruins started in 1916. Of Borænius' antiquarian work, only one of the forty-eight pages (in the modern Swedish translation) is actually about the buildings at Vreta. The rest of his text examines, for example, the name of the abbey, its foundation and founders, the Cistercian Order, the properties and incomes of the abbey and – not least – the royal graves in the church. About the building, Borænius says that it is difficult to describe, 'as it shows itself in another form than before. In some way I shall still try to present it, even if it has been forsaken for so long a time' (Borænius 1724/2003: 19).[1] According to Borænius, the building he is going to describe hardly exists anymore. What is left of it provides little information about what has been and is not attributed independent value of any kind. A huge tree has grown up in the interior of the abbey, and Borænius uses it to argue that the roof of the building must have been lost long ago – as it takes considerable time for a tree to grow so tall. Apart from this simple observation, based on the temporality of organic growth, the present state of the building is not used as a point of departure for any analysis of its original plan or the history of the edifice.

Borænius has applied his energy to the study of documents related to the abbey and to the inscriptions on the royal tombs. Words and text are what represent the links to the past, rather than the materiality that carries them. Both documents and inscriptions are reprinted in the thesis and obviously represent Borænius' main concern. His view corresponds well with Sweet's argument above and also with the more general lack of interest in material remains as transmitting information independent of literary sources, as pointed out above (cf. Chapter 2 in this volume). The abbey is considered for what it has once been and for the people who have lived and died there, not for what is has become or what it is at present. Its present state is nothing but deplorable: Very much inferior to the original and in itself devoid of any interest.

Greetings to the author on the occasion of his completed work confirm that the issue is not the physical remains of the abbey but rather the memories of past lives and devotion. The vicar of Vreta, Z.Z. Reuserus writes:

> How painful it is and how difficult to dig out of the hidden realms of history
> which seems to contribute to the honour of the Swedish and Gothic people,
> or to renew the memory of the ancient monuments. But the deed is equally
> beautiful and meritorious. In this way, models of virtue are veritably presented
> to our descendants, which they can imitate. The ancient monuments of our

fatherland, seemingly overgrown with greenery and oblivion are restored to their former glory. They are fittingly brought to light and to the sight of the people, even those who have never before seen them with their own eyes (Boraenius 1724/2003: 48).[2]

The task of the antiquarian is to preserve memory. At the same time, the greeting expresses very clearly that this idea of memory is closely related to an understanding of history as *magistra vitae:* The memory in question concerns the ancient glory of the fatherland and the meritorious lives of the 'Gothic people' who inhabit it.

Rudera: Decay, Vestiges and Remains

Sweet has made the important observation that the language and terminology available to describe the more or less decayed buildings and constructions was rather limited for quite some time (Sweet 2004: 242). The analysis of Schøning's work on the cathedral pointed out that part of his work consisted of constructing a terminology for the description of architectural elements. Even more important is the fact that a generic term for speaking about the buildings and constructions themselves was largely lacking: the word 'ruin' only gradually gained acceptance during the late eighteenth century. In the Scandinavian languages of Danish, Swedish and Norwegian, its occurrence is comparatively recent and mostly to be found from the nineteenth century onwards. In older texts, the Latin word *rudera* is used, or the Nordic equivalents *levninger* (vestiges) or *rester* (remains). The terminology reflects that ruins are not yet a separate category, neither as physical monuments, as historical sources or as aesthetic objects. Rudera is simply a matter of decayed or collapsed buildings. The vestiges are undefined in themselves and are mentioned only as by-products of what they have been.

The terminological shift from rudera to ruins will be the main interest of this chapter. The shift occurred in the latter part of the eighteenth century and will be taken here to reflect a new experience of time. The actual, physical remains of decayed and deteriorating built constructions became monuments in their own right. They were associated with values and meanings that were specific to their present state and only vaguely referential to what they had once been. What was seen as interesting was rather the temporal distance between then (the original building) and now (the ruin). It was this temporality itself that was seen as materialized in the ruin, in ways that an intact ancient building never could outdo. As monuments in their own right, ruins came to be the embodiment of time and of the difference and change brought about by it. The past was no longer an incomplete, but parallel, universe.

Little attention has so far been paid to the discrepancy of meaning between the two terms 'ruin' and 'rudera', neither in scholarly literature nor in translations of Latin texts: ruderae is normally translated as ruins, not as vestiges or remains. The modern Swedish translation of Borænius text says 'ruin' where the Latin original has 'rudera'. Another example is Erik Dahlberg's work *Suecia antiqua et hodierna* (see Chapter 3 in this volume). It contains more than 350 plates, presenting ancient and recent Swedish castles, fortresses, churches, abbeys and so on, all supplied with brief descriptions in Latin. When the texts were translated into modern Swedish in 1924, the Latin terms *ruderae, vestigiae* and *reliquiae* were all translated as *ruiner* (see Dahlberg 1716). Along with the terminology, the modern concept of ruins has been anachronistically transferred to a period when the remains of old buildings were nothing but silent vestiges (e.g., L.D. Cnattingius and N. Cnattingius 2007; Woodward 2001). The ideas and values conveyed by the modern term have become so self-evident as to appear inherent in sheer masonry and are projected from the material remains back into the past.

The absence of a proper terminology is noticeable in the answers to the 1743 questionnaire (Chapter 2 in this volume). The lack of terminology was not only accompanied by a lack of interest, it also conferred a kind of invisibility on the constructions in question: even large edifices were treated as if they did not exist. Some of the questions concerned royal castles and fortresses as well as 'antiquities'. The respondents frequently and vehemently stress that they are writing about decayed, demolished and abandoned buildings, implicitly without value or importance. Their answers consequently are quite short and signal clearly that what is being described are constructions to which little value of any kind is attached. *Rudera* is the generic term used in the texts.

The church of the former abbey at Gimsøy in Southern Norway is reported to contain the tombs of several noble persons, but we are also informed that the building 'for a long time has been left to decay, and according to a decision by the late honourable *geheimeråd* Mr. Adaler is no longer in use. In its stead a pretty wooden building has been erected' (Røgeberg 2003–05 1: 68).[3] This new, wooden chapel is mentioned by several civil servants of the region, and it is obvious that they see it as far more important and noteworthy than the remaining walls of the abbey. The new building was practically useful, functioning as the local chapel and therefore deserving of the words 'pretty' and 'stately'. It also seems more important to report the meritorious deed of the noble Mr. Adaler than to describe the old monastery. It is this deed, not the walls of the ancient building, that is 'historical', in the sense of exemplary. In this context, the decaying walls serve above all to mark the contrast between the useless and the meritorious.

The large mediaeval castle in the city of Tønsberg, south of Oslo, had also suffered from severe decay. In 1743 it is described as 'very ancient' and 'destroyed', after being ravaged by fire during the war with Sweden in 1503. The county judge (*stiftamtmann*) von Rappe writes that Tønsberg is

> [t]he most ancient town of Norway and was in its time large and famous, but has been destroyed and reduced to ashes by the large fire that ravaged it more than 200 years ago, and in the centre of the town there has been a castle that was erected on a mountain which can be seen at the end of the town, and on the same mountain vestiges of the mentioned castle can still be seen (Røgeberg 2003-05 1: 56).[4]

Even though Tønsberg is the oldest town in the country, and once has been both large and powerful, the ruins of the castle are not presented either as a *vanitas* symbol or as historic monument, but simply as rudera, vestiges, the remains of something that no longer exists – it is nothing but 'lime, bricks and stones', according to von Rappe (Røgeberg 2003–05 3: 346).[5] The construction has no practical use, and its remains carry no message save that of decay and demolition. At the time, the vestiges consisted of a wide circular wall with remnants of numerous towers, in addition to the remains of three large brick and stone buildings, among them a church. The castle hill rises almost eighty meters above the city centre. But despite its size and dominant position, the fortress remains practically invisible in the civil servants' answers to the questionnaire, it is barely mentioned. The vestiges did not belong to any clear-cut category and were not defined as interesting or meaningful, neither aesthetically nor relating to antiquarian work.

Even more invisible are the remains of the mediaeval cathedral of Hamar, in south-central Norway. The mediaeval town of Hamar had been abandoned and the cathedral left as an enormous hill of gravel and rubble, out of which poked the arched top of the southern arcade. The bishop's castle, situated east of the church, was equally derelict, but parts of it had been put to use as a barn. Some buildings of the Storhamar estate had also been built into the gravel heap that rose high above them. Nevertheless, von Rappe says that 'the farm Storhamar … is situated at Hedemarck in the place where the town of Hamar once stood, of which no vestiges no longer remain' (Røgeberg 2003–05 1: 70).[6] According to him, nothing is to be seen of the old glory. The arcade and the gravel hill do not seem to have caught his eye.

Ruin Romanticism

How and when did *rudera* become ruins? And what *is* a ruin, other than a decayed building? What defines it is obviously not the material decay itself, but a specific understanding of the destruction and the meanings of the processes that bring it about. The ruin is the product of a certain kind of discourse, a way of ascribing value and meaning to certain kinds of decay. This discourse was born in the eighteenth century and is integral to romanticism. It was informed by aesthetic theories of the sublime as well as the picturesque (e.g., Bale 2009), transforming the understanding of what had so far merely been considered for what it had been and deploring its present state. In his broad presentation of ruin motifs in Western painting, the art historian Michel Makarius demonstrates how ruin iconography and its meanings have changed over time. In Renaissance art, ruins frequently occur in nativity scenes. The stable is painted as the ruins of a classical building, with columns, arches and cornices. These elements serve several functions. They bear witness to Renaissance rediscovery of antiquity and the admiration for classical culture, but they also work as an allegory of heathendom defeated by Christianity. The decayed or collapsed buildings create a contrast to the new life and salvation promised by the Child (Makarius 2004). Even if these scenes convey an understanding of historical phases and change, their idea of history differs greatly from that of the eighteenth century. In these pictures the ruins do not speak about the passing of time, of the insignificance of human beings and the perishability of all worldly things. Their message is far more specific, about how different 'reigns' and traditions follow each other according to a divine plan. The pictorial elements do not refer to eternal, existential issues, but are specific indexical signs of the various traditions involved. In her study of the evaluation of ruins during the Renaissance, Sabine Forero-Mendoza points out that the lamentations over the lost grandeur of Rome only very rarely referred to specific buildings or to the exact topography of the city. Also, it is more the destruction as such, and its products of dust, ashes and spoils that are evoked, not the actual ruins. Poets and antiquaries alike lamented what had once been, but did not consider the existing ruins as independent monuments of the temporality involved (Forero-Mendoza 2002: 39ff).

During the Renaissance and afterwards only remnants of buildings from Greek and Roman antiquity were invested with this interest. Their message was related to the dominant view of antiquity and the ideas of the classical as representing something very different from a historical epoch in the modern sense of the word. Instead, antiquity was seen as a pattern and an ideal, the realization of values of timeless worth and validity transcending the fleeting changeability of human life and human history. In this context, ruins spoke about the loss of the perfect form and perfect beauty of classical art and architecture, and they also represented a call to restore these ideals. Hartog has argued that the Renaissance idea of restoration was very different from the modern. It meant to repair, reconstruct or recover, it might even mean to replace something that had been destroyed or ruined with completely new works. He sees this as specific to the historicity regime of the Renaissance: ancient buildings or pieces of art were not regarded as valuable because of their age, but because of their perfection. A restoration meant restoring this perfect state and did not by necessity imply the repair of decayed old pieces (Hartog 2003: 172f). In this sense restoring the perfection of antiquity simply meant bridging the gap – the Middle Ages – that had inserted itself between this period and the 'modern times' of the Renaissance. To this end, producing new works was just as efficient as repairing the old and decayed ones.

During the eighteenth century, the meaning of ruins changed radically. It was decisive to this development that the ruin now became an autonomous aesthetic object and a topic of independent aesthetic reflections. In 1765 the *Encyclopédie* defined 'ruin' as a pictorial genre:

> Ruin is a term in painting for the depiction of almost entirely ruined buildings: 'beautiful ruins'. The name 'ruin' is applied to a picture representing such ruins. 'Ruin' pertains only to palaces, elaborate tombs, or public monuments. One should not talk of 'ruin' in connection with a rustic or bourgeois dwelling; one should then say 'ruined buildings' (English version from Makarius 2004: 81).

The text points out that a ruin is not any decayed building but that the term refers to an artistic presentation of certain kinds of decayed and partly destroyed constructions. They are no longer explicitly classical, but still have to have a certain grandeur.

The aesthetics of ruins found in the *Encyclopédie* was developed by Diderot and closely related to the ideas of the sublime (Makarius 2004: 81f). The sublime, understood as a transcendental experience of greatness, was originally related to the appreciation of dramatic natural scenes and natural forces: mountains (above all the Alps), glaciers, volcanoes, maelstroms, thunderstorms, even earthquakes. In his essay 'A Philosophical Enquiry into the Origin of Our Ideas of the Sublime and Beautiful' from 1756, Edmund Burke argued that the sublime and the beautiful were mutually exclusive: beauty is that which pleases us, while the sublime has the power to compel and destroy. Makarius describes the sublime as an interplay between the attractive and the repulsive: 'The sublime ought thus to be understood as the esthetic and psychological expression of a fundamental principle: man and nature are subjected to conflicting *forces*' (Makarius 2004: 84, italics in original). He refers to the philosopher Georg Simmel, who points out that this principle is demonstrated in the ruin, which unites two opposite forces. On the one hand is man's 'will to erect buildings on the principle of verticality; on the other, nature tends to erode or flatten them' (Makarius 2004: 84). It should be added that when this understanding of the sublime is attached to ruins – differently from the case of, for instance, storms or volcanoes – the forces that are at work are not merely those of nature, but also of time. When it comes to ruins, experiencing the sublime is not a matter of witnessing strong natural forces that produce sudden and dramatic change, but of contemplating the slow and unrelenting processes working in time.

Diderot's poetics of ruins was above all developed in his texts of art criticism, published as *Ruines et paysage, Salon de 1767* (Bukdahl, Delon and Lorenceau 1995). His point of departure is paintings – 'ruins' as the genre is defined in the *Encyclopédie* – by the French artist Hubert Robert, who came to be known as *Robert des Ruines*. Compared with earlier years, Diderot here develops new methods for his criticism. Mixed with his description and evaluation of each work, he now presents more general reflections on philosophical and aesthetic questions (Bukdahl 1995: 5ff). The method is extensively applied to the discussion of Robert's pictures, where Diderot 'sketches a poetics of ruins with far more wide-reaching perspectives than those intended by the artist himself' (Bukdahl 1995: 10, my translation). He reprimands Robert because the paintings, according to his (Diderot's) view, contain too many figures and too many anecdotic genre scenes, saying 'M. Robert, you do not yet know enough about why ruins give such pleasure, regardless of the varieties of accidents they reflect'. To explain himself, he exclaims:

> The ruins arouse great ideas in me. Everything is shattered, everything perishes, everything passes. Only the world is lasting. Only time is lasting. How it is old, this world! I move between two eternities. Wherever I cast my glance, the objects that surround me announce an end ... (Diderot 1767/1995: 338, my translation).

Diderot's perspective turns the painting of ruins into a reflection upon basic conditions of human existence and not least on the temporal dimension. Literary scholar Else Marie Bukdahl underlines the close ties to Burke's discussions of the sublime and shows that Diderot's poetics of ruins heralds the coming of German painter Caspar David Friedrich's works from the first decades of the next century (Bukdahl, Delon and Lorenceau 1995: 12ff). Makarius, on the other hand, points out that Diderot's poetics of ruins have been highly influential in a more general context of cultural history: Today, the texts from 1767 may appear commonplace, even kitschy. The 'great ideas' aroused in Diderot have become common property, parts of popular romanticism, sentimental clichés. It may be difficult to understand the full originality of Diderot's thinking due to the process of naturalization that his ideas have since been subject to, Makarius argues. But just for this reason it is important to emphasize that the texts contributed heavily to transforming the ruins from *rudera* and more or less meaningful elements of scenery, to autonomous philosophical and aesthetic objects (Makarius 2004: 111).

Makarius' presentation of ruins in Western pictorial art has a close parallel in Carl Fehrman's discussion of ruins in Western literature. Like Makarius,

Fehrman emphasizes the role of the ruin as the *vanitas* motif in early romanticism. The ruin became a symbol of the futility and transitoriness of all human effort. Fehrman interprets this as the opposite of the preceding classicism and its cult of antiquity as a timeless ideal. Even if the ruins of early romanticism still were Greek or Roman, their meaning had changed. Their message was no longer centred upon the eternal ideals of classical culture and classical beauty, but came to treat more generally human, existential problems relating to life and death, time and transitoriness (Fehrman 1956). As part of this transformation, the temporality embodied in the ruins gained new and independent value. Temporality became sublime, the past distant and different, and the ruin a means to contemplate the processes that created these differences.

Sensibility and National Glory

The 'great ideas' that ruins inspired were gradually connected to the various national pasts of European countries, rather than to classical antiquity. Returning from their grand tour through Europe to Italy, the Northerners, in particular the British, started to discover the mediaeval ruins of their own countries. These buildings and their ruins had long been seen as far too lacking in harmony, too barbaric and irregular to be the objects of positive evaluations. But as classicism made way for romanticism, even the domestic Gothic ruins found their place in the aesthetic universe. In part, this was due to a reevaluation of the Middle Ages as a historical epoch and the fact the mediaeval ruins could be associated with the national pasts. In part it was also due to the preference of the romantic aesthetic for the irregular, the incomplete and the fragmentary – including ruins. Fehrman argues that ruins were not merely sublime, they might also hold a position within the other important category of romantic aesthetics: The ruin was the picturesque fragment incarnate (Fehrman 1956: 85ff).

Mediaeval ruins became a favoured element in poetry and painting, but also a much sought after blessing in the fashionable 'English' gardens. The ethnologist Tine Damsholt states that the new gardens served to stage the individual as emotional subject, 'as they were planned with the idea of arousing changing emotions and moods in the visitors. Specific kinds of scenery were linked to certain emotional effects, in such a way that a fixed repertoire of causal relationships between scenery and emotion was established' (Damsholt 2000a: 158, my translation). Ruins became part of this encoded language, in the same way as did grottoes, pagodas, hermitages, temples, pavilions and different kinds of altars, tombs and monuments. If mediaeval structures already were present, things were simple and the ruin was incorporated in the planning of the garden's paths and prospects. Less fortunate proprietors solved this problem by constructing sham ruins, in the same way as others installed artificial waterfalls, built grottoes and made empty graves surrounded by poplars and weeping willows (Fehrman 1956: 98f; Damsholt 2000a: 158).

It is not easy to discover how widespread the sham ruins actually were, among other things because the difference between them and other popular *fabriques*, like hermitages, Gothic follies and so on, was not always so clear (J.D. Hunt 2003: 41f). But whatever the case, the sham ruins drew much attention and soon gained a position as the very symbol of an exaggerated cult of sensibilities, where the sentimental had become more important than the authentic. It might therefore be fair to point out that the garden ruins – sham or real – originally were elements in a discourse on sensibility and subjectivity that was different from that of later periods and consequently that they were assessed according to other criteria. In the golden era of romantic gardens, the ruin was above all an aesthetic object. It should elicit certain – frequently rather well-defined – emotions and moods in the competent spectator. In the new gardens, the ruin – as defined in the *Encyclopédie* – was lifted out of the painting or the poetry and placed in real scenery. The experience was no longer based solely on the reading of a poem or the contemplation of a picture, but on the spectator's own promenade along garden paths. The ruins gained a new materiality, while their enjoyment at the same time was connected to the bodily experience of wandering in the garden, appreciating the turns and twists of the picturesque paths, and the joy of unexpected views. These experiences were prepared for through the planning of the garden, but their realization was wholly dependent on the spectator and his/her activity: The wandering was a prerequisite to interesting perspectives as well as strong emotions. What is evoked is the same aesthetic competence as in the enjoyment of poems and pictures, the same ability to be moved in specific ways by certain artistic expressions, and the same knowledge of a causal relationship between scenery and emotion. It was not as antiquarian, historian or mason that the spectator was supposed to appreciate the ruin, but as a sensitive and aesthetically competent subject. Referring to Foucault's theories on the constructions of subjectivity, Tine Damsholt describes the garden promenade as a 'technology of the self', i.e., 'a way to improve oneself via the emotions aroused by the garden' (Damsholt 2000b: 29). The garden architecture was part of the romantic cult of sensibility and – not least – of its ethical dimensions, where strong emotions were seen as the expressions of a noble character. Training oneself to express strong emotions in the right way – for example by crying and demonstrating compassion – became an important part of the development of the ethical subject (Damsholt 2000b: 27).

Problems concerning the historical authenticity of the ruins, and the corresponding ridicule of ruins which only imitate this authenticity, only occur when the ruins are perceived as historical testimonies and sources. As long as their value was the ability to arouse emotions and initiate certain kinds of philosophical reflections, any ruin may be considered genuine. Authenticity does not come from historical source value, but is rather an aspect of the spectator's emotions and the noble character thus expressing itself. The authentic ruin then is the one able to produce authentic – strong – emotions.

In Norway, General Erik Anker at Hamar was among the lucky proprietors who had an authentic ruin of his own. In 1831 he purchased Storhamar manor and farm with the ruined cathedral. During the latter part of the eighteenth century, a furnace had been established to produce lime from the rubble, but apart from that little had changed since 1743 (above). The cathedral was mainly a gigantic heap of stones. Schøning visited the site in 1775, and wrote:

> The entire church is now collapsed into a hill of rubble, apart from a few remains of the lower wall and a length of the western transept, or its inner wall that is carried by three massive stone columns, at both ends of which a piece is left. The rest has collapsed and has been demolished and carried away (Schøning 1980: 46).[7]

Schøning expresses his regret over the decay and says that it is a great harm to the region and the entire realm that the mediaeval town of Hamar never was rebuilt. It ought to be done, to the 'ornament and usefulness' of the country (Schøning 1980: 44).

Despite the lamentation over the pitiful state of the church, Schøning's text is very clearly about the material aspects of church and town, their lost glory and future usefulness. The ruin is neither an aesthetic object nor a *vanitas* symbol. But things were about to change. From the 1820s onwards, the old heap of rubble was termed a ruin. Excavations to clear more of the arcade also seem to have started in this period. Anker established a picturesque garden stretching from his house to the shores of Lake Mjøsa. Located on a point high above the beach the ruin became the centrepiece, now attracting the interest of artists and tourists. In 1828 the student K.O. Knutzen visited the site during a summer journey. Walking on foot, carrying only his backpack, he describes his lone arrival at the ruin one summers' afternoon. Passing by a small cottage inhabited by a simple rural woman, he approached

> some of the most remarkable ruins in Norway – the scarce remains of the once so powerful Hamar, which in its time was among the largest cities in the country. A beautiful road bordered by trees, almost an avenue, leads to the manor. From far away I could see the arcades that now are all that exists of the glorious cathedral of Hamar, and the only ruin which is left, as all other signs indicating that this has been the site of a city, are vanished … (Knutzen 1922: 65).[8]

At the manor he was met by its former proprietor F. Borchgrevink, who supplied him with some historical information about the town, but what really attracts his attention is the ruin itself. The cathedral must have been large, judging from the amount of rubble, Knutzen says. Nonetheless, at the centre of his musings are not the architectural details, but rather the atmosphere of the site and the emotions that are evoked. Rambling in the park, Knutzen presents the thoughts and feelings produced by the sight of the ruin:

> One is seized by wistful emotions on a site that *once*, in past times, has been the location of a *city* – a mighty, large and rich town, that now, with all its magnificent buildings, towers, churches and people has – disappeared without hardly any trace of past greatness! A ramble at the church-yard, when the moon shines in the quiet evening, when the birds are silent and nature asleep, is well fit to confront us with the transitoriness of human existence, and to make us observe the changes and revolutions in all things, but not so much as visit to a place where a large town has once been standing … For never have I felt more deeply the transitoriness of all things human and timely than now when I stood at the desolate site of Hamar, where no trace is left of former habitation. For nearly 300 years now the honourable vestiges of the cathedral have been standing, as for centuries to come they will remain a memorial from times gone by and be the sole sign that *here* a mighty town once stood (Knutzen 1922: 66, italics in original).[9]

The ruins of the cathedral no longer represent mere decay. On the one hand, they have become the symbol of the entire mediaeval town of Hamar and its sad destiny. On the other, both town and ruin carry a message that points beyond their mere physical state. The ruin is transformed into a symbol of *vanitas*, reminding the sentimental rambler of the inconstancy of all human life and effort. With his description, Knutzen presents not only the destination of his journey, but also himself as a person of sentiment and sensibility. He demonstrates his cultural competence as an emotional subject, capable of expressing a specific set of feelings and musings. The close connections between the emotions called forth by visits to church-yards and ruins have been pointed out by Fehrman, and are very explicit in Knutzen's text (Fehrman 1954). Not only are both kinds of sites conceived of as having the same kind of sentimental potentiality – though in unequal degree, according to Knutzen. The parallel also makes it clear that the ruin and the emotions it evokes are about human life and human existence, not, for example, about the qualities of stones and mortar or architectural styles and neither about the specific historic past.

Fehrman has pointed out that the growing interest in mediaeval constructions cultivated the national potentialities of ruin romanticism. The trend was particularly strong in the German states and was manifested during the nineteenth century. Fehrman writes:

> The ruin-like, the sentimental melancholy cedes the place. National, historic and heroic associations are evoked. The national current in German romanticism transforms the ruin in the direction of the heroic: it becomes a symbol of heroic times and heroic deeds (Fehrman 1956: 97, my translation).

This nationalization implied historicity, but it is also important to note that this history was understood in heroic terms. In this case the ruins did not bear witness to the transitoriness of all things, but spoke about the heroism of the past. The general symbolism of *vanitas* was supplanted by a more specific iconography of national history. Through its sheer material existence, the ruin in a very concrete way bore witness to national power and splendour – even if far away in the past. In these cases the timeless validity of classical virtue was replaced by a demonstration of national character and national history. Ruins no longer called for an imitation of universal classical ideals, but for a re-birth of national virtue and national deeds – the deeds of one's *own* specific ancestors, the greatness of one's *own* particular past. The link between past and present was no longer provided by the general exemplarity of the classical age, but by the organic bonds between forefathers and heirs.

This development towards more national readings can be traced in descriptions of the ruin at Hamar. In 1856 the writer Andreas Munch published a text with the title 'The Last Bishop of Hamar'.[10] The first part of it is not about the bishop, however, but describes Munch's own visit to the ruin in 1841. A 'strange destiny' seems to rest over the major cities of ancient Norway, Munch exclaims. Hamar, Oslo and Sarpsborg all have disappeared without traces. A new city has been built (from 1849) close to the ancient site of Hamar, but the old town has sunk into oblivion:

> But, even if later generations have neglected Hamar, then, as a compensation, poetic memory has spread its rich moonlight over it, and behind this mysterious veil its image dawns doubly noble. As a comfort in its loneliness, an incontestable witness of former grandeur Hamar still is in possession of a quite considerable ruin … (Munch 1856: 80f).[11]

Munch calls his journey to Hamar a 'pilgrimage', for 'history has its own religion and its sacred relics, to which the pious may come, kneel down and strengthen a hearth dried out by everyday life' (Munch 1856: 81). The pilgrimage took place on a sunny summer's day. Arriving by boat, Munch describes the landscape as majestic, romantic, green and fertile. In the middle of this scenery 'a reddish-grey, arched mass of stone, the ruins of Hamar!' The ancient town is presented as the beating heart of a rich rural landscape. As his night quarters Munch has chosen a small farm with the name 'Evensong', to where he is led by a young boy. The boy asks, 'I suppose you are going to see the walls?' but knows nothing more than that 'people say there once was a town there'. Wandering through a rather dense forest, Munch muses over the ignorance of the common people. The physical ruin of the cathedral, then, is closely accompanied by the (probably fictitious) name of the farm, the popular ignorance embodied in the boy and the density of the trees that have grown up were the town once stood. They all speak in a melancholy way of shadow, oblivion and lost secrets. Munch presents a brief description of the physical ruin and mentions that its present owner (Erik Anker) has carried out excavations to free some arches. Nonetheless, once again it is the views and the atmosphere that attract the most attention:

> Standing inside the ruin and looking through the arches, one has the most picturesque view of Lake Mjøsa. In the foreground large blocks of stones have been tumbled, somewhat farther away the mighty arcade is standing, which time has coloured in shades going from light blue to dark red and decorated with green herbs and plants; and finally, behind each of the enormous arches and framed by them as by a cornice, is breathing a lovely scenery of lake, green coasts and remote mountains (Munch 1856: 84).[12]

From these stones the past 'emerged', Munch writes, close and tangible. As in a dream he saw Bishops' chasubles, silken cloths and flying standards. From far away he heard the sound of song and strange voices. When he tried to draw near, it all disappeared, just to start over in another part of the ruin. Finally, Munch flees the church to contemplate the ruin from a distance as evening falls and the sun goes down.

Even Munch's text can be read as a piece of standard ruin romanticism. He is more attentive to nature and to scenery than Knutzen was, and less explicit on the *vanitas* motif. With small variations, however, Munch's text is a demonstration of the same kind of sensitivity and romantic competence. A difference lies in his references to history. Its presentation as a fleeting dream that can be chased but never caught fits well into the general romantic picture. In Munch's case this phrasing nonetheless also serves as an introduction to the narrative about the last bishop of Hamar, which is presented in part as factual history and in part as the same kind of romantic dream.

In 1537 when the Lutheran Reformation was introduced, Bishop Mogens of Hamar was arrested by the king's representatives and brought to Denmark. The events are known from the so-called Hamar chronicle, a text from 1553 that also reports on the numerous signs that preceded the dramatic events: The bells in the cathedral and all other churches in town started suddenly to toll; and a gigantic serpent showed itself in the lake. Highly important both to the anonymous author of the chronicle and to Munch in his story is the Reformation, and the arrest of the catholic bishops that also meant the end of national independence in Norway. After the country had entered into a union with Denmark in 1397, the bishops in the Council of the Realm (*Riksrådet*) had represented what remained of national authority. The king's resolution to introduce the Reformation by arresting the bishops thus had profound political impact. Correspondingly, the fleeting past that Munch chases and is at pains to grasp in his narrative is no random dream, but has a distinct political meaning. Hamar Cathedral is not just any poetic ruin covered with ivy and flowers, it represents a specific national past. When Munch was writing his text, Norway had gained new independence (from 1814) and entered into a period of vigorous nation building. The perception of its ruins as stages of a history to be recovered must be seen in this light.

When ruins became nationalized the challenge they posed was no longer to imitate, but to inherit and pass on. A ruin no longer was 'a concept of the pictorial arts', as stated by the *Encyclopédie*; it represented national history and supported national claims to power and influence. With this came also the establishment of modern antiquarian authorities, usually within national frames, as national history and national culture supplied the arguments for conserving and restoring ruins and other antiquities. In his text, Munch refers to the newly established Society for the Preservation of Ancient Norwegian Monuments (*Foreningen til norske fortidsminnesmerkers bevaring*; see also Chapter 5 in this volume) and expresses his hope that the decay at Hamar now will be stopped and the ruin will be better taken care of (Munch 1856: 86). Preserving ruins now meant safeguarding the national past; gaining knowledge about them correspondingly meant gaining knowledge about the nation. This also created an additional message. The ruin not only requested the present to emulate the heroes of the past. Conserving, restoring and investigating the ruins became praiseworthy in itself, heroic activity worthy of comparison with the deeds of the past.

Both as an antiquarian object and as a historical monument, the ruin is heavily rooted in romanticism. Not until it was established as the object of aesthetic reflections did the ruin appear as an antiquarian category. Before, it could be a site of memory and a potential repository of inscriptions, but it was in itself not the primary material of antiquarian study. It came to be the artists, not the antiquaries who first listened to the voices of the ruins and sought to interpret their message. Poetry and painting contributed to the antiquaries' discovery, and helped them turn *rudera* into ruins. The aestheticizing of the ruins preceded their historization and at the same time served as the necessary basis for interpreting them as the valuable remains of a national past and assigning the authorities the responsibility to take care of them.

However, the antiquarian and aesthetic assessments of ruins were never completely identical. The antiquarians' monuments were not merely aesthetic objects, but also sources of knowledge, concrete traces of a historic past. The antiquarians' approach brought demands for research and claims for preservation. Furthermore, it also brought a new understanding of authenticity, no longer rooted in the emotions of the spectators, but in the materiality of the bricks and masonry. The ruins started to speak with forked tongues, creating contrasts that are still present today.

In contemporary preservation work, the different aspects go hand in hand. On the one hand, ruins are expected to be visually enjoyable and also to be the sites of cultural events and historical spectacles. On the other, they are objects of scholarly study as well as historical monuments to be preserved. Events and experience are associated with the work of popularization, source value with protection and research. While preservation authorities must handle this duality on a practical level, it may more analytically be seen as a product of the composite origins of the ruin as an autonomous object.

NOTES

1. [E]ftersom den ju visar sig med annat utseende nu än förr. På något sätt ska jag ändå försöka skissera den, fastän den varit övergiven under så lang tid.

2. Vad mödosamt det är och svårt att gräva fram ur historiens dolda rum det som tycks bidra till att hävda svearnas och götarnas folks ära eller förnya minnet av de gamla monumenten. Men lika skönt och berömvärt är det också. På detta sätt framställs utan tvivel dygdemönster för de efterkommande, som dessa kan härma. Fäderneslandets gamla monument liksom övervuxna med glömska återställs skönt till sin tidigare glans. De dras passande fram i ljuset och till människornas åsyn, även de människor som aldrig tidigare sett dem med egna ögon.

3. [E]r for mange aar side bleven forfalden, og deretter af afgangne geheimeraad Adaler i grund sleifet, men i dens stæd een smuch træebygning opsatt.

4. Den ældste bye i Norge og i siin tiid har været heel stor baade af begreb og handling, med ved den byen for over 200 aar siden overgangne jldebrand er den bleven fortæret og lagt i aske, midt i byen har staaet et slaatt som har wæret opsatt paa et bierg der nu ved enden af byen lader sig tilsyne, og findes paa samme bierg endnu mange rudera af bemelte slots bygninger.

5. [K]alck, steen og mur.

6. Hammer gaard ... beliggende paa Hedcmarchen paa det stæd hvor Hammer bye i fordum tiid haver staaed hvoraf nu ingen widere tegn haves.

7. Den heele Kirke ligger nu nedfalden i en Steen-dynge, naar man undtager nogle faae Levninger af den nederste Muur ved Choret og en Længde af Kirkens vestre Kors, eller dens indere Muur, som bæres af 3de meget tykke og massive Steen-Pillarer ved begge Ender af hvilken staaer tillige et Støkke tilbage af Muren.

8. [N]ogle af de merkværdigste Ruiner i Norge – de faa Levninger af det engang saa mægtige Hammer, der i sin Tid var en af Landets største Byer. En smuk, med Træer beplatet Vei, jeg kan næsten kalde den en Allé, leder til Gaarden. Allerede langt fra saae jeg den Søilerække, det eneste der er tilovers af Hammers prægtige Domkirke, og den eneste Ruin, der er tilbage af Hammer, da alle Tegn til at her har været en Bye, ere forsvundne …

9. Det er en vemodig Følelse man gribes af, naar man staar paa et Sted, hvor der *før*, engang i den fremfarne Tid har været *en Stad*, – en mægtig, stor, rig Bye, der nu med alle sine herlige Bygninger, Taarne, Kirke og Indvaanere er – forsvunden næsten uden Spor af fordums Storhed! En Vandring paa Kirkegaarden, naar Maanen skinner klart i den stille Aftenstund, naar Fuglene tie og al Naturen sover, er vel særdeles skikket til

at stille Mennesket dets Forgjængelighed ret klarligt for Øine, og at gjøre det opmærksomt paa Tingenes Af- og Omvexlinger, men dog langt fra i den Grad som et Besøg til et Sted, hvor en stor Stad engang har staaet … This aldrig har jeg dybere følt den menneskelige, de timelige Tings Forgjængelighed end nu, da jeg stod paa Hammers øde Tomter, der nu intet Spor viste mere til fordums Beboelse. Næsten 300 Aar have nu de ærverdige Levninger af Domkirken Staaet, og endnu staae i Aarhundreder som et Minde fra de fremfarne Tider, og som eneste Tegn paa at *her* stod engang en mægtig Bye!

10. Den sidste Biskop i Hamar.

11. Men, hvis ogsaa Menneskene og Efterslægten have forsømt Hamar, saa har Mindets Poesi, som til en Erstatning, bredet sin rigeste Maaneskinsglands ud derover, og bag dette mystiske Forhæng dæmrer dens Billede dobbelt prægtigt. Og til en Trøst i sin Eensomhed, til et uimodsigeligt Vidne om fordums Storhed besidder Hamar endnu en ganske anseelig Ruin …

12. Naar man staaer inde i Ruinerne og seer ud gjennem disse over Mjøsen, har man et yderst pittoreskt Syn. Forgrunden dannes af store, vildt omkastede Steenblokke, noget længere borte har man den mægtige Søilerad, som Tiden har skatteret fra lyseblaatt til dunkelrødt, og behængt med grønne Urter og Væxter; og endelig, bag enhver af de kolossale Buer, og indfattet ad disse som af en Ramme, aander et herlig Landskab af Sø, grønne Kyster og fjerne Bjerge.

5

Mediaeval Monuments

The nineteenth century can rightly be called the age of the historic monument. This applies to what the French historian Maurice Agulhon has termed the 'statuomanie' of the period, which is his name for the veritable sea of public monuments and memorials that were erected in towns and villages in honour of historical events or deserved citizens during the nineteenth and early twentieth centuries (Agulhon 1988). Equally important in the present context is that the designation also describes the growing interest in preserving or restoring ancient constructions, in Riegl's terms making unintended monuments out of the remains from the past, as well as taking care of the intended ones that still existed. The historical value, which, as Riegl points out, had been acknowledged since the Renaissance, grew increasingly important. Slowly it was also augmented with the idea of age value, which is Riegl's term for the growing awareness that an ancient object 'reveals the passage of a considerable period of time' (Riegl 1903/1982: 24; cf. Chapter 1 in this volume). The age value is also termed developmental value, and Riegl says: 'Historical value, which was tied to particulars, transformed itself slowly into developmental value, for which particulars were ultimately unimportant. This developmental value was none other than the age-value' (Riegl 1903/1982: 29). Even if Riegl designates the twentieth century as its main period, the idea of age value can be seen to emerge earlier, as was demonstrated, for example, by the new interest in ruins as expressions of the passing of time discussed in Chapter 4. In the following, we shall also see how age value gradually became part of the nineteenth-century discovery of mediaeval remains. In this chapter, the efforts to document and preserve the stave churches will be discussed as one instance of Europe's discovery of its mediaeval architecture and at the same time as illustrations of the shift in the way ancient buildings were spoken of in the nineteenth century: this period saw the waning of traditional antiquarianism and the growth of a modern historical approach that studied processes of development over time and searched for national particulars.

During the nineteenth century, the term 'historic monument' came to refer to a wide and growing range of artefacts and constructions, also involving a range of activities related to them – from excavation and exploration via preservation to the erection of public memorials. In the Scandinavian languages, the terms *oldtidsminner* (literally, ancient memorials), *oldsaker* (ancient objects) and *oldtidslevninger* (ancient remains) also were frequent. The word 'antiquities', on the other hand, gradually went out of use as a generic term in these languages and came to be reserved more or less for the sphere of antique dealers and collectors and in some cases for individual museum items.

During the same period the study of historic monuments as well as the work with their preservation was institutionalized. The new scholarly disciplines of art history and archaeology were established at the universities, and the old discipline of history underwent a transformation from its traditional rhetorical and pragmatic form to its modern, critical and source-based version (e.g., Koselleck 1985; B.E. Jensen 2003: 123; Eriksen 2007). Hand in hand with this professionalization of knowledge production came the establishment of associations and institutions responsible for the care and preservation of monuments. Most often this took place within a national framework. The explicit goal was to care for the *nation's* historic monuments in the same way as the new academic history had the development of nations and nation states as its primary interest.

The newly gained independence made nation building a major project in Norwegian society during the nineteenth century. The process changed the public discourse from the patriotic to the national mode. Ethnologist Tine Damsholt describes eighteenth-century patriotism as an ideal of society as based on a contract between sovereign and citizens and implying a certain set of reciprocal obligations. Warrantor of the common good, the sovereign's duty was to make this the chief object of his considerations. Conversely, the care of the sovereign was what enabled the citizens to fulfil their duties, which above all meant demonstrating civic virtue: the willingness to subsume one's own ambitions under the common good and work for its realization (Damsholt 2000a: 123f). In principle, patriotism looked the same in all countries. It did not make national particularities or 'culture' a part of what was supposed to make people love their fatherland. Neither did it demand that all inhabitants of the realm should share the same nationality (or language). What mattered was the willingness to take on civic duties and display civic virtue. Historian Odd Arvid Storsveen has argued that more specific notions of 'national patriotism' also can be distinguished. This is his term for the development in Norway in the late-eighteenth-century period preceding independence. Even if the concepts of common good and civic virtue were still the general principles expressed in the political discourse in Denmark-Norway, he points out that they were gradually tied to ideas about a common good specific to Norway and about distinct Norwegian virtues (Storsveen 1997: 18f). With nineteenth-century nationalism, this cult of national particulars became the driving political force.

Concerning antiquities – or monuments – the development led to a grad-ual transformation of perception and evaluation. The patriotic conceptualiza-tion had worked with terms and categories that made antiquities appear as local specimens representing such universal phenomena as 'heathen religion', 'war craft', 'justice' or 'burials' (the work of Iver Wiel, discussed in Chapter 2 is a good example). New perspectives turned the same objects and sites into weighty expressions of national particulars. History was important to the na-tional project in general because it represented a link to the periods before the union with Denmark: during the Viking and high Middle Ages, Norway had been the dominant force among the Scandinavian kingdoms. Nineteenth-cen-tury popular culture was sought for proof of still living connections between the present and this glorious past, as was also the vernacular language. And while the antiquaries of the eighteenth century had looked for traces from the 'ancestors', as these were known from the Norse literature, the historians and archaeologists of the nineteenth century now added the Middle Ages.

The Discovery of the Stave Churches

Despite Schøning's heavy volume on the cathedral in Trondheim (Chapter 3 in this volume), the discovery of mediaeval architecture in Norway is normally credited to the painter J C. Dahl (1788 1857). Living most of his active life in Dresden and pursuing his artistic career in a German and international context, Dahl is still considered to be a fundamentally national artist in Norway. The country's first major landscape painter, he is above all known for his large and dramatic pictures of mountainous areas in western and central Norway. On a journey to his fatherland in 1826, Dahl was enthralled by the stave churches. Today, twenty-eight buildings of this kind remain of the about a thousand cal-culated to have been built in Norway during the Middle Ages (Anker 1997). A large number of them were left to decay after the Black Death in 1349. The Lutheran Reformation in 1537 reduced the total number of churches in the country and made several old buildings superfluous. When Dahl made his first journey, about ninety-five stave churches were still standing, and Dahl became intensely aware that their number was dwindling. Between 1850 and 1885, a further thirty-two churches were demolished (Anker 1997: 15). An act from 1851 regulated the proportion between the size of a church and the total number of its parishioners, which implied that several old churches were too small. As the stave churches were also thought to be old-fashioned, dark and primitive, communities jumped at the opportunity to replace them with new buildings, often in the then fashionable neo-Gothic style.

Dahl made himself a spokesman for the preservation of the remaining stave churches. In the wake of the increasing institutionalization later in the century, his initiatives have been written into a grand narrative of national awakening, with Dahl positioned as the father of historical preservation work in Norway. His interest in mediaeval buildings and his call for preservation has unquestioningly been seen as reflecting an understanding of the term similar to the modern (see, e.g., Brøgger 1914; Bang 1987). Closer investigations of Dahl's work and his way of arguing nonetheless make it more accurate to see him as a figure of transition between two periods (Wexelsen 1973). While his arguments and strategies clearly were linked to the antiquarian tradition of former periods, they also express new ideas specific to the nineteenth century.

Dahl's initial move was to send the young painter F.W. Schiertz to Norway to make drawings of stave churches. The aim was to publish a book of plates. This choice of action was highly traditional. Understanding 'preservation' as the making of drawings and prints was exactly what antiquaries and artists had done for centuries, as Françoise Choay has pointed out with her term 'iconographic preservation' (Choay 1999: 70; and Chapter 4 in this volume). Consequently, Dahl's idea of making drawings of the stave churches did not by necessity imply a wish to preserve the buildings physically, and it is not obvious that he understood 'preservation' in more modern ways during these early years (cf. also Wexelsen 1973: 73f). Nonetheless, even if the drawings initiated by Dahl and made by Schiertz were not part of a plan for physical preservation of the buildings, they were far more accurate and much more focused on a correct rendering of details than any earlier depiction of the wooden churches had been. It might have been Dahl's gift for visual perception that first made the churches catch his eye, but the images finally produced nonetheless differed from older presentations of the churches as mere picturesque scenery. The collection was the first attempt at presenting systematic visual knowledge about these mediaeval buildings.

The series of drawings ended up being less comprehensive than what Dahl had envisioned. When it appeared in three volumes in 1836–37, the collection presented the churches in Borgund, Urnes and Heddal. It was published in Dresden, with the title *Denkmale einer sehr ausgebildeten Holzbaukunst aus den frühesten Jahrhunderten in den innern Landschaften Norwegens*. The wording signals the remoteness of these churches in both temporal and geographical terms and makes exoticism a primary quality: the buildings are from the earliest centuries and situated in the most unwelcoming regions of this mountainous northern country. Nonetheless, they are monuments (or memorials: Denkmale) of a highly developed art of construction. Apart from the drawings the publication contained an introductory text. Originally it was to be written by the theologian and historian Andreas Faye, but the final text was composed by Dahl himself, influenced by the German art historian K.F. von Rumohr (Aubert 1920: 218). Faye had sent Dahl a draft in 1836, without knowing exactly which churches were to be included in the collection. A version of this text was published in the popular journal *Skillings-Magazinet* in 1837 after Dahl had chosen not to continue the collaboration (Wexelsen 1973: 78f). Faye then gave his article the title 'Gaara Kirke i Bø i Tellemarken' (Gaara Church in Bø in Telemark) and also presented a drawing of the exterior of this (now lost) building. Between them, the two texts by Dahl/Rumohr and Faye, respectively, are the earliest scholarly texts published on stave churches. They both merit attention as basic elements in the discovery of mediaeval architecture in Norway.

Faye gained renown as the first person in Norway to publish a collection of popular legends. His book *Norske Sagn* (Norwegian Legends) appeared in 1833 and was inspired by the work of the brothers Grimm. On his journey to Germany in 1831 he had also met Dahl, and the friendship between the two men was to last for the following decades. Faye later published a number of historical works, and he contributed to the founding of one of Norway's earliest public museums in his home town of Arendal in 1832.

Despite the title, the main part of his text on Gaara church is a rather general discussion on historical monuments in Norway, among them stave churches. Faye observes:

> Strangers who travel in Norway, and Norwegians who have visited foreign countries, will without doubt agree that Norwegian scenery is equal to that of most other European countries, both when it comes to majesty, variety and grace; but among things that are wanting, they commonly regret Norway's poverty of beautiful monuments and ruins, which contribute so much to embellish many a southern region and make e.g. a journey through Italy, Switzerland and the countries of the Rhine so interesting. These remains from the remote past do not only please the eye, but due to the legends that often are told about them, they also give the imagination rich matter for pleasurable diversion (Faye 1836: 177).[1]

One reason for this deficiency, Faye says, is the long period of the union with Denmark, when the Danish authorities strove to exterminate the memories from Norway's glorious past. Another reason is the fact that '[i]n ancient times most churches and other buildings were built of wood, which more easily is destroyed, and which when destroyed does not leave picturesque ruins like the more solid stone buildings' (Faye 1837: 178).[2] Nonetheless, ancient buildings, among them stave churches, can still be found in the most remote areas of Norway, together with costumes, customs and even language that reflect a remote past and make the inhabitants of these regions 'strange, living parallels to the people we meet in our ancient sagas …' (ibid.).[3]

Faye then proceeds to describe barrows, standing stones and other monuments and refers to Odin's much cited words that 'for men of consequence a mound should be raised to their memory, and for all other warriors who had been distinguished for manhood a standing stone' (Ynglinge saga, Chapter

8:11; and Chapter 2 in this volume). He does of course know that while the stave churches are Christian, the barrows, stones and so on are pagan. But what matters most to him is that they are all, including the way of life of the peasants of his own time, 'ancient'. The different periods tend to merge into the more general category. This is not least obvious in the passage that actually relates to the church at Gaara. About one-half of this very short text is a description of two large standing stones in the churchyard. According to Faye, they most probably mark an ancient site of a cult or court of justice, as the earliest Christian churches frequently were erected at the ancient *tingsteder.*

The references to barrows and stones supply a link to Norse literature. Not only was the majority of historical and antiquarian knowledge in Faye's time based on this corpus, the study of the texts of ancient 'history writers' was also considered by far the most trustworthy way to such knowledge. In this way, Faye's text resembles very much the texts of the eighteenth-century antiquaries, even though the intention is to present a mediaeval church. Moreover, while his way of speaking about historical monuments seems inspired by the emerging ideas of a nationality and national cultures, Faye's text reflects the patriotic discourse of the former period. What matters is not so much the national particulars but the issue of whether Norway can be favourably compared to other European countries when it comes to scenery, history and visually agreeable monuments and ruins. If it is to stand its ground in this international contest, Norway needs more monuments, not to develop a distinctively national character.

Material Evidence – a New Approach

Dahl's introduction to the collection of plates also speaks of the stave churches in rather general terms (Dahl 1837: unpag.). He points out that even if they have survived the centuries, 'der Geist der Aenderung und Neuerung' will now lead to the complete disappearance of this kind of monument (Denkmale). Then follows an attempt at analysing the different elements of the buildings. Dahl argues that the churches are of a composite character. Their ornaments reflect heathen models and prove that Norse culture not only developed the poetic, but also the plastic arts. The construction and not least the plan, for their part, are named Byzantine. Apart from establishing a connection to Christian Constantinople, this accorded well with generally accepted ideas and refers to the theory that Norway originally had been populated by the descendants of Odin, who arrived from the east, via Russia. A narrative of these events had been developed by Schøning in his history of Norway from 1771. But Dahl also makes clear what distinguishes the Norwegian from Russian churches. To the difference in doctrine comes the fact that while the eastern buildings are timbered, the Norwegian ones are framework constructions. Furthermore, Dahl adds a processual perspective, saying that nearly all the churches have lost their original design due to changes and decay over time. Best preserved are those situated in remote areas. Echoing Faye, he writes that in such regions stylistic features similar to those of the churches can be seen in vernacular architecture, tools and even in popular costumes.

Despite their common lack of precise knowledge about the churches and their attempts at compensating for this by drawing on saga literature, the two texts have important differences. The introduction to the work of plates expresses a far greater understanding of historical change. It does not merely note that the churches are about to disappear, but makes the additional observation that most of them have been changed over time. While these more general arguments may result from Rumohr's influence, the attempts at stylistic analysis of ornaments and decoration must be based on Dahl's own impression of the churches that he had actually seen. Taken together, the perspectives in the introduction to the plates can be said to refer to what Riegl called a developmental value: an awareness of processes of change working in time rather than an interest in specific events or persons of the past.

Even if it is not obvious that Dahl thought of physical preservation of the stave churches as early as the 1820s, he reacted to their increasingly rapid disappearance. From 1839 he started a campaign to save the stave church in Vang in Valdres (central Norway) from demolition. When he did not succeed in this, Dahl bought the church and sold it to the Prussian King Friederich Wilhelm IV. It was reerected in Silesia in 1844. In 1842 Dahl also joined the debate on the restoration of the cathedral in Trondheim and argued against the architect's idea of changing the plan of the church by taking down the choir and moving it to another position. In the same period, Dahl started working for the mediaeval fortress of his hometown of Bergen, not least the large construction that is now known under the name of Haakon's Hall (Håkonshallen). Built during the thirteenth century, it was the place of celebration for the wedding between the future King Magnus Haakonsson and the Danish princess Ingebjørg Eriksdatter in 1261. When Dahl 'discovered' it, it had long been used for storing grain, while its history and original use were unknown.

In 1841 Dahl issued a public invitation to restore the building and presented his plans with quite a long text in the local newspaper. He refers to history as *magistra vitae:* history makes the great men of the past – once the honour of the nation and the ideals of their time – appear to us as if they were still alive. Their works ought not only be the comfort and joy of the nation, but should encourage us to great and good deeds and make us gratefully preserve their memory (Dahl quoted in Wexelsen 1973: 169). Among the admirable works of the forefathers are their magnificent buildings. Travel and study have taught us to admire the buildings of classical antiquity and the culture of Egypt,

Greece and Rome, Dahl says. We also know 'the style and character of the brilliant Gothic buildings, whose magnificent remains can be found in Germany, France, England and Spain, but we still pass silently and uncaring by the great monuments that we ourselves have from our ancestors' (Dahl quoted in Wexelsen 1973: 169).[4] This must be changed. It is our duty to 'preserve and make usable' these remains while there is still time. The expression leaves no doubt that in this case Dahl's intention was a physical preservation of the building and did not merely refer to the tradition of iconographic preservation. Indeed, the aim of his invitation was not just to stir up interest for the mediaeval building, but actually to raise money for the works. Dahl pointed out that the city of Bergen had no building fit for grand festive occasions. Premises for royal visits or assemblies for the town's citizens were lacking. For this reason, the interior decoration of the ancient hall ought to be made in accordance with 'the taste and needs of our own time', but in a way that 'bespeaks the ancient spirit and character' of the building (Dahl quoted in Brøgger 1914: 13f). Historian Einar Wexelsen has pointed out that this argument disagrees with Dahl's stance against changes made in the cathedral in Trondheim. His explanation for this lack of consistence is that Dahl was compromising to achieve his goal of raising interest and money for the building in Bergen (Wexelsen 1973: 164). But it can also be argued that Dahl's argument was a genuine expression of his own view. It refers clearly to the old tradition of preserving ancient buildings by giving them new functions. It is not obvious that Dahl, any more than his contemporaries, saw the point of repairing a building to make it a mere monument. The invitation was published widely. Dahl also used his influence with local members of Parliament, but despite his energetic work and distinguished position, his project for restoring the hall did not obtain funding from the state or much support from private citizens.

In 1842 Dahl's friend, the poet and pedagogue Lyder Sagen included the case in an article entitled 'Historisk vandring i Bergen og dens nærmeste Omegn' (A Historical Tour of Bergen and its Vicinities), published in the scholarly journal *Urda*. Sagen describes the melancholy he feels walking in a city where so many kings and earls once lived, of whom hardly any memory is left. The few 'memories of the past' that still exist, ought to be preserved. It is not obvious what Sagen means by 'memories' in this context. On the one hand, they are clearly tied to actual sites and buildings in the city and are presented according to the route of the tour. Sagen mentions the fortress, the Great Christ Church with its royal tombs (demolished at the time of the Reformation), and proceeds to other locations that in some way or another can be related to persons or events known from national history. On the other hand, it is still not the actual buildings or material locations themselves that are 'memories'. They rather work as points of reference for the evidence that can be found in texts.

Into his article Sagen has inserted a passage written by Dahl about the fortress. The difference between the ways the two friends describe the ancient buildings is remarkable. The explicit aim of Sagen is to present his friend's antiquarian expertise as well as his (artistic) enthusiasm for the old buildings. Probably less intended by Sagen is the demonstration of a new way of considering 'antiquities'. The passage by Dahl starts by pointing out the picturesque, i.e., visual qualities of the ancient fortress. Dahl then goes into detail about its tower (Rosenkrantztårnet) and says that '[i]ts construction, of solid and for its period beautiful execution, which seems yet to resist the centuries, indicates a work of the 11th or early 12th century, and has been very little changed' (Dahl quoted in Sagen 1842: 263).[5] Continuing to the banquet hall, Dahl says that he believes the building to be 'a work of the second half of the 12th century, it is one of the most beautiful buildings of Norman architecture from Mediaeval times, reminding one of similar buildings from England, Normandy and some parts of the buildings that still are left from the Norman period in Sicily' (Dahl quoted in Sagen 1842: 264).[6] He then embarks on a description of the building as it could be seen.

What distinguishes Dahl's text is the way he builds his arguments and evaluations on what can be inferred from the material evidence represented by the building itself, rather than on texts describing persons or events related to it. Furthermore, the information gained by examining the building is actively used in an attempt to date it more exactly – it is not merely presented as 'ancient'. Even if Dahl may have been wrong concerning the hall (today it is reckoned to be somewhat younger), this makes his approach radically different from that of most earlier antiquarians. Stylistic criteria are what constitute Dahl's tool of analysis. Contrary to the way Schøning saw the cathedral in Trondheim, where differences in style were mainly seen as an expression of an organic life cycle of the cathedral itself (Chapter 2 in this volume), Dahl combines the stylistic analysis with a comparative method, which enables him to relate the buildings in Bergen to European architecture of the same period.

As was the case with the discovery of ruins (Chapter 4 in this volume), the new appreciation of mediaeval buildings, here articulated by Dahl, was based in an aesthetic and visual approach: what could actually be seen and visually enjoyed became as important as what old texts might say. At the same time, physical remains acquired independent evidential value. Once established, this material evidence also appeared to produce answers to questions that had not been asked before. They were no longer about specific persons and events. The new issues were stylistic influence, the gradual diffusion of new forms and ideas and the observable differences that could be related to the passing of time.

J.S. Dahl and the Society for the Preservation
of Norwegian Ancient Monuments

Despite the lack of success of his previous initiatives, Dahl did not give up his efforts to preserve mediaeval buildings. He had already initiated societies for the promotion of art in Norway. In Dresden he was a proud member of the Royal Saxons *Alterthumsverein*. His next idea was to start a similar society in Norway. Dahl is usually credited for having founded the Society for the Preservation of Norwegian Ancient Monuments (*Foreningen til Norske fortidsminnesmerkers Bevaring*), even if much of the actual work was performed by his younger friend, the painter Joachim Frich. A public invitation was launched on Constitution Day 1844. Once again general enthusiasm was lacking, but the society was nonetheless established in the capital some months later. Its first name was the Society for the Maintenance of National Monuments.[7] A statement of intent was adopted, declaring the aim of the society to be

> to *trace, investigate* and *maintain ancient Norwegian monuments,* in particular those which illuminate our people's ingeniousness and love of art in the past, and make these objects known to a general public through *images* and *descriptions.* For this reason, the society intends, within the limits of its funds, to *support journeys in the fatherland* and promote the *publication of works* that contribute to the above-mentioned aims (Brøgger 1914: 24, italics in original).[8]

The text as well as the society's name include the maintenance of monuments. Historians of the society have never been in doubt that this implied physical preservation, which has been – and still is – an important aspect of the society's work (Brøgger 1914; Lidén 1991). A closer investigation of the text and the subsequent events will, however, show that the picture is not quite that simple. On the one hand, the text above mentions images and descriptions as results of the society's work. This does not of course in itself preclude actual interventions, but the following passage is highly significant: the society will use its limited means to support relevant journeys and publications. If the physical restoration of buildings was intended, it would clearly have had to be mentioned among the projects that the society planned to fund. As it is excluded from the paragraph, it seems probable that the original idea was to continue the tradition of iconographic preservation. On the other hand, the question of what to do with ancient buildings that were falling into disrepair and going out of use soon claimed attention.

The first initiative for a physical preservation of a stave church did not come from the society itself, but from the vicar at Heddal stave church in Telemark. In 1848 he asked the society for artistic and architectural assistance in the renovation of this church. The project was developed by the architect J.H. Nebelong, and the restoration work was carried out in 1851. The work was criticized from the beginning. In its annual report for 1851, the society expressed some doubts about the possibility of restoring a church as a monument and at the same time making it functional as a church (Lidén 1991: 31). Dahl vented his displeasure by saying that Nebelong had turned the building into a 'pastry temple' (*konditor-tempel*) (Dahl quoted in Brøgger 1914: 39). The same year, there was another case. The mediaeval stone church of Aker in Oslo was to be replaced by a modern building. The society's board wanted the church documented in drawings before it was demolished, but at the annual general meeting a protest against demolition was adopted. In this case, the general opinion also favoured preservation, and the building was finally saved with funds partly raised by the society.

By the means of these cases the idea of physical preservation of buildings and monuments gradually was brought to the fore. Over the years the society ended up buying several stave churches to save them from being demolished by the local authorities who were building new churches. This made physical preservation an issue. It is still worth noting that in the early discussions, the issue of antiquarian intervention was always closely linked to questions of continued use and function. It is generally accepted even today that the best way to preserve a building is to keep it in use, but in the early years of the society nobody at all seems to have imagined the possibility of implementing preservation work aimed solely at monumental and historical values.

One other aspect of practical work never entered into the society's consideration or activities. Among Dahl's own arguments for supporting the society was his wish to improve contemporary architecture, not least that of churches. As early as 1829 he had described the neo-classicist architect H.D.F. Linstow's drawings for new church buildings as 'barns'. In a public statement from 1844, Dahl presented the Society for the Preservation of Norwegian Ancient Monuments as a union 'for the preservation of our more noble and national church buildings, working to ensure that less profane designs are developed for the new and modern churches that are being constructed, than what has so far been the case' (Dahl quoted in Brøgger 1914: 20).[9] He added that the society would develop plans and drawings for these kinds of new constructions and work to have the old ones suitably repaired (Brøgger 1914: 21). The wording makes it clear that for his part, Dahl was no longer aiming for the mere iconographic preservation of old buildings, but also that his notions of antiquarian work were deeply embedded in ideas about use and utility. Preservation work and repairs, even when historically motivated, should serve the present and the future and not merely by offering symbols. According to Dahl, the work to design new buildings was part of this historical initiative, as was also his early project to adapt the mediaeval banquet hall in Bergen to modern needs (above).

Dahl's suggestion has been taken to mean that he wanted the stave churches to be models for modern architecture due to their specific national qualities

(Brøgger 1914: 10ff). His words about the 'noble and national church buildings' seem to support this view. A national and highly romantic style in wooden architecture was indeed articulated during the late nineteenth century, and Dahl has been seen as a precursor of this development. However, it should be noted that Dahl criticized the neoclassical 'barns' designed by Linstow for looking profane, not for lacking national qualities. The critique of Nebelong's 'pastry work' in Telemark, on the other hand, indicates a basic dislike of a strongly romantic style – the very opposite of classicism. As a whole, Dahl's remarks make it difficult to divine what kind of church architecture he actually wanted.

Swedish historian of museums Magdalena Hillström has pointed out that programmes of nation building, in terms of what later became hegemonic, often have been read into nineteenth-century projects that actually were governed by other rationalities and ideologies (Hillström 2010: 584). This may also be the case with Dahl. It is not obvious that the word 'national' carried the same meaning for him as it acquired later on. In its older patriotic meaning the term could be used to refer to a nation's share of universal values and its ability to be on a par with others, rather than to features distinctive to it in particular. Faye's article about the stave churches (above) is a case in point. According to him, the stave churches supplied Norway with an equivalent to the picturesque ruins and monuments that could be seen in other countries. The churches were uniquely Norwegian, but their national value was found just as much in the fact that they compensated for the lack of stone architecture and made it possible for the country after all to equal others when it came to beautiful scenery and interesting monuments.

Dahl's ideas were complex. On the one hand, his perception of ancient buildings was radically new, with its great weight on visual and material evidence. The insights he inferred from this evidence, his analytical use of observations about style and his interest in history as stylistic development rather than persons and events were equally innovative. On the other hand, and despite his great respect for the original constructions, Dahl's evaluation of the buildings and his ideas of restoration differed from those that were developed later in the nineteenth century. As restoration came to mean physical intervention, historical authenticity became an acute issue. The emerging understanding of nationality as something particular and distinctive also changed older notions. Taken together, these ideas gave new motivations for preserving ancient remains as monuments, not merely as useful constructions. It also meant that artefacts and buildings came to be investigated with the explicit aim of uncovering nationally distinctive traits. The development can be read out of A.W. Brøgger's text at the seventieth anniversary of the society. To him it is beyond doubt that nationality and authenticity are what historical preservation work is all about, no less than that he takes it for granted that this has always been the case.

History and the Nation

After Dahl's initial work, the first more scholarly study of the stave churches was carried out by Lorenz Dietrichson, Norway's first professor in art history. During the summer of 1884 he made a very systematic tour of the European regions still known to possess mediaeval wooden churches. The aim was to investigate the relationship – if any – between these buildings and the stave churches in Norway. Dietrichson's first text on the topic, presenting the findings from the journey, was published in 1885. After a few more articles, a large work on the construction, origin and history of the Norwegian stave churches appeared in 1892. The aim of what follows is not to analyse this work in its entirety, but to use some of Dietrichson's texts to illuminate the new ways of referring to these mediaeval buildings and to discuss the new conceptualizations of the problems they represented – as well as the answers they could give. The perspective builds on those introduced by Dahl, not least when it comes to the heavy emphasis that is put on material evidence. However, it also represents other and new ideas concerning the conceptualization of change and the terminology used to describe it.

The starting point for Dietrichson's work was the idea that the construction and decoration of the churches originated from the same areas as the earliest inhabitants in Norway, i.e., from Russia and Asia. The idea, first presented by Dahl (cf. above), had been repeated by a number of German scholars. According to Dietrichson, the most important arguments supporting it were the fact that wooden churches existed even in Russia and that the contacts with the eastern areas had been maintained during the Middle Ages (Dietrichson 1885: 1f). Nonetheless, his investigation does not only add nuances to the theory, it also represents another approach to the problems. The article from 1885 starts with a presentation of the literary sources that had something to say about wooden churches in the Orient as well as the Occident. The second and largest part of the text is concerned with the 'monuments' themselves and presents Dietrichson's own study of the buildings he has visited. This structure, with its emphasis on literary sources, might seem traditional, but as we shall see, Dietrichson's argument gives it a new turn.

The presentation of the textual evidence does not retain the narrative form that in most cases structured the literary sources themselves. Instead, Dietrichson extracted the information that directly concerned buildings and omitted the narrative frame. The information is not given in the generalized way favoured by the older antiquaries when they were to describe for instance the cult or constructions of 'the forefathers'. Dietrichson does not aim to produce a system of universals. His presentation is strictly chronological, and he always seeks to give the specific period or date for his information, as well the exact locations for the churches and other constructions that are mentioned.

The chronology follows the process of the christening of Europe, beginning in the Roman world of early Christianity and ending in northern Europe in the twelfth century. This strategy gives the presentation a high degree of historic specificity. However, equally important is the way Dietrichson avoids an emphasis on the deeds and intentions of individual agents. To older historical and antiquarian studies, this often was a main point, also enhanced by the narrative character of the source material (cf. Chapter 2 in this volume). Dietrichson rather presents human agency as cumulative and processual. This implies that even if his text is based on narratives of saints, bishops and kings, his presentation is not one of events, intentions and good or bad rulers. The powerful individuals are seen in a context of historical forces, and more anonymous figures like monks, missionaries, builders and artisans, raiding Vikings and invading barbarians are given very active roles. In this way, the real protagonist of Dietrichson's text is not the historical individuals, but the wooden church as a type. Moreover, the historical forces do not only *produce* buildings, but *express* themselves in changing forms and styles. This activity is expressed in organic terms of growth and decay. The objects are imagined as 'moving' and behaving according to the regularities of biologically themed processes: church types 'wander' from one place to another, ornaments 'penetrate' new regions, forms and styles 'grow' and 'flourish' when they find fertile soil.

The second part of Dietrichson's text starts with a presentation of wooden churches in eastern regions: Russia, Hungary and West-Slavonia. The Russian churches are most thoroughly analysed, due to the theory of their close relationship with the Norwegian ones. However, Dietrichson draws one conclusion for the entire area: these churches are very different from those in Norway. They employ cob joints, while the stave churches use standing timber. Several of them are also of a rather recent date. Furthermore, Dietrichson argues that while the Norwegian churches belong to the Roman, occidental basilica type of building, the eastern, in particular the Russian churches, belong to the oriental type of central buildings (Dietrichson 1885: 37). Dietrichson then goes on to the few wooden mediaeval churches that can still be seen in Germany. Even here he finds important differences in the construction principles. Nonetheless, he concludes that the German and Norwegian buildings belong to the same cultural sphere, that of Roman influence.

An investigation of the church in Greenstead, some miles outside London, is the final part of Dietrichson's work and supplies his decisive arguments. The church had been mentioned by several scholars as related to those in Norway and is presented as the most important clue to the mystery of the origin of these buildings. Despite its acknowledged importance, Dietrichson first has to confront the problem of localizing the church that no antiquary seems to have visited since 1747. Aided by literary sources, he finds the building in Essex and by the same means identifies it as a chapel originally built for the body of St. Edmund, most probably no later than 1012 (Dietrichson 1885: 79). In Dietrichson's time, only two walls were left of the original construction. Inspecting them closely, Dietrichson not only finds that the earlier descriptions are inaccurate, but also that the building actually has the same kind of construction as the Norwegian ones. Moreover, he argues that the principles of construction used in Greenstead must be identical with what a number of written sources – among them Bede the Venerable – term 'mos Scotorum', and which Dietrichson himself has identified as the specific Irish way of building churches. The point here is not only that the churches are built from standing material fitted into a frame, but also that the wall planks consist of very heavy timber, produced from oak trunks hewn into two halves. Dietrichson concludes that he has solved the mystery of the origin of the Norwegian stave churches. As England and Norway both were christened from Ireland, their most ancient churches do not merely show the generic connection to the Roman world which also can be found in Germany, they also and more particularly are shaped by the Irish tradition (Dietrichson 1885: 80ff).

Equally important in this context is the method that Dietrichson develops to arrive at his results and the novelty it represents when compared to traditional antiquarianism. Dietrichson does indeed build on literary sources. He also plays the game of identification when trying to locate the church in Greenstead, relying quite heavily on narrative testimonies concerning St. Edmund. Nonetheless, this identification is never his final aim, and the literary sources do not represent any undisputed authority. Rather, Dietrichson lets his own observations and the knowledge he can infer from them correct what has so far been written about the buildings. Also, it is his close investigation of the construction in Greenstead that gives him the key finally to understand what the mediaeval texts mean by 'mos Scotorum' as a way of building churches. Again, this emphasis on observational data implies that the vital elements of explanation are styles and forms. It is the various ways of building churches, i.e., their construction principles, architectural organization and stylistic expressions that appear as the prime historical agents. Saints, bishops and kings are important so far as they initiate projects or are the objects of cult, but the factors actually shaping the buildings are different.

Dietrichson claims to have established as a general rule that in all Christian regions, the principles of church construction have been received from the respective mother church. His next step was to explain more precisely how the Anglo-Saxon churches had influenced architecture in Norway (Dietrichson 1888: 119). Compared with the stave churches, Greenstead is a very simple construction, and Dietrichson asks where the fully elaborate form was developed: in England or in Norway? The question has important implications, as it turns the history of the stave churches into a matter of national particulars. Dietrichson very quickly identifies some elements as specifically Norwegian.

The roofs are constructed according to principles not found elsewhere. Dietrichson compares their rafters to elements used in traditional Norwegian boats. The roof is said to have its very steep angle to make the snow fall off easily, but Dietrichson underscores that it is also a decisive part of the distinctive aesthetic of the churches (Dietrichson 1888: 123ff). The principles of construction identified as specific to the Norwegian churches are quite complex, and Dietrichson asks whether they really can have been developed in the country *after* the originally Anglo-Saxon church buildings had been introduced. If so, why are there no traces of the simpler forms that must have preceded them (Dietrichson 1888: 126)? His answer is that heathen cult buildings must have been constructed according to the same principles. Basing his argument mainly on saga literature, he argues that in a number of cases these buildings were later converted into churches. Dietrichson then presents a list of twelve items all pointing out similarities between the heathen *hov* mentioned in the sagas and the still existing stave churches in Norway (Dietrichson 1888: 144ff). The conclusion produced by this argument is that the two kinds of buildings are practically identical. This great similarity between early Anglo-Saxon churches and heathen Norwegian *hov* is said to be due to a reciprocal influence during the Viking period. Before this, Dietrichson says, no cult buildings whatsoever existed in the country, and the rituals of the heathen cult took place in the open air. Through their contact with Christian regions, the Vikings learnt how to construct cult buildings long before they adopted the new religion. When this finally happened, the art of erecting stave buildings had already reached a high degree of perfection.

Dietrichson's argument is flawed by the fact that no physical remains of a heathen *hov* have been found. Also, none of the existing stave churches in Norway are reckoned to have been built immediately after the Christianization took place in the early eleventh century, but are for the most part one or two hundred years younger. It is thus very difficult to verify the link postulated by Dietrichson in his early work, and he later moderated this part of the argument (Dietrichson 2010). However, important in the present context is the fact that the arguments presented in this text add a distinctly national dimension to the questions about the origin and age of the stave churches. While his first article situated the churches in a wider European and Christian context, Dietrichson's second text has the identification of national particulars at its core. They answer the questions about *where* the more advanced elements of stave building developed. The ship-building and weather conditions specific to Norway supply the answers, and the churches become intrinsically national due to their close kinship with the indigenous way of living and the natural surroundings. By the same manoeuvre, Norway no longer appears as a mere passive recipient of cultural forms developed elsewhere, but becomes an active force able to elaborate and embellish the simpler forms created in other countries. The argument corresponds well to Dietrichson's theory of Norwegian art history more in general, seeing its distinctive development as a response to specific natural conditions (Dietrichson 1906 and 2010).

Dietrichson speaks of the stave churches as monuments, not as antiquities. He also seeks to identify their national aspects and tends to see them as an expression of distinctive national principles. The churches are aesthetic and constructive products of Norwegian nature and way of life. At the same time, his perspective is highly processual, and 'development' is a very dominant term in his argument. The development is portrayed as nearly organic. It expresses itself in styles and forms, and it transforms buildings and gives them ever new shapes. The vitality gives forms and styles an agency of their own, and lets them take possession of the buildings and change them.

A Change of Regimes?

The 'discovery' of mediaeval art and architecture correlated with the terminological change from antiquities to monuments. Following Riegl, this implied a growing interest in establishing unintended monuments, i.e., turning ancient constructions and even objects into monuments by means of physical preservation. As we have seen, the idea that restored buildings still should serve some practical function seemed to prevail during the first part of the nineteenth century. Gradually the idea of independent monumental functions emerged. Contrary to intended monuments – be they ancient or modern – the unintended monument did not so much commemorate a specific person or event. Using Riegl's term, the new monuments bore witness to 'the passage of a considerable period of time' (Riegl 1903/1982: 24; and above). This new interest in age value and historical development meant that material remains acquired an independent evidential value. It could even be employed to correct or illuminate textual sources, as was the case when Dietrichson used the church in Greenstead to understand the expression 'mos Scotorum'. To gain this new kind of evidence, observation and fieldwork were required. Correspondingly, to preserve a building, images in books no longer sufficed, but became a matter of physical intervention.

These changes refashioned the assessment of ancient artefacts and buildings, the way they were spoken about and treated. They also have more general implications as one expression of the temporalization of history that occurred during the nineteenth century, particularly its later decades. Koselleck argued that the old *magistra vitae topos* in historiography started to dissolve during the second half of the eighteenth century. No longer understood as a collection of examples – to be followed or shunned – history came to be seen as a process of continuous development. Changes and transformations were more important historic issues than individual narratives (Koselleck 1985). Danish historian Bernard E. Jensen has underscored that it was not until the late nineteenth century that the past itself became the historians' obvious field of study, and the discipline of history became the investigation of processual change over time (B.E. Jensen 2003: 123). The terminological shift from antiquities to monuments reflects a deep transformation of the idea of history and the cultural organization of temporal experience.

NOTES

1. Saavel Fremmede, som reise i Norge, som Nordmænd, der have besøgt Udlandet, ere udentivivl enige i, at Norges Natur baade i Stolthed, Afvexling og Ynde, kan maale sig med de fleste europæiske Landes; men blant andre Savn beklage de almindeligen, at Norge er saa fattigt paa skjønne Oldtidslevninger og Ruiner, som bidrage saameget til at forskjønne mangen sydlandsk Egn og gjøre f.Ex. en Reise igjennem Italien, Schweiz og Rhinlandeene interessant. Disse levninger fra en svunden Tid forlyste ikke blot Øiet, men give Fantasien ved de Sagn, som gjerne ere knyttede til dem, rigt Stof til behagelig Underholdning.
2. En stor Deel af Oldtidens Kirker og andre Bygninger vare af Træ, som lættere ere udsatte for Ødelæggelse, og ødelagte ikke efterlade de maleriske Ruiner, som de solidere Steenbygninger.
3. [M]ærkelige, levende Sidestykker til de Folk, som færdes i vore gamle Søgur ...
4. Stilen og Characteren i de herlige gothiske Bygninger, hvoraf saa pragtfulde Levninger fines i Tydskland, Frankrig, England og Spanien; – men vi gaae tause og ligegyldige forbi de store Mindesmærker, som vi mellem os selv have fra vore Forfædre.
5. Dens Construction og solide og for den Tid skjønne Bygningsmaade, der synes endnu at vilde trosse Aartusinder tyder paa et Arbeide fra det 11te eller Begyndelsen paa det 12te Aarhundrede, og er temmelig uforandret.
6. [E]t Værk fra den sidste Halvdeel af det tolvte Aarhundrede; det er en af de smukkeste Bygninger af normannisk Bygningskunst fra Middelalderen, hvilken erindre om deslige Bygninger i England, Normandiet og enkelte Dele af Bygninger, der endnu ere tilbage fra hiin Normannernes Tid paa Sicilien.
7. Foreningen til Nationalmonumenters Vedligeholdelse. The name was later changed to Society for the Preservation of Norwegian Ancient Monuments (Foreningen til Norske fortidsminnesmerkers Bevaring).
8. [A]t *opspore, undersøge* og *veldligeholde norske fortidsmindesmerker,* især saadanne som oplyse folkets kunstfærdighed og kunstsands i fortiden, samt gjør disse gjenstande bekjendte for almenheden ved *afbildninger* og *beskrivelser.* Foreningen vil derfor, saavidt dens midler tilstrække, *understøtte reiser i fædrelandet,* og befordre *udgivelsen af verker,* sigtende til ovennævnte øiemeds opnaaelse.
9. [T]il Vedligeholdelse af de ædlere og nationale Former af vore Kirkebygninger, og til at virke for, at de nyere efter Tidens tarv byggede Kirker faae et mindre profant Udseende, end de hidindtil opførte.

6

Museums to Preserve Our Past

In 1825 a museum was opened in Bergen, on Norway's western coast. Apart from the collections of the Royal Norwegian Society of Sciences and Letters in Trondheim and those of the new university in the capital (from 1811), this was the country's first public museum. Behind it was W.F.K. Christie, a man of considerable political experience, but without any scientific training. After returning to his home town after a parliamentary career, he spent his energy on a number of projects to improve the urban infrastructure and to build up a civil public sphere. Following Christie's example, similar museum initiatives were taken in other regions and provincial towns. Public museums were established in two waves. The first saw the opening of museums in Kristiansand in 1828 and Arendal in 1832, in addition to the one in Bergen. After some quiet years, a new wave commenced in the mid-1860s, with Aalesund museum opening in 1866, followed by Tromsø in 1872, Stavanger in 1877, Bodø in 1888, Skien in 1891 and finally Tønsberg, Kristiansund and Vardø museums in 1894. A major part of the collections in these museums consisted of natural history items. Ethnographic material was also important, and in all cases local ships from these coastal cities were supplied with lists and instructions when sailing overseas. And finally, these museums collected what they still called antiquities. The emphasis on natural and ethnographic material greatly influenced the way this group of objects was understood and discussed. To modern museum visitors, finding antiquities in a museum is no great surprise. Rather, museums are generally regarded as the 'natural' place to keep and preserve objects cherished for their age and historical value. As we shall see, such ideas emerged only in the late nineteenth century.

When the last three of the above-mentioned museums were established, the concept they represented was quickly becoming outdated. In 1894 another new museum also had opened, signalling a different conceptualization of museums as well as the artefacts they contained. Norsk Folkemuseum (National Museum of Cultural History) in Oslo was the first open-air museum in Norway and also the first museum to make objects of traditional popular culture its main concern. It was rapidly followed by a number of other museums adopting the same principles. Among the largest is Maihaugen at Lillehammer, opened in 1904, but a huge number of other local or regional museums of this kind was also established during the first decade of the twentieth century, and they rapidly became paradigmatic (Eriksen 2009). What was fundamentally new about these museums was the kind of objects found relevant for collection. Age now became a dominant museum value. Despite this emphasis on history, the new objects did not simply represent an extension of the traditional category of antiquities. The reverse was rather the case. Older museum principles were eclipsed by new historical perspectives, and the older groups of artefacts were gradually redefined. The new museum type that appeared from the 1890s was historical rather than systematic. This implied that old artefacts became a larger and more important part of their collections, but more basically the turn towards history represented a change in museum principles. Age became a key to the value that the objects were ascribed, but was also fundamental to the ways they were interpreted and displayed. Historical context and processual change replaced the system as the meaningful frame for understanding museum items. The shift is traceable in a great number of European museums and collections and can be seen as the museological response to the general breakthrough of historicism (Hooper-Greenhill 1992). As a general trend, it led away from universal museums to a greater disciplinary specialization, in this way also reflecting the differentiation taking place in the academic world. In the new museological landscape, collections of cultural history gained in importance.

Systems, Specimens and Antiquities

The museums of the early nineteenth century were systematic. This does not – of course – imply that they all were very well ordered, but that objects were collected and treated as samples taken from a system and referring back to it. They were specimens, whose primary value lay in their adherence to a system and their place in it. Conversely, the system itself was the place where the relevant information needed to understand the item was to be found. This rationality is easily understandable when it comes to natural history, as it is in this way that we still think about animals, plants and minerals. In ethnographic museums we are likewise used to meeting objects being organized systematically according to their place of origin. As Camilla Mordhorst has argued concerning the erudite collections of the seventeenth century, the material that the objects were made from was the more important systematic element, which placed the ethnographic collections in a continuum with natural history (Mordhorst 2009). Ethnographic material was collected to show what human ingenuity could make out of the resources of nature, and also to show how different natural conditions made humans solve identical problems in different ways: how to carry water, prepare food, construct boats or protect their heads against the weather. Variety and difference were geographical, not historical. During the eighteenth century, the predilection for tables and systems of mutually exclusive categories, described by Foucault in his investigation of what he calls the classical *épistémè*, gave this rationality a new turn but did not introduce historical ways of thinking about difference. This systematic rationality prevailed in Norwegian museums until the very end of the nineteenth century.

What made it possible to treat antiquities as parts of a system was that even if they were 'ancient', they were not usually thought of as representatives of different periods of the past. As we have seen in the discussion of antiquarian work (Chapter 2 in this volume), the ancient objects were above all related to the narratives of sagas and other Norse and mediaeval literature. In this way they represented a world of their own, and even if it was remote, it was also temporally 'flat'. It had no internal temporal structure but was rather organized according to the different persons and events in the literary sources. Conceiving the past in these terms, its structure did not differ too much from that of natural history systems. As has already been pointed out (Chapter 3 in this volume), the enigmatic character of the past largely stemmed from its incompleteness, not from any deeply perceived historic difference. Conceiving the past as a kind of system could work as a heuristic tool when the aim of investigations was to increase completeness. While antiquaries regularly sought to connect objects and constructions with persons known from literary texts, and saw this as one of the main tasks of their work, they also tended to think in universals. Artefacts and constructions were related to generic concepts like 'cult', 'battlefield', 'banquet' or 'site of justice', supposedly equally relevant to all heathen groups and enabling cross-cultural as well as cross-temporal interpretations. Even this gives a basis for conceptualizing antiquities as specimens of a system, like natural history objects.

The systematic way of thinking implied that local particulars were not in themselves interesting. Particulars were not used to emphasize local distinctions, but rather seen as contributions to the system or generic category, making it larger and more interesting. Even this could apply to natural history specimens, ethnographic material and antiquities alike. Identifying a new species of roses or butterflies made their genera larger, while on the other hand it was the idea of genera that made it possible to identify new specimens. Finding new species or specimens of arrow heads, axes or standing stones correspondingly contributed to their respective genera. The particular circumstances of the findings did of course enter into the picture, but were subordinated systematic principles (and literal sources) as a key to erudite understanding.

The early museums in Norway were established with the explicit aim of contributing to the construction of a new civil society and a modern public sphere. Establishing museums meant contributing to the construction of a new public sphere in a modern civil society. During the nineteenth century, this project was pronounced in distinctly national terms in Norway. The needs of the new state were articulated and provided for. An overall aim of this work was to supply the country with institutions and systems equal to those of other countries, however, not to make them different by emphasizing local distinctions. In a number of aspects, this early phase of nation building was close to the older values of patriotism, with its emphasis on universals and loyalty to the state. The new museums generally were defined as institutions of public education. In the earliest text on museum theory published in Norway, the poet and critic J.S. Welhaven defined museums as

> well-ordered collections of educational and interesting material from the field of natural history and the arts. From their close study will emerge an intimate knowledge and love of science, which letters alone only rarely produce, and here lies the true impact of museums for the present period, that is known to denounce all kinds of feigning systems and with all its energy turns towards reality. In this way they join forces with the institutes of higher education, and fail more or less their purpose by serving ostentation or mere curiosity (Welhaven 1833/1991: 183).[1]

In a number of cases, the educational tasks of the new museums were expressed by connections to local schools or libraries. Some of the towns that opened museums also had newly established theatres, newspapers and reading societies. None of these institutions were established to make a show of local particulars or local history, but rather to give the locals their share of things that reached beyond their small communities, be it art, science or education. When the provincial towns took pride in their museums it was not because they celebrated local culture, but because the new institutions made the town contribute to a civil conversation between modern societies of educated people.

For a long time, developing a national culture meant being able to assert oneself among other nations by sharing common values and being measured by the same yardstick. Gradually this universalism was to dissolve.

National Awakening

The Scandinavian version of the historical turn in museums was the open-air museum. The first museum of this kind opened at Skansen in Stockholm, in 1891, as an extension of Nordiska Museet (the Nordic Museum) established by Arthur Hazelius in 1873. Three years later, in 1894, Norsk Folkemuseum outside Oslo followed suit. The ideas behind this institution were clearly articulated by Moltke Moe, who was also the country's first professor in folklore studies and the ideologue behind the museum. Inviting people to the foundation of the new museum, he explained:

> The aim of this collection is to give the Norwegian people a picture of the life that was lived in Norway down through the centuries, our fathers' ways of building houses, their furniture, their tools and utensils, their dress, in short the entire environment in which they moved and lived, and about which the memory now is gradually fading (Aall 1920: attachment 1).[2]

In this museum, objects were to be valued for their age and for representing a world and a way of living that was now disappearing. The perspective implied a considerable extension of the kind of old objects that were regarded as interesting in museums. To the 'antiquities' of the 'ancestors' were added objects of a far more recent date, reckoned to represent 'our people', in actual practice coming from traditional peasant culture. In his text on museums from 1833, quoted above, J.S. Welhaven had explicitly rejected peasants' artefacts as interesting for museums. He complained that some collections were filled up with 'piles of insignificant parchments' (probably concerning peasant property) and even 'loads' of primstaffs. As 'antiquities' these traditional wooden calendars had no value, according to Welhaven, as they still were used by peasants at the end of the seventeenth century (Welhaven 1833/1991:188 note 2). For the same reason, however, the primstaffs became highly cherished objects in the new collections of cultural history. In this context they above all demonstrated cultural continuity. On the one hand, the calendars were inscribed with ancient runes, on the other, they had been used in peasant culture until quite recently. Proving this kind of continuity between the present (or recent past) and the Viking or mediaeval periods was an important part of the project of building a national culture in the new state. At the same time, and more fundamentally, the reevaluation of objects from peasant culture illustrates a new way of conceptualizing history. It was no longer a collection of examples – the narratives of heroic ancestors from a remote past – but was turning into a matter of process, development and change. The artefacts were part of this process.

Moe's invitation to found Norsk Folkemuseum referred very explicitly to 'the Norwegian people' as a collective. One reason was the intention of the new museums to collect artefacts from the entire country, not merely the Oslo region. An even more important aspect is that nationality is treated as a unifying and actively working force. Representing bonds so strong that the centuries of Danish rule had not broken them, nationality is presented as something that creates continuity between 'then' and 'now'. It also unites people of different social classes in the present: as Norwegians all have the same fathers – whose way of life it is important to know. It is to the advantage of this community that the museum is prepared to work. The people or the nation is seen as a living organism taking its vitality from the bonds between past and present and from ancient culture that once was equally shared by all, and now to be preserved and cherished. The former inhabitants of the country are our close kin, and their artefacts and buildings are the memories of our own family.

Moe's text continues with a description of the new museum. The plan was to acquire property just outside the city centre and collect 'typical' buildings from rural districts all over the country. The exhibitions were going to show distinctive features of both nature and culture in the various regions. A new and purpose-built museum building was to be erected to display 'images of the life of the higher social classes'. Although a group apart, the phrase communicates that even the elite belongs to the national community! The museum's aim is twofold. Moe writes that 'a collection of this kind will be of great utility for the investigations of the history of our country', but also that the museum will 'awaken and strengthen our national feeling by widely distributing knowledge about the development and way of life of our nation' (Moe quoted in Aall 1920: attachment 1). In this way, the museum communicates with two different groups: scholars and the general public. For the latter, the use of the museum will above all serve to develop national feeling by keeping alive the memories of the 'fathers'' way of life.

These ideas were further developed at the museum's foundation meeting. Moe commenced his speech by claiming that 'a living interest in the history of the fatherland has always existed among our people. From the days of the sagas until the present have the life and history of the past held their grip on our thoughts in a very specific way' (Moe quoted in Aall 1920: 3). Above all, the history of our own country has excited us because it is about the 'fathers', their lives, their toil and their struggle against natural forces. And the more 'we' know about this, the more 'our' national feeling will increase, Moe states. The connection between 'us' and the 'fathers' is presented as very close in his words. Not only are we interested in their history, such an interest has 'always' distinguished the Norwegian people. What unites us appears to be both history and an interest in history. The people, the nation and its history represent a natural continuum. The museum will contribute to a further development of this organic community. Moe claims that what gives a museum of this kind its real significance is its impact on the national feeling of the people, and in this connection he refers to the motto of the Nordic museum in Stockholm: 'know thyself'. He then adds:

> A mirror of the life of the people is what the museum holds up to the present age, and the better our generation knows its past, the better it will know itself. A Norwegian museum of cultural history will give common people of our nation an understanding of our national life and our cultural development and a feeling of unity among us as well as with past generations – which certainly will yield returns in the future (Moe quoted in Aall 1920: 4).[3]

The museum's task is to produce knowledge, but the knowledge is presented in new ways. The older systematic museums were supposed to give an insight into scientific work and to encourage studies. The knowledge of the new museums is presented as far less intellectual and more intuitive and emotional. And while the older museums frequently had some connection to higher education or to clubs and societies that were dominated by the local elites, new groups were now addressed. Moe emphasizes that the museum of cultural history will be useful for 'common people'. For a large part, it will be their culture that is on display, and it is also in them that a national feeling is to be 'awakened'. This may be seen as an expression of the open and democratic character of the museum, an aspect that is often claimed to define museums in modern societies and distinguish them from the traditional collections of princes and learned men (e.g., Vergo 1989; Bennett 1995). Correct as this may be, it is also obvious that the museums of the new historical kind were addressing a public with another kind of competence. To visit and enjoy the new collections, erudition or higher education were not required. What was important, on the other hand, was an intituitive – and appearently natural – power of empathy and feeling of belonging. The museums had become projects of identity, and the value of their artefacts was found in their ability to embody community, continuity and a historically defined sense of cultural belonging.

Between Temporality and Topography

The ideas articulated by Moe in 1894 were not entirely new, but had taken some time to find their clear expression. Different terminologies and lines of argument had been tested. They concerned what kinds of objects might be found interesting to museums, but it is equally important that the reason for incorporating new kinds of objects was disputed. As we shall see, their age was neither the only nor the earliest argument for building museum collection with artefacts from peasant culture.

When a new museum, still of the systematic type, was established in the provincial town of Skien in 1891, the expressed aim was to build '[c]ollections of natural history and ethnography from all countries, though above all to start with new and old pieces of decorative art from our own country' (Moe quoted in Livland 1987: 161).[4] These words added a new dimension to the traditional systematic programme of natural history and ethnographic collections. Artefacts from 'our own country' were singled out as particularly interesting and actually ranged above the other groups of objects. A very direct reason for this new interest was that foreign antique dealers and wealthy collectors were buying peasant artefacts for export (cf. Sveen 2004). Skien is located close to the valleys of Telemark and not too far from Setesdal, two regions very rich in traditional folk art: paintings, textiles, silver work and wood carvings. In addition to the general disappearance of traditional rural ways of life in the wake of modernization, this commerce brought a very acute experience of loss. Nonetheless, the arguments that stated exactly *why* these artefacts should be collected and preserved in museums were not yet quite clear. What kind of values did they represent, apart from the pecuniary? Why had such items become important and how were they conceptualized? As we have seen, neither Bjerregaard in the 1740s nor Welhaven in the 1830s saw the point in preserving objects that were more or less identical with those still in use by peasants of their own time. The situation had changed, but the voices that now made themselves heard still seemed to be searching for the right terms and the most efficient way of expressing an experience that had not yet acquired its definitive form.

The invitation to start a museum in Skien states that 'Telemark is a main centre for our national decorative art, and is still prepared to offer numerous samples that it would be desirable to preserve before they have completely disappeared' (Moe quoted in Livland 1987: 161).[5] The term 'national decorative arts' refers above all to ideas expressed by the art historian Lorentz Dietrichson (cf. Chapter 5 in this volume), who was one of the men behind the Museum of Decorative Art and Design that had been opened in Oslo in 1876. An international phenomenon in the period, these new museums of applied arts built historical collections of objects intended as models for contemporary artists and artisans to help them develop their craft. The idea was to encourage production of good-quality artisan work as an alternative to the cheap and ugly industrial manufactured goods that gradually replaced the traditional ones. For the Museum of Decorative Art in Oslo, Dietrichson had argued the value of folk art and objects from peasant culture, which also came to be an important element in the Norwegian Arts and Crafts Movement (Glambek 2003). However, Dietrichson did not find every object from peasant culture to be interesting or valuable. The artefacts were judged according to aesthetic criteria, and only those of artistic value were found relevant for a museum. Age was subordinate to beauty, and even if the idea of 'folk art' defined peasant objects as a category of its own, it was fundamentally judged according to the same criteria as other pieces of decorative art.

The word 'samples' (*prøver*) in the text quoted above is also worth noting. In the systematic museums, items were normally designated with this term. It refers very directly to the principles that governed these institutions, implying that single objects always per definition were samples. Each item referred to the system and elucidated it and was itself explained by its position in the system. To employ the term when speaking about objects defined as art can be said to express a somewhat tentative approach to these objects and a still uncertain feeling about what kind of museum value they might represent.

Other lines of argument to explain why artefacts from peasant culture should be collected by museums were also tested. Already in the 1840s, W.F.K. Christie had suggested that the museum in Bergen should collect objects from peasant culture in western Norway. The initiative came to naught, however, and collections of 'national ethnography' were not established in Bergen until the early 1890s (Aall 1920: 1). In the capital, a struggle arose between Dietrichson's view and the alternative approach represented by the leaders of the university's ethnographic collections, Ludvig Kristensen Daa and his successor Yngvar Nielsen. Both argued that objects of 'national ethnography' should be collected without regard for aesthetic values. In 1881 Nielsen succeeded in getting a small public grant to buy these kinds of items for the museum. As argued above, items in ethnographic collections fit easily into systematic thought. A geographic organization of the objects according to their place of origin became more important as ideas of cultural fields or circles were developed. In this picture, national ethnography was no anomaly, but rather a way of articulating the idea of national culture in spatial terms.

However, none of these approaches – the aesthetic, the systematic or the geographical – considers the objects' temporal aspect. Also, it seems that none of them were felt to be completely adequate to give grounds for including peasant objects in the museums. What was new in Skien was that the objects were seen as historical in a modern sense, which made them different from the traditional category of antiquities. The region could 'still' offer objects that ought to be 'preserved' before they 'disappeared'. The expressions show an awareness of processual change and development. Even if the argument was linked to the very acute issue of export and commerce, it also communicates a growing awareness of history as processual and of artefacts as products of such processes taking place in time.

An experience of loss and a corresponding longing for a lost or fading world is constitutive to the modern historicity regime (Hartog 2003). This was also a driving force for the new museums and distinguished their rationality from that of the older kind. Even if both types of museum were interested in precious and rare objects, the new museums put far greater emphasis on objects that were rare – or becoming so – due to their age. This idea of history acquired its own particular expressions in museums collecting traditional peasant artefacts. Art historian Einar Sørensen has pointed out that the new way of thinking quickly became so self-evident that the principles governing the collecting hardly ever were discussed. The museums declared that they wanted 'the best' artefacts from peasant culture, but frequently without articulating what they meant by this qualification. In practice the idea of 'the best' involved a complex composite of age and beauty. Peasant culture was seen as old, but also as intrinsically static. Until it had started to 'dissolve', it was considered to have stayed more or less constant over the centuries. The paradoxical result was that even quite recent artefacts from peasant culture might be collected. The underlying idea was not an interest in contemporary culture, but rather an idea that any object defined as part of rural tradition was intrinsically 'old', regardless of its actual age. Artistry and beauty added to this particular idea of age or tradition. Such objects were felt to document the dramatic difference between the volatile presence experienced by the collectors and the supposed stability and long continuity of peasant culture. Traditional artefacts were taken to reflect a way of life reaching back to the Middle Ages (Sørensen 1990: 7). This stability was now threatened by historical processes of change.

From this perspective, modernization meant dissolution and destruction. The peasant culture still existed, some of its artefacts could yet be saved, but time was running short. Bearing such ideas in mind, museum work acquired a new sense of urgency and was frequently spoken of in terms of rescue operations. Consequently, the new museums with their emphasis on peasant culture did not illustrate history in the more general sense of events and change over time. Rather, they investigated one specific set of such events and changes: those related to the breakthrough of industrialization and the great transformations of rural society that followed in its wake. The museums were established as memorials to traditional rural culture, but became themselves monuments of modernity. As such they are vehement expressions of the modern historicity regime as described by Hartog, above all characterized by longing and the feeling of loss.

Peasant objects were collected without much contextual information. They were considered interesting in themselves, as representatives of types and forms, most often related to regions or cultural circles. As a contrast, Sørensen argues that in the case of objects from urban culture, connections to historical persons, leading local families and specific historical conditions were accentuated (Sørensen 1990: 7). The rural communities were felt to possess a culture that was ancient and authentically national, while urban people were seen as 'modern'. Their culture was distinguished by novelties rooted in foreign and imported influence. The variations in rural culture, on the other hand, were seen as created by local topography and geography, separating one valley or region from the next and defining cultural 'circles' or regions (Sørensen 1990: 8f). While nature had moulded rural culture, historical processes and human activity were what had set their ever shifting stamp on the urban way of life.

On a very concrete level, similar ideas can be read out of the first Norwegian handbook in museum work, published in 1925 by Hans Aall, director of *Norsk Folkemuseum*. The book is a guide to the most practical aspects of museum work, like the registration and labelling of objects, the organization of boxes and drawers, and the construction of shelves. The very mundane contents make the book seem far from ideological, and the solutions that are recommended appear as nothing but the outcome of entirely practical considerations. Nonetheless, behind the recommendations about, for instance, how to mark the objects (no loose labels) and what kind of register books to use (hardcover), categories and principles with profound implications for the understanding of the collections are present. On the topic of registration, Aall writes:

> when organizing the catalogue cards in each main group, we normally follow the rules [from the Scandinavian museum society], with subgroups arranged alphabetically and within each of them urban objects in chronological order and rural ones in a topographical (Aall 1925: 22).[6]

This principle also applies to the arrangement of the objects themselves in magazines as well as displays. Urban artefacts are to be placed in chronological order, rural ones to follow topography. The idea behind the chronological principle is to 'show the visitors how the conception of style as well as the domestic equipment and decoration have changed over the centuries. This development has not been uniform or concurrent in all parts of the country' (Aall 1925: 29).[7] The oldest rural artefacts and those from districts marked by 'urban influence' may also be arranged according to this principle. However, the idea that rural artefacts from the eighteenth century or later – in practice the major part of the collections – should be arranged topographically to demonstrate their inherent 'local character' is becoming prominent during this period. Moreover:

> In both the main groups [rural and urban] we do only include what is sufficient to present the actual historic period or the distinctive features of the respective valleys. For this reason, the urban exhibition rooms will acquire a more historical quality, while the rural rooms will resemble geographically arranged collections of folk art (Aall 1925: 30f).[8]

The work becomes an exercise in the practical use of preestablished categories. The categories seem quite natural, as if they emerge from the artefacts themselves, but in fact actually represent very specific ideas about culture and history. Aall's text communicates that it is *because* rural culture is local and urban culture is historical that the museum ought to arrange its collections according to these principles. The task of the museum is to emphasize these intrinsically distinctive features. Objects that do not contribute to presenting the historical character of urban culture and the topographic character of the rural, on the other hand, are not to be included.

Museums collecting rural artefacts thus ended up with historical perspectives that also drew on systematic principles. It was the new awareness of temporal change and subsequent loss that brought the rural objects into the museums. Genuinely new principles were active, and the inclusion of peasant objects cannot be seen as an extension of any existing group of museum items.

The logic that governed the older categories was tested out, but not found to give adequate reason for the inclusion of objects from peasant culture. Nonetheless, when the new objects had been included, the single items were treated in a way close to the old systematic principles. History became the context and was what gave the motivation for collecting the objects. Nonetheless, the idea of history as processes of change remained mainly contextual: it did not penetrate into the understanding of each single item, which still were seen as 'samples'. Once defined as historical, the objects were rapidly transformed into representatives of 'the past', 'tradition' or simply 'national culture'. The terminology shows the same development. The term 'peasant antiquities' (*bonde-antikviteter*) was used during the early years of the new museums, but it was relatively quickly relegated to the commercial market of dealers and collectors. In museums of cultural history, the same artefacts simply became 'museum objects' or even just 'objects'. These names say nothing about age. The lack of terms designating peasant objects as historical, despite this being what had brought them to the museum in the first place, correlates with how they were treated. Even though an awareness of historical processes was the museological context for these items, the knowledge they were thought to present emphasized history only in very rough terms.

Conflicts and Invisibilities

In some cases, the new museological principles led to conflicts. The small provincial town of Ålesund, on the northwestern coast of Norway, supplies a good example of the changes in museum rationality. From 1931 this city had two museums. The work of the Aalesund Museum, located in the town itself, reaches back to 1866. The Sunnmøre Museum, taking its name from the region, was opened in 1931 outside the urban centre. The older museum originated as a permanent exhibition of model boats and fishing equipment, planned to inspire and educate local fishermen and contribute to the modernization of their trade. During the 1860s, the headmaster of the local Latin school also built a collection of archaeological and natural history items, and in 1901 the municipality proposed that 'an ethnographic museum for the historical development of the way of life, the industries, customs etc. in the region of Sunnmøre and vicinities' should be established (Braaten 2003: 10).[9] As we see, the plans were quite traditional. The proposal reflected the ideas of the older systematic museums and had important educational aspects. Objects of local history were still spoken of in ethnographic terms.

The city and the museum were consumed by the great fire of 1904. The plans for reconstructing the museum focused on the importance of 'life and history in Sunnmøre' and stated that the collection should commemorate 'the life and work of the fathers'. The phrases probably reflect feelings of loss in the wake of the catastrophe, but can also be read as an expression of new museological ideas that reflect the general emergence of museums of cultural history (Braaten 2003: 25). Despite such declarations, however, the new museum that resulted was still a traditional one. Artefacts from peasant culture were collected, but were not exclusively local, and seem to have been valued mainly as art. Fishing equipment and natural history items still had priority. When the museum acquired a new building in 1930, the natural history collections, including the Arctic material, were placed on the ground floor, the fishing equipment on the first and the rural objects in the attic. The collections as well as their arrangements clearly reflect the rationality of older museums types.

In 1950 the museum's statement of intent was amended. The institution was now explicitly said to represent the city of Ålesund, only the fishing history covered the entire region. Local schools were offered the natural history items. The Arctic and ethnographic collections were still kept at the museum because of their relevance to 'the fishing and hunting traditions' of the region (Braaten 2003: 46). Peasant objects were also sorted out on this occasion. The new profile was motivated by the work of the more recent Sunnmøre Museum. The initiative for this museum was taken by local branches of Noregs Ungdomslag (Norway's Youth Society, NYS), an organization on the political left. The society was dedicated to a new appreciation of peasant and folk culture and for a cultural mobilization from below. NYS organized song and dance shows and theatrical performances and was involved in education. Local branches often built their own assembly houses for meetings, debates and study (Hodne 1995). The movement counted some leading authors among its adherents and also promoted the use of New Norwegian, a language constructed by Ivar Aasen and based largely on dialects from western Norway. It had particularly strong support on the western coast, including the region of Sunnmøre.

During the early years of the twentieth century, NYS engaged itself in museum projects. The new museum type, with its emphasis on popular rural culture corresponded well with its general agenda. At Sunnmøre several of the local branches started collecting objects and even buildings. When the new regional museum was established in 1931, this material was gradually transferred to the new institution, turning it into a museum that truly mirrored the whole region (Molvær 2003: 124ff). The Aalesund Museum had for some time been looking for a suitable site for a new open-air section, and the competition from the successful new institution was bitterly felt.

Over the years, a number of initiatives to encourage the two institutions to collaborate, or at least agree upon some principles of division of labour, failed due to each museum's fear of ending up subordinate to the other. Harsh words were said. The Aalesund Museum was accused by its opponents of representing urban snobbery and being ignorant of authentic Norwegian culture. For their part, the leading men of the older museum contemptuously spoke of the 'porridge museum' outside the city and bragged that champagne and canapés were served at their receptions (Grytten 2003: 160). The open-air museum was compared to a theatre, while the urban one considered itself more like a university (Molvær 2003: 139). A number of differences were set into play in this conflict. They concerned contrasts between urban and rural culture as well as different museological principles. The old systematic museum of universal knowledge was rivalled by the modern museum of cultural identity. The town museum represented traditional erudition and an urban bourgeoisie, while the open-air museum exhibited the kind of rural culture that was assigned a very important position in the construction of national culture, built on regional participation. The new museum exhibited the founders' own culture and history. Its buildings and objects came quite literally from their forefathers, for a large part they had been donated by families engaged in the museum work. It had an open-air stage, a restaurant and an assembly square for dancing and entertainment. It was open, welcoming, democratic and inclusive.

The old museum fought a losing battle. Provincial and amateurish as the 'porridge museum' might have been when it started, its ideas and work corresponded well with modern ideas of nation building and current museological principles. In a history of Norwegian museums written in 1944, it was judged to be 'beautifully situated', doing 'excellent work with its old buildings and collections'. As 'one of our best' it is assigned a leading position in the national museological landscape. The old institution in the city, on the other hand, has 'quite rich and good collections, rather aimlessly put together' (Shetelig 1944: 288ff).

The open-air museums rapidly became paradigmatic due to their number as well as their rhetorical efficiency (Ågotnes 2007: 50f). They supplied the kind of knowledge that was eagerly sought by the nation-builders of the twentieth century. Their dominant position soon led to the general impression that the older museums were 'aimlessly put together'. The rationality that originally had governed them was very quickly eclipsed by principles reflecting the new historicity regime. More or less successfully, the old institutions adapted themselves to the new situation. Objects originally collected to illustrate universal, systematic knowledge were reinterpreted as historical. A case in point is the museum in Tønsberg, south of Oslo, established in 1894 and reorganized in 1939. An open-air section displaying rural houses from the region was now planned. The museum's pride, a large collection of Arctic and Antarctic animals, among them some huge skeletons of whales, was installed in a new building constructed for this purpose. However, what had so far been a collection of natural history was now employed for exhibition of whaling and seal hunting and – not least – for a presentation of the local protagonist of this trade: Svend Foyn, whose invention of exploding harpoons started modern industrial whaling. Natural history was turned into local history. The harpoons appeared in a continuum with the ploughs and other equipment in the rural, open-air section, and the large skeletons were presented as the results of a local trade comparable to farming. The museum had turned from whales to whaling.

This example reflects the general principles. Old objects were transferred to new narratives about national culture, local distinction and cultural identity. Their age, history and local connections became their defining aspects. Not all parts of the old collections were equally fit to follow the new principles. Most adaptable were the antiquities. Even if systematic thought had been important, their age had always been a key to what made them relevant for collecting. The new ideas accentuated this aspect. Modern archaeology contributed to this temporalization, producing gradually more detailed knowledge about relative and absolute chronology. In this way, antiquities were no longer merely 'ancient'. The object, or group of objects, was also seen as the product of different periods and a variety of historical conditions. Moreover, the antiquities – now termed *oldsaker* (ancient objects) – could easily be seen as distinctively local, representing the oldest part of 'our' history.

The situation of the natural history objects was more complex. In some cases they could be transformed into representatives of a local trade, as in Tønsberg. The museum in Ålesund also kept its collections of natural history due to their alleged relevance for the local fishing trade (above). Another solution was to define the entire museum as one dedicated to natural history alone, as was the case in Kristiansand and in part in Bergen. Despite these strategies, a number of objects from the original collections still can be found in the museums of cultural history, not least large, stuffed animals. Stowed away in magazines and corridors these space-consuming objects remain monuments of forgotten museological principles.

Ethnographic collections have suffered a corresponding loss of meaning and have represented even larger problems than the natural history objects. The old museums in coastal towns still possess large quantities of ethnographic objects, hardly fit to serve as elements in displays of local culture and identity. They are not 'ours', they are not 'popular', and nobody knows if they are old. In some cases the objects are put forward simply as curiosities, in other cases ethnographic material is displayed as souvenirs. They are presented as examples of the kind of things that 'our boys' brought home with them from the seven seas and thus in their way a part of local culture. In fact, they are the kinds of objects that most clearly demonstrate the effects of the new historicity regime in museums.

Museums and History

The museums of cultural history led to a kind of democratization. The contents of the new museums did not refer to universal and somewhat abstract fields of learning, but to 'our own' culture and history, defined with a basis in national, regional or local communities. The contents implied new strategies. In principle what was now collected and exhibited was the culture of the intended audience, defined in a continuum reaching far back in time. This was most clearly expressed in the cases where the Youth Society was involved in the work, making the groups of museum founders, donors and visitors merge into one. But also more generally, the new museums were founded and led by people whose identity was based on the cultural forms that were exhibited. These changes gave the museums new tasks. While the older museums aimed to disseminate scientific knowledge and encourage studies in learned disciplines, the new museums were to create recognition and contribute to 'awakening'. Members of the nation – or the region or the local community – should learn about themselves and their origins and develop or strengthen their identity. The museums remained institutions of knowledge, but acquired an additional aspect of celebration.

These new tasks assigned new roles to both visitors and museum workers. In the older museum, the museum represented the expertise, placed hierarchically above the visitors. The expertise administered by the new museums was of a different kind and could at any time be eclipsed by a competent visitor. A local person, preferably old, who could tell stories about former ways of life or add information about the artefacts in the collection would represent more valuable – because more authentic – knowledge than the theoretically trained museum worker. To a certain extent, every museum visitor, coming to see 'our own' culture in the museum, can take on this role. Sharing an identity means sharing the kind of knowledge that the museum most fundamentally 'is about'. Historization opened the museums for quite new kinds of objects because it defined museum relevance in new ways. No collection will ever be complete, but the old collections did at least refer to an enclosed and finite universe of systems. The collections of the historical museums proved to be incomplete in new ways. Providing roots for people in a changing world appeared to be a more comprehensive and challenging task than originally envisioned. As time went by, the artefacts entering the museum gradually became correspondingly variegated.

NOTES

1. [O]rdnede Samlinger af belærende og sandsvækkende Gjenstande fra Naturhistorien og Kunsternes Gebet. Af den klare Beskuelse danner sig her en levende Fortrolighed og Kjerlighed til Videnskaben, som de døde Bogstaver sjelden kunne frembringe og heri ligger Musæernes sande Betydning for vor Tid, der bryder Staven over allehaande fingerende Systemer for med al Kraft at vende sig mod Virkeligheden. De slutte sig

saaledes til Instituterne for den høiere Dannelse og forfeile defor i større eller mindre Grad deres Hensigt ved at tjene under Ostentationen eller den blotte Skuelyst.

2. Hensigten med denne Samling er at faa bevaret for det norske Folk Billedet af det Liv, som i de senere Aarhundreder har været ført i Norge, vore Fædres Bygningsskikke, Bohave, Husgreaaad, Dragter osv., kort i det hele det Milieu, hvori de bevægede sig, og hvorom Minderne lidt efter lidt forsvinder.

3. Et speilbilde av folkets liv er det jo som Folkemuseet stiller frem for nutiden, og jo bedre vår slekt kjenner sine forutsetninger i fortiden, dess bedre vil den kjenne sig selv. Et norsk folkemuseum vil gi brede lag i nasjonen en forståelse av vårt nasjonale liv og vår kulturutvikling og en følelse av samhørighet både innbyrdes og med de fremfarne slekter – som sikkerlig vil gi renter for fremtiden.

4. Samlinger til Naturhistorie og Etnografi fra alle Lande, dog for det første begynnende med vort eget Lands eldre og yngre Kunstindustri.

5. Thelemarken er et af Hovedpunkterne for vor nationale Kunst-husflid og det sidder endnu rede med mange Prøver paa denne, som det vilde være ønskeligt at faa bevaret, før end de ganske forsvinder.

6. [V]ed ordningen av kortene innenfor de enkelte hovedgruppene følger vi i almindelighet reglenes [from Skandinavisk museumsforbund] bestemmelser om å ordne de fleste undergrupper alfabetisk og innenfor disse igjen bysaker kronologisk og bondesaker topografisk.

7. [Å] vise de besøkende hvordan stilfølelsen og hjemmenes indre utstyr og utseende skifter fremefter århundrene. Denne utviklingen har ikke vært helt ensartet eller foregått samtidig over hele landet.

8. I begge disse hovedavdelinger gjelder det at vi kun tar med det som trenges til å karakterisere de enkelte tidsrum og de forskjellige dalførers særkultur. Byrummene får derfor et sterkere tidshistorisk preg, mens bygderummene nærmer sig geografisk ordnede samlinger av folkekunst.

9. [E]thnografisk museum, omfattende Søndmøres og tilgrændsende bygders udvikling gjennem tiderne i levesæt, næringsdrift, sæder, skikke etc.

7

Monuments and Memorials

Without much distinction, the term 'historical monument' has been used from the nineteenth century onwards to refer both to ancient objects and constructions turned into monuments and to monuments erected to commemorate somebody or something. Both types – intended and unintended monuments – came to work as publicly accessible materializations of collective memory, national as well as local.

An important reason for this merging of two kinds of monument was the idea of age value and its position within the historicity regime emerging in the nineteenth century. According to Riegl, the idea implies that objects cherished for their age no longer were defined as simply ancient, but came to be understood to reveal or even embody 'the passage of a considerable period of time' (Riegl 1903/1982: 24). This temporality was then identified with continuous processes of change and development and even ascribed a kind of agency: it *passed*. Organic metaphors often were chosen to articulate this experience of time as something causing movement and processual change (cf. Hafstein 2000; Chapter 5 in this volume).

It was this recognition of age value that above all made it relevant to physically restore and preserve buildings, artefacts and constructions from the past and in this way to turn them into monuments. What separated them from the traditional intended monuments referring to important events or great men was the commemoration of time or temporality itself. Starting with the discovery of ruins as aesthetic objects in the eighteenth century, the recognition of age value successively influenced the growing interest in mediaeval culture and was also highly significant to the historization of museums during the nineteenth and early twentieth centuries. Defined as monuments rather than antiquities, the preserved buildings and artefacts now commemorated the passing of time, but could also serve as a means to bring it to a momentary halt. The monuments were designated as a contemplation of the organic bonds uniting past and present as well as of the 'time passed by'.

The recognition of age value also had an impact on intended monuments. Sharing the term 'monument', the two kinds came to influence one another in ways that made the celebratory dimension of the intended monuments merge with the temporal aspect intrinsic to the unintended ones. Age value made it relevant to designate ancient buildings, sites and objects as monuments, but also defined even intended monuments as commemorating events and persons *from the past*. Originally erected to honour great men, celebrate important events and secure their eternal and unchanged memory, i.e., outside any specific temporality, monuments were now conceived as commemoration of persons and events existing within historical temporality. They were celebrated for the importance of what they *had done* or what *had happened*. It is important to note that the 'statuomanie', analysed by Maurice Agulhon as distinctive to modern bourgeois society and emerging from the latter decades of the nineteenth century, is orchestrated in this historicist key (Agulhon 1988). The public monuments that were erected in great numbers during this period were seen as celebrating persons and events conditioned by a historical context – not as representing timeless virtue. Often rhetorically the more elaborate of the two, intended monuments have strongly influenced commemorational discourse in general. Not least this has been the case from the early twentieth century up to the present due to the development of a commemorational language related to the two World Wars and to the Holocaust and the immense number of monuments and memorials erected in their wakes.

To elucidate this merging of two monumental discourses, this chapter will explore some aspects of the Norwegian cultural memory of World War II. In addition to the monuments actually erected to commemorate sacrifices during the war and the German occupation of the country from 1940 to 1945, a large number of objects and sites referring to this epoch have been turned into monuments rather more as 'time witnesses' whose primary memorial quality is that they are authentic remains of past reality.

From Royal Glory to Civic Virtue

A general history of public monuments is outside the scope of this book. Nonetheless, some points of particular relevance need to be presented. In Mediaeval and Early Modern Europe, public monuments were either religious or erected to commemorate the deeds, lives and deaths of princes and the aristocracy. They embodied the power of monarchs and noble families, defined public space, provided continuous royal presence in different parts of the domain and installed deference in the subjects. Funeral monuments in churches spoke of dynastic continuity and buttressed claims of property, power and privileges. These monuments made public space their own in celebration of agents and forces beyond the reach of most people: God and royalty. Monuments stated to whom commemoration was due, as well as what space they rightfully should occupy. They asserted clear distinctions between the object of commemoration and the subjects offering it. Monuments were the privilege of princes and spoke of authority above the secular and temporal.

Not until the eighteenth century did this begin to change. In his book *Naissance du Panthéon,* Jean-Claude Bonnet argues that a 'cult of the great man' emerged during the Enlightenment, gradually supplanting the idea of kings and nobles as the only ones worthy of admiration, eulogies and commemoration (Bonnet 1998). The 'great man' could be a politician or a military hero, but just as often he was an author, a *philosophe* or – gradually more important – a public benefactor. Contrary to the old monuments' celebration of unbridgeable difference, the new were symbols of community, Bonnet points out: '[t]he glory fit for the new era installs a solidary community and a strange kind of closeness which is remarkable as the most singular trait of the cult of the great men during the eighteenth century' (Bonnet 1998: 40).[1] A decisive point in the French tradition that Bonnet investigates was reached in 1758. That year, the French Academy established a new topic for their annual competition in eloquence. Instead of presenting the usual panegyric to the king, the competitors were invited to give a eulogy to a great man of the nation. The idea was very well received, and for a number of years the annual event presented authors and philosophes with an arena and a genre where they could articulate their views on greatness, virtue and heroism. The genre developed gradually. It was taken to serve both political and literary strategies and was eagerly adapted by a number of the young and ambitious persons who later would play active roles during the Revolution: Condorcet, Marat, Robespierre and de Staël. One reason for its popularity was that the genre did not produce '[a] dusty row of epics exclusively turned towards the past', but proved an effective and forceful weapon for discussing the present as well as the future (Bonnet 1998: 111).[2] Despite the fact that this minor rhetorical genre later sank into oblivion, it is Bonnet's conclusion that it played an important role in the shaping of a new kind of heroism. The Pantheon of stone, inaugurated in the former church of Sainte-Géneviève in Paris in 1792, was preceded by a 'Panthéon in paper', he contends.

In his analysis of the 'statuomanie' of the nineteenth century, Maurice Agulhon delves deeper into the political radicalism of the monuments that came to be erected to commemorate the lives and deeds of the new kind of hero. What was at stake was not just a new kind of heroism, but also new ideas about society, authority and citizenship. He points out that the sheer number of statues in modern societies makes it difficult to understand how dramatically radical the new public monuments to persons who were neither royal, noble or saints once seemed. Erecting monuments to individuals whose merits were both personal (not inherited) and secular was an expression of the same kind of liberal humanism that later developed into the politics of democracy (Agulhon 1988: 143).

The new kind of public monument, emerging in Europe from late eighteenth century, signalled a redefinition of public space, turning it into a public sphere of a distinctly modern kind. The monuments were erected by citizens to celebrate and commemorate fellow citizens for their 'civic virtue'. The term was popular in patriotic discourse and is usually defined as those personal qualities and habits that are important for the success of the society or community. Above all it was identified with a willingness to place the common good above personal convenience (Damsholt 2000a: 102, 124; Chapter 6 in this volume). The new kinds of monument presupposed a general consensus that the distinction was deserved. For the same reason, it came to be important that the costs of the monument, at least symbolically, were carried by the community. Fundraising for the erection of a planned monument became a prerequisite not only for economic reasons, but to signal the general will to contribute to the distinction of a deserved fellow citizen. The monuments thus materialized new civil understandings of society as a union of equal, free citizens and of public space as the lawful stage for the life of this society.

Standing Stones and Universal Values

As a remote Danish province, Norway was bestowed with very few monuments of the older kind. Some civil monuments were erected after the country gained its independence in 1814, but initiatives did not rise in number until the early twentieth century. The dissolution of the personal union with Sweden in 1905 and the centenary of the Constitution in 1914 were accompanied by strong waves of nationalistic enthusiasm. The decades before World War 1 brought an increasing number of monument initiatives, culminating with the celebrations in 1914. Monuments honouring local delegates to the Constituent Assembly of 1814 were inaugurated throughout the country that year. Memorials of the 1808–1814 war, leading to national independence, were also erected, as well as other monuments celebrating earlier events in national history. Taken as a whole, the monuments from the late nineteenth and early twentieth centuries contribute to creating an image of national history as a continuum, existing independently of the country's four-hundred-year-long subordination to Denmark. They communicate that during this long period, the national will for liberty and to defend the fatherland had never been extinguished. With this as the backdrop, the rather suddenly achieved independence in 1814 appears as the natural culmination of a long, heroic tradition.

Norway remained neutral during World War I, but as much as 50 per cent of the merchant navy that continued its activities during the war was sunk by mines and torpedoes. In 1926 a huge memorial hall shaped like a pyramid was constructed in Stavern, a coastal village with a fort and naval base. The names of the nearly two thousand seamen who had lost their lives were inscribed on tablets along the interior walls. Even if this was not, formally speaking, a monument to fallen soldiers, the design seems very directly inspired by the war graves and war memorials that had been constructed on the Continent and in Britain.

Nonetheless, it was World War II that led to the real boom in memorials in Norway. At present, every local municipality in Norway has this kind of monument and frequently quite a number of them. As an example, approximately half of the nearly fifty public monuments in the northern city of Narvik refer to World War II. The city's strategic importance during the war and the fact that it was the last free Norwegian town after the German invasion in April 1945 means that Narvik is not the average in this context. But the number of monuments still demonstrates the strong impact this historical period had on Norwegian cultural memory and public space. In the capital itself, fifty-two monuments referring to World War II exist at present, not counting allied and Norwegian war graves (Tvedt 2010: 646ff).

The background for this commemorational practice is the ideas of war that emerged with nationalism. The soldiers of the new nation-states were no longer a tool of the sovereign monarch, but citizens defending their own country. Based on this rationality, fallen soldiers were the martyrs of the nation, citizens who had given their lives in its defense (Mosse 1990: 19). While military monuments traditionally had celebrated only the victorious (and noble) officers, this new understanding gave ample reason for the commemoration of the rank and file who had sacrificed their lives. While this way of thinking about the role of the soldier goes back to the French Revolution, the turning point in types of monuments and commemorations came with World War I. Thomas W. Laqueur points out that '[i]n January 1915 – one can date this remarkable change with a precision not usual in cultural history – a new era of remembrance began: the era of the common soldier's name or its self-conscious and sacralized oblivion'. The British Red Cross started to search for graves, mark them with a cross, identify the soldiers and register their positions (Laqueur 1994: 152). The same year, France sanctioned a law that granted all soldiers the right to a proper grave (Mosse 1990: 46). Soon, all parties engaged in the war followed this practice, which, among other things, finally produced the endless rows of white crosses marking the graves in the area of the Western Front, including the memorials of the battles at Ypres, Verdun and the Somme. As George L. Mosse has pointed out, a veritable cult of the fallen soldier emerged, developing its own language of symbols, memorials and rituals. Martyrdom and sacrifice were major themes, but what Mosse calls an 'appropriation of nature' also became important. Uniting itself with the nation's soil, the life and blood of the fallen soldier were turned into symbols of future growth, indicating that the sacrifice was not fruitless (Mosse 1990: 107ff).

The construction of war memorials in Norway started shortly after the liberation in 1945 and is still going on. One reason for the continued and long-lasting activity is the gradual changes in the understanding of whom and what are to be commemorated and of what qualifies as casualties of war or as active resistance work. For this reason new groups and individuals have received their memorials, while at the same time ever more sites, constructions and artefacts have come to be considered as monuments. Monuments have been inaugurated on the five- or ten-year anniversaries of the liberation during the entire postwar period. Several of them are the scenes of annual commemorational ceremonies on Constitution Day and Liberation Day, 17 May and 8 May respectively.

The earliest memorials honour the victims of the two months of actual war in Norway after the German invasion on 9 April 1940. Monuments were also erected to commemorate the king's flight through the country after the invasion, closely followed by the enemy who wanted him to resign, or – when it became obvious that he was not going to do so – tried to kill him and the crown-prince through heavy bombing. The location of these early monuments follows the route of the campaign in 1940. A third group of monuments from the most immediate postwar years commemorates fallen members of the resistance movement. From a feeble start, resistance against the occupation and the Nazi government grew stronger after 1942 and included both civil and military actions.

One of the earliest monuments commemorating the resistance has also functioned as a national war monument in more general ways. The first anniversary of the liberation was celebrated with the inauguration of the 'monument to fallen Norwegian patriots' at Akershus fortress in Oslo. The site had considerable symbolic value, as the fortress had been one of the most dreaded prisons during the occupation, and a number of executions had been carried out there. Located at the very place of execution, the monument commemorated forty-two resistance men who were shot during the winter of 1945. Moreover, it was also intended as a symbolic burial place for all fallen members of the resistance movement, whose graves were not always known. The monument itself carries a short phrase from a well-known poem by Arnulf Øverland, originally written during the war. It has no names, but an inscription saying, 'In this place, Norwegian patriots were shot during the war 1940–1945.'[3] Cultural historian Kyrre Kverndokk has argued that the choice not to cite the names of the forty-two executed men, nor to fix the events that are commemorated to the winter of their deaths, makes the monument point beyond its specific time and place. Using the words 'Norwegian' and 'patriots' and referring to the entire war period, the monument does not only include other resistance fighters, but more or less all Norwegians who had run the risk of identifying themselves with the resistance during the five years of occupation (Kverndokk 2011: 105). Kverndokk also points out that the exclusion of individual names together with the design of the monument as a symbolic grave give clear references to the tradition of war graves developed after World War I and the cenotaphs dedicated to unknown soldiers (Kverndokk 2011: 104).

Corresponding monuments honouring local resistance men and women have been inaugurated all over the country. The initiatives have come from municipalities, neighbourhoods and in some cases from institutions and government services commemorating their former employees or schools their pupils. During the postwar years, the various veteran organizations gradually became very influential in the field. In all cases, the deceased are conceptualized as 'our' people and 'our' fallen. The community that is invoked in this way refers in part to the specific place and in part to the larger, national community. Inscriptions may unite these dimensions by naming the home town or village of the deceased and at the same time state that they 'gave their lives for Norway' or add 'Norway thanks you'. The fallen soldiers and resistance men and women are commemorated both as members of the local community and as agents in national history.

A number of these earliest monuments are designed as simple standing stones, quite roughly hewn and with minimal decorations except names, dates and a phrase expressing remembrance and gratitude. This makes the monuments resemble graves, an aspect that is further accentuated when the stones are placed in or by the churchyard. However, another aspect is the close resemblance to ancient standing stones. Eighteenth-century antiquaries referred to these stones as having been produced in a direct line of tradition following Odin's call to erect standing stones at the graves of all men of consequence (Chapter 2 in this volume). Even if these words no longer were taken to have had such a literal impact (and the Norse deity Odin was no longer considered a historical person), the tall hewn stones still carried strong symbolic weight. Choosing an identical design for the monuments erected after 1945 meant inscribing the lives of those who were commemorated into a proud national narrative of greatness and courage. Moreover, this was not the first modern use of standing stones. Several of the monuments erected in the first decades of the twentieth century commemorated the 1808–1814 war, and even they were often modelled according to this tradition.

In some communities monuments from the two wars (1808–1814 and 1940–1945) have been erected side by side. This is the case in Bagn in Valdres, one of the locations of actual fighting during the campaign in 1940, where two proud standing stones can be seen in the square outside the church. One reason for this arrangement is no doubt a wish in both cases to give the monument the best possible location, resulting in the same choice of place. Nonetheless, an additional effect is produced by the juxtaposition and by the fact that the two stones have very similar designs. Seen together they communicate a message of continuity and connections not merely between them but also to ancient history. The monuments do not really bespeak the fact that they have been erected approximately fifty years apart, neither that one of the commemorated events has taken place about 150 years before the other. The roughly hewn stones of the two monuments look natural – as if taken directly out of Norwegian rock – and ancient. These qualities appear as just as important as the specific events that are being commemorated.

The standing stones above all commemorate the death and sacrifice of soldiers and resistance fighters. While their inscriptions tend to emphasize the national struggle against the enemy, other monuments do more to transform the meaning of this sacrifice into universal values. Even these monuments can bear lists of names, but as memorials they communicate a message pointing beyond the destiny of the single individual. As with the standing stones, the struggle against the German occupation and the Nazi regime is referred to as a fight for freedom or liberty, but it is also portrayed in a more generalized way as a fight for democracy, for human dignity and human rights, or for peace and justice. The earliest examples of this kind of iconography communicated their message largely by using allegorical figures, while the more recent ones usually are quite abstract. The development reflects more general changes in artistic expression, but what these monuments nonetheless have in common is the interpretation of World War II as a drama pointing beyond any specific historical context and of the fight against Nazism as having universal implica tions. The early use of allegorical forms indicates that this interpretation of the war dates back to the immediate postwar period, but it is probable that its position has grown even stronger later. Over time the experience of grief and loss has grown less acute, but it is still felt imperative to keep up the memory of the war and not least to pass it on to new generations. To do so, a message emphasizing the values that the struggle against Nazism most profoundly 'were about' becomes vital.

An example is the monument inaugurated in the small community of Vefsn in the county of Nordland in 1990. According to Einar Grannes, who had taken the initiative, the words liberty, democracy, justice and human dignity, which were inscribed on the monument, 'are intended to place the struggles into a historical and cultural context that is larger than the nation, and to emphasize the ideological aspect as the core element of the fight against Nazism'. Grannes also underlined that 'World War II was not a battle fought between large and powerful states' but a struggle that 'concerned us all. It was a struggle for the abstract and elevated goal that gives meaning to life and lifts the human spirit above the level of slaves' (Grannes 1992: 5; 31).

The more specific references to events and persons from the war have not disappeared from these monuments. For example, for all its insistence on universal values, the memorial at Vefsn is dedicated to 'our fallen'. What is important is the will to see the historic events as representatives or examples of universal values. The standing stones linked the events of World War II to 'history', understood as a long, continuous line of national pride and the will to fight for independence. The monuments celebrating universal values use another strategy to connect specific events to an overarching set of values, reducing the national implications and emphasizing what is common to 'the human spirit' or other universally held values. Nonetheless, in both cases specific events and persons from the war period are lifted out of their immediate temporal context and seen as examples of something larger. This manoeuvre does not imply a reduction of the specific events, nor subordination. Rather, on the one hand, it sets forth the events or persons that are celebrated as ideal cases, as examples to revere, admire and – if necessary – follow. On the other hand, the historical examples serve to confirm the validity of the ideals and universal values, stating that they are not just abstract principles but something that real people actually have fought and died for.

All of Us – Resistance as a Collective Project

While individual names were an option with the earliest monuments, they have become a requirement for the more recent and now define war memorials as a genre. Kverndokk argues that the Vietnam Veterans Memorial (1982) in Washington, DC, has been a decisive force in this development, which he sees as an international trend. One consequence is that older monuments, originally not without individual names, now are supplied with additional plates or inscriptions. Another is the number of new monuments with lists of individual names of persons, for example from a school, a neighbourhood or a place of work.

Who are the persons listed on the new monuments? As a general trend, the development means that more names of women and children are on the lists and the monuments. While the early monuments mainly commemorated the activities of male soldiers and active resistance fighters, the more recent communicate to a much higher degree that the war and German occupation concerned the entire civil society and had its casualties among all groups. This development may have been further enhanced by the fact that the Norwegian word *offer* means both sacrifice and victim, thus making it possible to blur the distinction between the deaths of soldiers and civilians during war: they are all victims as well as martyrs.

The new monuments with their lists of individual names thus reflect an increasing individualization but also an extended definition of resistance. They may be less explicitly nationalistic in their design and inscriptions than the older ones, but both individually and as a whole they very effectively convey a message of resistance and anti-Nazi activity as a collective project, uniting all the nation's citizens. In some ways this development also affects the older monuments, which no longer appear to commemorate deeds that stand alone but rather are integrated, if unique, parts of a collective, national project.

Another effect of the increasing number of monuments is that activities, institutions and bodies, which were quite loosely organized and had a fleeting and unstable character during the war, gain stability and presence of a new kind. One example is the illegal press. During the war, a considerable number of persons were engaged in the work of spreading information, not least after all private radios were confiscated by the Nazi authorities. The 'papers' most often produced were simple duplicated sheets containing news transcribed from BBC broadcasts. In a number of cases the papers were distributed only for a short period because the small cells making them were arrested or had to go underground. In 1984 a monument was erected to 'the illegal press' in a public park in Oslo, close to the University Library. The monument was created by the artist Skule Waksvik after an initiative from the veterans' association. The monument commemorates and honours the important and often dangerous work carried out during the occupation. However, it also works in another way. The monument does not merely conserve the collective memory of the illegal press as it was back then, it also makes this press a body in the present – and perhaps even a more substantial and solid body than it ever was before. This is not to say that the work of the press during the occupation was not important. Nonetheless, it was a consequence of its historical possibility conditions that it could not be a united and solid organization during the period when it was effective. As such, the illegal press did not exist during the occupation other than as a rather random selection of ephemeral prints and copies. Establishing the veterans' association and erecting a monument turns this activity into something that it originally was not, while at the same time claiming social reverence for this retrospectively constructed institution.

Time Witnesses

The continuous work of inaugurating new memorials has also led to non-intended monuments gaining in importance. Sites and constructions where important events took place during the war have been endowed with memorials ever since 1945, but a new trend is turning such sites into memorials themselves. Bagn in Valdres is again an example of this. The standing stone commemorating the battle there has already been mentioned (above). It was erected by the local church soon after the liberation. In 1986 even the battlefield itself, at the farm called Bagnsbergatn, was inaugurated as a memorial by King Olav V. While the stone *represents* events that are commemorated, the actual battlefield *presents* the event; it is invested with another kind of authenticity.

Moreover, as the idea of resistance work has expanded to include more activities and new groups of individuals, the number of relevant sites has grown correspondingly. Initiatives to convert such locations into publicly accessible memorials have been an important feature of the memory work during the last two to three decades. One element of the Norwegian resistance was the small cells of boys and men doing secret military training in preparation for a final fight to liberate the country. Known under the name 'Milorg' (the Military Organization), such groups were connected to the allied forces and received parachute drops of equipment and men. Huts and cabins in the forests were used for storage and as hiding places. The work was dangerous because it was illegal, and German reprisals if they were discovered were severe. Just as important when it comes to memorials is that these cells – 'the boys in the forest' – are among the most mythical and heroically laden element of the Norwegian resistance, conveying a message that Norwegians contributed to the allied victory in World War II simply by exercising their most fundamental national instinct: hiking and skiing.

In later years a number of the hiding places of these groups have been made into monuments. Parachute drop sites are marked with plates, the dilapidated cabins and huts have been restored, and information boards have been erected. Even here the veterans' associations are important agents, together with local history societies. Originally, the sites of the resistance cells were chosen for their isolation and secrecy, and making them publicly accessible therefore includes setting up signs to show directions and clearing and marking paths. The sites are frequently connected to new or already existing trekking routes, a fact that makes them appear as destinations or attractions for hikers. The monuments supply a distinct meaning to the landscape, instructing the hiker to experience it in a specific way. The memorial sites are integrated in natural scenery and an activity already conceived as distinctly national. Moreover, this activity merges with that of the resistance fighters.

At Finnskogen, a vast forest region along the Swedish-Norwegian border, a cabin called *Gjestgiveriet* (the Inn) was rebuilt and inaugurated as a memorial in 1990. During the occupation it served as a place of shelter for Milorg and was also used for secret radio communication. The cabin was discovered by the Germans in 1944 and burnt down. Two men were wounded in the battle. The description given by the Norwegian Trekking Association contrasts the originally secret location of this cabin with its present state, when 'the parking lot and the flag pole speak of more peaceful times'. This place is now part of a trekking route crossing the region and serves as one of the regular overnight accommodations and resting places run by the association. The visitors' entries in the guest book indicate that it also works as a war memorial. They refer to the past, compare then and now and – not least – compare themselves and the resistance men, both trekking in the forest. In Uldal in Gudbrandsdalen, the Milorg cabin *Reiret* (the nest) has also been restored and opened to the public. Compared to 'the Inn', this place is more of a museum, less a resting place for hikers. But even to reach this attraction one has to embark on a hike. The cabin lies in a very remote place, and despite the signs that have been erected, it is quite difficult to find – and part of the story is that the Germans never found it.

These nonintended monuments lack the elaborate rhetoric of the intended ones and rarely have complex iconographic programmes. Their actual design and their location are determined by past events and historical conditions, not by an artist or an executive committee planning to design a memorial. On the other hand, these monuments carry with them an authenticity of their own. They are – or are supposed to be – genuine parts of the past, representing history and historical persons in a quite direct way. They are time witnesses in a way that the intended monuments erected in retrospective commemoration cannot be.

At the Museum

Norway's Resistance Museum opened in 1970 as part of the celebration of the twenty-fifth anniversary of the end of World War II. As such it is an intended monument. Nonetheless, as a museum exhibiting objects from the period in question, it also has important aspects of the nonintended monument. The museum turns ordinary and at times random objects from the period and events in question into objects of commemoration. In this way it illustrates the general trend of merging the categories of intended and nonintended monuments. The exhibition also demonstrates how this merging of categories has a deep impact on the message that is conveyed. When 'ordinary' objects from a past period are made into monuments, they acquire an additional symbolic value. The recontextualization makes them point beyond themselves and their own history and conveys a message of a more general kind. They are no longer 'just old'; their very – and frequently fragile – materiality is imbued with higher meaning. On the other hand, the meaning of monuments and memorials are enhanced when they are made up of 'real' history. The age and authenticity of the objects or constructions in question mean that the persons and events that are to be commemorated are not just represented by the monument, but are literally present. This is the time witness effect: the past is mediated by the means of a presence.

The Resistance Museum itself puts great weight on the fact that authentic material and symbols, i.e., from the period, have a dominant place in the exhibition and are a main instrument to communicate its message. The exhibition itself is organized chronologically. It follows the development of the war, but at the same time turns the chronological structure into a narrative one. Visitors are led through a well-defined route constructed of corridors and narrow passages with little possibility to escape or follow their own whims when visiting the museum. The route is defined by the walls and structures of the building, but is accentuated by the use of iron bars and heavy chains. This design makes the most of the available space, but it also creates an experience of restricted freedom and lack of choice. Once they have entered 'the five dark years' – the common rhetorical term for the German occupation – the visitors have no possibility of getting out quickly unless they press against the chains and concrete. The showcases and other museum installations are designed according to the same ideas. Heavy, rough wood or solid steel are the prevalent materials, emphasizing the impression of seriousness, darkness and gravity. Apart from conveying a message of the occupation as a dark period, the choices of materials and design also seem to indicate that in these rooms, nothing is going to change. The exhibition is very solid. It is not to be taken down, and its message is not open to negotiation. The museum resembles a monument erected to commemorate something 'forever' rather than an academic institution presenting the results of new research or discussing different perspectives and interpretations.

In the vestibule, old newspapers announce the outbreak of the war in Europe, contrasting this with the still peaceful life in Norway. Entering the exhibition, visitors are confronted with an installation of guns formed in the shape of a swastika. The darkened room contains information about the German plan for the invasion of Norway. There is also an image of Vidkun Quisling, leader of the Norwegian Nazi Party. An extract of his radio speech is played: Quisling announces his new 'national government' taking over the country. The museum caption is: betrayal. From here, the exhibition tells about the battles during the spring months and follows the king and crown prince on their flight toward the northern (and still free) parts of Norway and from there to England.

After this start, a narrow and low-ceiled corridor leads the visitor down a slope. The construction is made to hide a step, but also to symbolize the nation's loss of liberty and the entrance to the dark and difficult years of occupation. This section tells about the Nazi government and the attempts of the Norwegian Nazi party to reorganize civil society according to their political principles. A new caption informs the visitor that 'resistance grows'. Through iron bars and solid timber the visitor obtains a glimpse of the guns that people in Norway are said to have put aside after the military defeat in the spring of 1940 and which here are made into a symbol of the emerging resistance. This creates a continuous line from the fighting in 1940 to the resistance movement. When this emergence is juxtaposed with the Nazi takeover of society, an impression is created that these two developments were equal in both strength and influence as early as the summer of 1940. The fact that Norwegian resistance took somewhat longer time to emerge is not mentioned here.

The low-ceiled corridor ends abruptly in a wall with four steel plates. Pictures of three men show the earliest losses of the resistance movement; they were shot as spies in August 1941. Below their portraits, the steel plates are perforated by bullets. The fourth column has the shape of a cross and carries an explanatory text. The installation lets history merge with commemoration. It is definitely a memorial in honour of the three men, but in the museum context it also functions as an image of the evil forces reigning over the country: an individual life is not worth much. The people are to be subdued and individuals who do not obey will meet their final destiny. At this point the exhibition makes a sharp turn and continues downstairs. School children visiting the museum are told that 'now you are going underground. From here, everything is illegal'. Above the stairs hangs a large picture of the manor house where the Norwegian Constitution was signed in 1814 – an icon well-known to most Norwegians. Here it is shown behind iron bars.

The exhibition on the upper floor can be read as an overture. It tells what happened and how this led to the situation where the Norwegian resistance was formed. The resources used are of a regular historical nature, mixing different kinds of sources like old newspapers, radio speeches and pictures with the curators' explanatory texts. The merging of history with commemoration, indicated in the monuments to the resistance men, becomes far stronger in the next part of the exhibition. Not least is this the case because the number of artefacts from the period increases. They are used to tell the story of the resistance and its development as a movement, but also to make this movement present by displaying artefacts that do not only refer to it but were part of it.

In two vaulted cellar rooms different aspects of life during the five years of occupation are described. The first presents the resistance movement, also known as 'the Home Front'. Along one wall the structure of the organization is presented; the other is about illegal information work and shows a number of illegal newspapers and other printed material. Ways to hide private radio receivers when the authorities wanted to confiscate them are also shown. By pushing buttons the visitors can listen to the recordings of what was available to people who managed to keep their radios. Out of the darkness ring the voices of Churchill and of the exiled King Haakon VII, the voices of the free world. The real highlight of this exhibition is a reconstructed cellar of a resistance man, showing a selection of resistance props in their 'natural context'. The display shows a mixture of regular trekking equipment, like a pair of skis, a rucksack and some clothes, and the tools of illegal information work: a typewriter, a radio, a stencilled newspaper and the apparatus to produce it. The mixture is far from random. The outdoor life referred to by the skis, rucksack and so on is a vital element in national culture and identity, and these objects are thus nothing else than what any Norwegian might be supposed to keep in his cellar. When they are combined with the artefacts of resistance work, a message emerges that the resistance man was 'anyone' and 'all of us', or rather that all Norwegians were resistance men, judging from what they kept in their cellar. This becomes possible because the mixture of artefacts indicates that resistance activities – apart from producing and distributing illegal information – for a large part consisted of doing what 'every' Norwegian 'always' does: living a life of outdoor sports, trekking and skiing.

Not until the second room are we presented to the German occupiers. One wall describes the German organization in Norway. The fact that its authority was without legitimacy is emphasized: the *Reichskommisariat* is symbolized by a copy of the book containing all Norwegian laws pierced by a bayonet. The opposite wall presents the terror of this regime. The execution of the two resistance fighters Hansteen and Wichstrøm is presented, together with portraits of a number of Gestapo men, each with his 'attribute' – different torture instruments. In contrast to the executed resistance men, the Gestapo representatives have neither name nor rank attached to their portraits. Despite the use of pictures, they are not presented as individuals, rather representing the different faces of evil. A model of a prison camp in Norway is also shown, together with a map of the German system of concentration camps in Europe. Dolls in male and female prison costume respectively are shown, and behind them is a container of poisonous gas. The texts explain that the costumes are authentic. Equally authentic is a sheet from the diary of Peter Moen. This young resistance fighter managed to produce an entire manuscript of his last days in prison by perforating sheets of paper with a drawing pin and hiding them in his cell.

Leaving the exhibition in the basement and moving upwards to light and liberty, the museum visitor passes information about a now well-structured resistance movement. Its different groups and tasks are presented in small showcases and films.

'Uniting the forces', a caption declares at the top of the stairs. The northernmost county, Finnmark, is liberated, Quisling tries to mobilize new forces, and Hitler commits suicide. The tempo picks up. The Norwegian forces are presented; the king inspects them. Some final sabotage operations have been pressed in before liberation. The visitor sees the lights in the vestibule where peace 'breaks out'. A calendar sheet shows Tuesday 8 May. The Resistance movement declares that 'our struggle has been crowned by victory' and takes over Akershus fortress from the Germans. The king returns and opens the Parliament. The visitor passes a reproduction of Edvard Munch's painting 'The Sower'. It is difficult to miss the point.

As has already been pointed out, the museum is a monument, commemorating the Norwegian resistance. It is constructed as such by quite extensive use of objects not originally intended as parts of any monument. The museum conveys historical knowledge about a specific period and set of events. On the one hand, it celebrates the courage and effort of the Norwegian resistance fighters. On the other hand, it also signals the close relationship between these individuals and all Norwegians of the period – given that they were good patriots (or *jøssing*, as the contemporary term was). The link is created by frequent references to a shared cultural identity in which a love of nature and outdoor life is at the core. It is no less important that this is not merely a historical phenomenon. The 'typical Norwegian' that is portrayed as a resistance fighter due to his national qualities and general love of outdoor life is not a character of the past. He is meant to invite identification and – if necessary – imitation. This is the message of the museum, made most explicit when school classes are visiting. Never again must our country fall prey to foreign invasion. So the children are told. And it is up to them to prevent such a disaster from occurring again – they represent the nation's future.

Even a regular memorial could convey this message by the means of inscriptions, symbols and not least through the reference to the persons or events that are commemorated. Nonetheless, the time-witness effect adopted by the museum as well as by other more recent monuments forcefully enhances it. At the same time, this ascribes a new value to the objects and constructions that are employed in the strategy. They become important not merely because of their age and the temporality they manifest, but also because of the message they are supposed to transmit from the past to the present and even to the future. This use of old objects and this reason for cherishing them points beyond the age value described by Riegl as fundamental to modern society and also beyond the modern historicity regime discussed by Hartog. These artefacts become valuable and important because they relate directly to the present as a gift from the past. They are being transformed from monuments to heritage.

NOTES

1. Loin de diviser, la gloire qui convient aux temps nouveaux instaure une communaté solidaire et une étrange proximité qui est l'aspect le plus marquant comme le plus singulier du culte des grands hommes au XVIIIe siècle.
2. Loin d'être une poussiéreuse rhapsodie tournée exclusivement vers le passé, le genre de l'éloge se révélait donc une petite machine de pouvoir qui intéressait le présent le plus immédiat et l'avenir de la cite.
3. På dette sted ble norske patrioter skutt under krigen 1940–1945.

8

Cultural Property, Cultural Heritage

In 1925 a booklet was published in Bergen with the entreating title 'Tordenskiold Back Home to Norway. Answers from Norwegian Women and Men'.[1] It was published by a society called *Norrønafelaget Bragr*. The name, as well as the archaic-like form of the New Norwegian language used in the texts, indicates an advocacy of a left-wing programme of nation building parallel to that of the Norway's Youth Society (Chapter 6 in this volume). The book contained a number of letters or brief commentaries, all solicited from a question posed by the Bragr society: would Norwegian men and women support a claim to move the sarcophagus holding the mortal remains of the naval hero Tordenskiold from Copenhagen to the newly restored Nidaros Cathedral in Trondheim? The respondents were not random contributors. Among them were well-known authors and church authorities and other leading figures in society. A considerable number were ardent champions of the same cultural and political movement as Bragr itself, most notably the author Hulda Garborg. The bishop of Trondheim and the cathedral's architect were given an additional question: what did they think about the idea of establishing a national mausoleum in the cathedral, a Pantheon for Norwegian heroes, to be inaugurated in 1930, when Norway was to celebrate its nine hundred years of Christianity? Nearly all respondents were positive to Bragr's ideas. The bishop and architect nonetheless pointed out the need to discuss the exact placement of a mausoleum, considering that the cathedral was to be used for regular religious service. The bishop was somewhat reluctant to admit war memorials into the sacred building but conceded that 'a single, brisk soldier like Tordenskiold' hardly would do any harm.

Peter Wessel Tordenskiold was born into a prosperous bourgeois family in Trondheim in 1690. He ran away from home as a young boy and made a rapid career in the Royal Navy during the war against Sweden. After distinguishing himself under the battle at Kolberg in 1715, he was ennobled and took the name Tordenskiold (literally, 'Thundering Shield'). More triumphs followed, most notably at Dynekilen in 1716 and Marstrand in 1719, both locations along the western coast of Sweden. After this last battle Tordenskiold was appointed a vice-admiral, which was his rank when the war ended and he went abroad in 1720. Not long after he was killed in a duel with the Swedish colonel Staël von Holstein. Military officers in Denmark-Norway were forbidden to fight duels, so this death brought no honour. The body was brought to Copenhagen and the sarcophagus placed in Holmen's Church, the traditional burial place of officers from the Royal Danish Navy.

The sarcophagus is still there. Bragr did not succeed, and Tordenskiold never returned 'home'. What sentiment was behind the claim? Why spend time, money and other resources on moving a marble coffin containing the remains of a person more than two hundred years dead from Copenhagen to Trondheim, from Denmark to Norway? The obvious answer is that Tordenskiold was a hero. He was also – at least according to the Bragr society and the fifty-seven Norwegian men and women who answered its call – a *Norwegian* hero. The problem they encountered was that according to the Danes, Tordenskiold was a *Danish* hero. And the two countries were no longer one kingdom.

Bragr's initiative may be seen as a mere historic trifle, as curious and obsolete as its archaic language and romantic name, inspired by Norse mythology. The cathedral in Trondheim never became the national Pantheon of their dreams, and Tordenskiold is still resting in Copenhagen among his fellow officers from the Royal Navy. However, this also serves as a point of departure for exploring debates and arguments that have become increasingly more acute over the years: issues of repatriation of cultural property, of ownership rights to cultural goods and symbolic objects and – even more generally – of the values that are ascribed this kind of cultural capital. This chapter will investigate some ideas about value and temporality that are basic to such issues, and, perhaps even more fundamentally, highly important elements of the notion of heritage.

In the present world, claims for return of cultural property are part of an immense international discourse, not least targeting Western museums (see, e.g., Skrydstrup 2009; Cuno 2008; Gillman 2010). Ethnic groups, new states and former colonies do not only all claim their land, but also the cultural property that has been exported by Western collectors and museums mainly during the nineteenth and early twentieth centuries. At the heart of the discourse and the international legislation to which it has given birth, stands the work of UNESCO. A start was made with The Hague Convention from 1954, concerning the 'Protection of Cultural Property in the Event of Armed Conflict', established as a response to the situation created by World War II. At present, the Convention on the Means of Prohibiting and Preventing the Illicit Import, Export and Transfer of Ownership of Cultural Property from1970 has been ratified by about ninety states. The convention has been followed up by the work of The Intergovernmental Committee for Promoting the Return of Cultural Property to its Countries of Origin or its Restitution in Case of Illicit Appropriation, established in 1978. The committee has worked systematically to develop international standards for presenting claims and organizing returns.

There are significant differences between the work of UNESCO and the project initiated by Bragr, not merely in scope and dimensions, but also due to the elaborate (and bureaucratic) terminology developed by UNESCO and now permeating the rhetoric of this field even more generally. Nonetheless, the aims are very much identical: the return of cultural property to its rightful owners – a former colony, now an independent state. Not least thanks to UNESCO, the basic rationality of this kind of claim has become generally acknowledged, even in cases where the specific claim is contested. Energy, both inside the UNESCO system and in other settings, is spent on disputing the legitimacy of claims, on tracing objects, discussing conditions for return and eventually arranging for it to take place. The reason *why* somebody should insist on – for instance – ownerships rights to the mortal remains of a two-hundred-year-old dead man is hardly ever made an issue.

Bring Him Home!

What did the 'Norwegian women and men' more precisely say in their answers to Bragr's inquiry? How did they express themselves? Quite unanimously, they supported the proposal: Tordenskiold was a Norwegian and belonged to Norway. Some of them also presented more elaborate answers and arguments. Tordenskiold was referred to as a 'full-blooded Norwegian' (Bragr 1925: 18) and as an 'undeniably typical Norwegian' (Bragr 1925: 19). The captain K.E. Johnsen sent a long text arguing that Tordenskiold was a true Norwegian, in blood as well as being, despite the facts that he was trained in the Royal Danish Navy and made his career there. It was not true, as the Danes claimed, that Tordenskiold 'owed everything to Denmark'. Quite to the contrary, Denmark owed (the Norwegian) Tordenskiold its gratitude, the captain argued (Bragr 1925: 10ff). The author Hulda Garborg wrote:

> Yes, starting to move home the remains of our ancient heroes is, in my view, both beautiful and right. The translation itself becomes a symbolic act, shaped by the respect for a great historic memory, and gives hope of increasing national strength. Let us have the fine chieftain into the Nidaros cathedral, where he naturally belongs (Bragr 1925: 27).[2]

The answers published by Bragr are based on the supposition of a deep and natural relationship between Tordenskiold and other Norwegians, in his own time as well as later. These bonds are produced by a common home and a shared bloodline as Norwegians. The answers evoke ideas about qualities that all Norwegians (potentially) possess and which Tordenskiold embodied to an extreme degree. He was, the respondents say, 'an honest and decent Norwegian' (Bragr 1925: 32); 'the chief, the big idol, the bold and fearless sailor, the resolute, vigorous and valiant warrior' (Bragr 1925: 9). In short, he was 'too good a Norwegian to rest in Copenhagen' (Bragr 1925: 35). The basis of the claim is historical: Tordenskiold is a part of Norwegian history and memory. Equally important is the fact that it is also organic: Tordenskiold embodies qualities and values shared by all Norwegians. There are bonds of blood and kinship between him and his compatriots.

The recipient of the claim for repatriation would be the Danish state, which accordingly was ascribed the role of the opposing party. Most of the respondents underscore that the matter must be solved by the means of peaceful negotiations. They express their hope that the Danes will understand the Norwegian claim and sympathize with it, even acknowledge it as rightful. Such an attitude will strengthen the bonds of friendship between the two nations, the argument goes. However, there is no denying that the hero has been treated badly by the Danes. This is part of the argument why his remains should now be removed. The lawyer A. Lindboe says:

> Is there a Norwegian alive who, when he bares his head in front of the sarcophagus in the sinister chapel at Holmen, will think that the hero has been laid to rest in a dignified way? The Danes have not wanted it any better. We will (Bragr 1925: 22).[3]

The school director Thomasen-Overvik expressed similar feelings:

> I am of the same mind as those who will move Tordenskiold home. He could be used to trash the Swedes when the Danes were scared and ran away. But they did not allow him a proper burial when he had passed away. He has been there far too long. Let us bring him home! (Bragr 1925: 23)[4]

The Danes are left little honour in these arguments. They used Tordenskiold when they needed him, but treated him badly in return. When alive, he was harassed by the Danish nobility, the respondents argued, and condescendingly nicknamed 'the Norwegian sailor', despite his high rank and noble title. He was denied a proper burial as well as of the honour that was rightfully his. Nonetheless, the Danes insist that he is theirs, which implies – so the argument goes – that they still treat Norway as they did in Tordenskiold's own time: as an inferior province. Danish refusal to answer the claim will bring shame upon the Danish nation because it implies continuing the old colonial repression of Norway. Repatriation, on the other hand, will not only serve Norwegian needs by returning the hero to his true home, but also serve to cleanse Denmark of its old misdeeds – against Tordenskiold and Norway.

At the core of the argument is the idea that the country has been robbed of its honour and historical memories during the four centuries in the union with Denmark and that a return is Norway's lawful right. The scarcity of such memories makes any existing historical trace all the more valuable, and getting them 'back' is imperative. Moreover, the return is in itself a matter of setting old injustices right. By recognizing Norway's right to Tordenskiold's mortal remains and to the honour they represent, Denmark will amend some of the hardships that were conferred on the country as a Danish province. Repatriation will indicate that Norway's subordinate position is now history and that at present the relation between the two kingdoms is one of equality and mutual respect.

The relational aspect is significant even on a more general level. On the one hand, its rationality centres on the nation or group that can claim a unique right to the artefacts or remains in question. On the other hand, like other ideas about nations and national cultures, it contributes to an international network of mutually recognized rights and negotiations over rights (Löfgren 1993). Repatriation of cultural property is a kind of discourse that nations, ethnic and religious groups and so on engage in to present claims and/or relate to the claims of others. The values that are at stake are of a strongly symbolic nature. When the contested objects also have, for instance, aesthetic or economic value, this dimension is less obvious, but it is nonetheless worth noting the intrinsically symbolic character of even such cases. Claims, negotiations and eventual repatriation contribute to a mutually obliging network of arguments and relations. More than a mere side effect of the repatriations and/or economic compensations that actually may take place, the maintenance of this network can be said to be the key to the international work on cultural property.

From Property to Heritage

The impetus for the UNESCO efforts relating to cultural property that commenced after World War II came from situations caused by armed conflict. During the following decades its rationality was appropriated by former colonies, third world countries, minority groups and so on, which meant that it was transferred to new political contexts. On the theoretical level, corresponding ideas became part of the postcolonial discourse. The development did not only imply an extension of the argument about cultural property into new settings, it also gradually changed the ideas of what kinds of objects could be defined as such property. Originally referring to artwork and historical monuments of more traditional kinds, the concept of cultural property has expanded to include any object that a nation or group wants to claim to be important to its identity and self-understanding. Accompanying this conceptual extension, the notion of cultural heritage has also developed. The folklorists Regina Bendix and Valdimar Tr. Hafstein point out that the concepts of cultural property and cultural heritage both emerged through The Hague Convention from 1954. Nonetheless, they 'constitute parallel rather than identical modalities within the patrimonial regime' (Bendix and Hafstein 2009: 5). Their argument is that UNESCO has developed separate legal instruments and bodies for the protection of cultural property and the safeguarding of cultural heritage respectively. The important distinction is that

> cultural property is a national concept at its inception, used in the context of claims for the return or restitution of historical artifacts from one state to another. Cultural heritage, on the other hand, is the preferred term in contexts that stress the general safe-guarding of artifacts, buildings, sites, and, most recently, cultural practices (Bendix and Hafstein 2009: 6).

Bendix and Hafstein conclude that while cultural property belongs to an 'exclusive "us"', heritage belongs to an 'inclusive "us"'. They also describe cultural property as a 'technology of sovereignty', while claims to cultural heritage rather can be said to be a technology of governmentality:

> Teaching people to have a heritage, to value it, and keep it safe, requires the intervention of outside experts and training of local ones to reform the practices of local populations and reframe their relationships to habitat and habitus in terms of heritage (Bendix and Hafstein 2009: 6f).

Bendix and Hafstein nonetheless point out that even if the distinction between the concepts are rather clear-cut in the international legal instruments that govern them, the two fields tend to merge in popular understanding and actual practice (Bendix and Hafstein 2009: 6). The Tordenskiold case, discussed above, is a good illustration of the fact that claims for repatriation are closely tied to issues of sovereignty and national recognition. Nevertheless, when the respondents insisted that having Tordenskiold's sarcophagus in Trondheim would inspire future generations of Norwegians to imitate his skills and qualities, the arguments also include elements from a heritage discourse of governmentality: the claim is that access to their cultural heritage will serve to shape individuals as national subjects, helping them to internalize the same cultural values and moral qualities.

The merging of ideas on cultural property and cultural heritage may also stem from more theoretical considerations. John Henry Merryman, an international expert on art and cultural property law, bases his argument on what he calls 'two ways of thinking' about such cultural goods: a cosmopolitan and a nationalistic perspective, respectively. Strongly on the side of the cosmopolitan position himself, Merryman argues that this means thinking of cultural property as 'common human culture, whatever their places of origin or present location, independent of property rights or national jurisdiction' (Merryman 1986: 831). Opposed to this is 'thinking about cultural property … as part of national cultural heritage. This gives the nation a special interest, implies the attribution of national characters to objects, independent of their location or ownership, and legitimizes national export controls and demands for the "repatriation" of cultural property' (Merryman 1986: 832). He also argues that in terms of the nationalist position, 'protection' of cultural goods in reality means retention. This does not merely imply that some nations 'hoard' objects 'beyond any conceivable domestic need' (Merryman 1986: 847), but also that there is no guarantee that the objects will be properly conserved or protected from decay and damage. Nonetheless, this position is the stronger today.

To Merryman, the important distinction is not what separates cultural property from cultural heritage, but the two perspectives themselves. Words and concepts change meaning depending on the perspective in focus. Protection may mean retention or safeguarding, trade may be an illicit activity or a means of exchange, and the value of the objects may stem from their intrinsic national qualities or from artistic, historic or scientific interest. Merryman's work has been influential, not least concerning art and art museums. Not surprisingly, his line of argument has its warmest adherents in what he himself calls the 'cultural market nations', which mainly are Western countries with large museums and economic resources that would make acquisition of new objects possible had it not entailed the risk of what is now defined as 'illicit trade' (see, e.g., Cuno 2008; Gillman 2010).

In all Scandinavian languages cultural heritage – *kulturarv* – is a comparatively recent term. Historian Bernard Eric Jensen, who has investigated the Danish case, reports that until 1955 the word did not appear in the national dictionary and was still infrequent into the mid-1990s. A very rapid diffusion then took place from the end of the decade. The first appearance in a Danish encyclopaedia occurred in 2001. The following year it was also included in a supplementary volume of the national encyclopaedia. Furthermore, 'cultural heritage' was chosen as the name of a new administrative unit in Denmark, established in 2002, when elements from the two ministries of Culture and Environment were merged. The so-called Heritage Agency of Denmark (Kulturarvstyrelsen) was established as an umbrella organization, covering both bureaucracy and education, most notably through a coordinated Ph.D. programme for architects, librarians, artists and preservationists (B.E. Jensen 2008: 8). Similar systematic surveys have not been produced for the other Nordic countries, but Jensen suggests that with minor differences, the development in Sweden and Norway is paralleled to Denmark.

Jensen argues that the term cultural heritage works in a number of different, though related discursive fields. On the theoretical level, the term belongs to a vocabulary of social constructivism in the wake of the cultural turn. In this context, it is descriptive and inclusive and designates all culture that an individual or a group have received from others and concerns certain signifying practices occurring in all aspects of individual and social life. The second field of discourse is that of the professionals working with preservation, in museums, archives, libraries and so on. In this context, the term has a sense that is both practical and bureaucratic. It concerns work in or with cultural heritage as well as its administration. The third field identified by Jensen is the political arena (B.E. Jensen 2008: 13ff). Even if his examples refer to specific Danish debates, a more general relevance cannot be doubted. Heritage, as the term originally was used by UNESCO, was political from the start and has become no less so through its application to questions of multiethnicity, repatriation, post-colonialism and a number of other contemporary political issues. Jensen points out that even if these three fields may be separated analytically, it is not equally obvious, in a given situation, which of the meanings of 'heritage' is in play. He still has no doubt that when it comes to making heritage the catch-word it is today, the political use of the term has been the most influential. The immense success of the term is due to its popular appeal and its capacity to mobilize general enthusiasm and create interest. It is nonetheless impossible, Jensen argues, to use the term politically without at the same time touching upon highly contested issues related to such areas as identity, community and democracy in contemporary societies (B.E. Jensen 2008: 18). While the term has become popular due to its ability to create interest and encourage defence and preservation of shared cultural goods, it has also created a veritable minefield of challenges and conflicts.

Even if 'cultural heritage' as well 'cultural property' appear in The Hague Convention from 1954, the term cultural heritage did not really commence its career until 1972, when UNESCO introduced the Convention Concerning the Protection of the World Cultural and Natural Heritage and established the World Heritage List (WHL). At present, the convention has been ratified by 187 states. The list includes 936 sites, or 'properties', among them 725 cultural, 183 natural and 28 so-called mixed sites in 153 countries. The Norwegian sites on the list are the old mining town of Røros (Sør-Trøndelag county), the stave church at Urnes (Sogn og Fjordane), the architecture of Bryggen in Bergen (Hordaland), the rock carvings in Alta (Finnmark), as well as the Vega islands (Nordland), and the fiord landscapes of Geiranger and Nærøy (Møre og Romsdal). In addition, Norway is one of the ten countries embraced by the Struve Geodetical Arch, which is also on the list. This is a chain of survey triangulations stretching from Hammerfest in Norway to the Black Sea.

The World Heritage Convention builds on preceding documents. Apart from The Hague Convention, already mentioned, the so-called Athens and Venice charters are important in this respect (from 1931 and 1964, respectively). However, both these documents were about the preservation of 'historic monuments', and the Venice charter was expanded to also cover groups of buildings and 'sites'. This charter employs the word heritage twice. In the eight-years-younger World Heritage Convention, admittedly a somewhat longer text (seventeen pages), the same word occurs seventy-five times. The convention name as well as this frequency should indicate that a definition of the concept would be found in the document – or at least an explanation why what had so far been called 'historic monuments and sites' now had turned into 'heritage'. Articles 1 and 2 of the Convention establish what qualifies as cultural and natural heritage, respectively. Both groups contain three categories. For cultural heritage they are monuments, groups of buildings and sites. Natural heritage is specified as natural features, geological and physiographical formations and natural sites. The 'sites' category of cultural heritage is presented as 'works of man or the combined works of nature and man, and areas including archaeological sites which are of outstanding universal value from the historical, aesthetic, ethnological or anthropological point of view' (WHC 1972). Rather than a definition, this is an enumerative description.

If no explicit definition can be found in this document, or in later texts related to the WHL, important clues are found in the Convention's preamble. It starts *noting* 'that the cultural heritage and the natural heritage are increasingly threatened with destruction not only by the traditional causes of decay, but also by changing social and economic conditions which aggravate the situation with even more formidable phenomena of damage or destruction' and goes on to *consider* 'that deterioration or disappearance of any item of the cultural or natural heritage constitutes a harmful impoverishment of the heritage of all the nations of the world', as well as that 'in view of the magnitude and gravity of the new dangers threatening them, it is incumbent on the international community as a whole to participate in the protection of the cultural and natural heritage of outstanding universal value, by the granting of collective assistance which, although not taking the place of action by the State concerned, will serve as an efficient complement thereto' (WHC 1972, emphasis in the original).

The more specific reason for these observations and considerations can be found on the website presenting the history and background of the WHL:

> The event that aroused particular international concern was the decision to build the Aswan High Dam in Egypt, which would have flooded the valley containing the Abu Simble temples, a treasure of ancient Egyptian civilization. In 1959, after an appeal from the governments of Egypt and Sudan, UNESCO launched an international safeguarding campaign. Archaeological research in the areas to be flooded was accelerated. Above all, the Abu Simbel and Philae temples were dismantled, moved to dry ground and reassembled.

> The campaign cost about US$80 million, half of which was donated by
> some 50 countries, showing the importance of solidarity and nations' shared
> responsibility in conserving outstanding cultural sites. Its success led to other
> safeguarding campaigns … (WHC [n.d.]b).

This cannot only be read as a narrative of the events leading up to the convention, but also as a very concrete performance of the principles – or 'considerations' – presented in its preamble. Extensive interventions of regional or even global consequence, due to war, large-scale construction work or changes in climate and natural conditions, demand equally large projects for safeguarding and protection. The rhetoric of cultural heritage and world heritage has been developed from these premises. The global ambition has been high, both when it comes to defining monuments and sites from the entire world as valuable and to developing terms and concepts that can supply a firm basis for international interventions.

The establishment of the WHL has been criticized. Its European bias has frequently been pointed out, not least because due to this, the term 'universal outstanding values' easily becomes identified with European history and culture alone (Smith 2006). The list has also been accused of supporting a highly commercialized heritage industry, offering historical idylls to naïve tourists (Hewison 1987). The focus on buildings and monuments has also in itself been criticized for being Eurocentric. This was one of the reasons why a new convention on 'intangible heritage' was established in 2003. However relevant these criticisms might be, it is important to note that when the 'historic monuments and sites' occurring in older documents rather suddenly were turned into 'heritage' it was as part of a strong effort to incite action and create new responsibilities. This was in part accomplished through the continuous references to 'universally outstanding values', an expression clearly emphasizing that safeguarding the monuments, buildings and sites in question was too important (or too resource-demanding) to be the responsibility of one nation alone. Moreover, the new terminology also articulated a specific kind of responsibility: that of an inheritance. The crux of 'heritage' as a concept is that it does not merely describe monuments, buildings and sites as important in themselves because they are old, beautiful or represent some other value, but because they come with the obligation of property as owned goods: it is *ours*. As heritage, it is part of our own resources on which *we* build our *own* existence.

Bendix and Hafstein (above) pointed out that despite clear distinctions in the legal instruments used to handle them, 'cultural heritage' and 'cultural property' tend to merge. In the discussion inspired by Merryman's work, the point has been that both property and heritage can be seen from either a cosmopolitan or a nationalistic perspective. A reason for this merging of concepts (whether it is found in the practical contexts referred to by Bendix and Hafstein or on a theoretical plane as in Merryman) is that they share a common basic assumption. Both describe the cultural goods in question – artefacts, buildings, sites or traditions – in terms of *ownership*. What defines the objects or sites is no longer age ('antiquities') or historical consequence ('monuments'), but interest. The terms property and heritage do not describe the objects (or buildings or sites) they apparently refer to, but state a specific relationship to them, shaped by interest. Moreover, this interest is explicitly located in the present. Even if age and historical importance still contribute to the value of the objects, what more than anything else defines both cultural property and cultural heritage is that somebody in the present acknowledges them as significant and valuable to him or her. Cultural property cannot exist without proprietors, cultural heritage not without inheritors.

The rationality of both concepts links them to the life and interest of living subjects in their roles as proprietors and heirs. As Hartog has argued, this implies that the terms can be seen as prominent expressions of the historicity regime of our own time: that of presentism. As was argued in Chapter 1 (in this volume), presentism is characterized by 'an extreme and immediate historization of the present or the very close past' (Hartog 2003: 207). Hartog also describes presentism as '[t]he contemporary experience of a perpetual present, fleeting and nearly immobile, seeking despite everything to create its own historical time' (Hartog 2003: 28).[5] One of the strategies employed in this effort to create historical time is the construction of heritage. According to Hartog, one reason for the eagerness to take action is the experience that it may soon be too late, that the past – and even the near present – is falling apart due to the acceleration of continuous change (Hartog 2003: 206). Hartog himself relates this pattern of reaction to what he calls a 'crises of time', which according to him is the essence of any shift of historicity regime. The explanation may also be read in accordance with the more general argument in classical modernization theory that returns to history, traditions or religion are answers to the loss of meaning, or even 'deprivation', caused by modernity. Nonetheless, the presentism that lies behind heritage work can also be understood in less negative terms, not as a compensatory response to lack or loss, but simply as the genuine expression of an experience of temporality that is distinctive to our own time.

A fundamental feature of this experience of temporality, clearly visible in the ideas about cultural heritage and cultural property, is its embodiedness and the organic terms and metaphors it inspires. The past is not merely defined, even colonized by the present, but also seen from the position of *somebody's* present. Even if the subject in question may be a group or a nation rather than an individual, it is most often understood in quite organic terms as having a life and body of its own. This is due in part to the rationality of heritage, or inheritance, as a specific kind of property. What defines it is that it is acquired on the death of some predecessor and is supposed to be passed on to future generations. Another reason for the organic metaphors is that a conception of the nation or other identity groups in terms of living bodies, with their birth, life, progeneration (and even eventual death) already is an integrated part of the rhetoric surrounding such entities.

This intrinsically organic character may also be part of the reason why even human remains so often are understood as elements in cultural property or heritage. Religious beliefs and traditional rituals concerning death and burials will lie behind demands for repatriation of human remains. Moreover, the claims are often politically motivated, and the repatriation can in itself work as a rite of conciliation, for instance in the relationship between an ethnic minority group and the state. However, both these kinds of arguments – religious as well as political – gain strength and support from the notion of heritage and its emphasis on bonds of kinship between past and present agents. The demand for a repatriation of Tordenskiold's mortal remains occurred before this terminology had developed. Nonetheless, the arguments (above) demonstrate an understanding of a synecdochal relationship between Tordenskiold and the national community: his body is part of the nation's body. There is an organic relationship between him and his fellow Norwegians, easily spanning the two hundred years that separate them.

Unique, but Not Particular

As it is the originator of the immensely popular, if ambiguous, term, UNESCO's system of world heritage merits closer inspection. To gain inscription on the World Heritage List, sites have to represent what is called 'universally outstanding value'. This vital concept is presented in the 'Operational Guidelines', the document that serves as the manual of the system:

> Outstanding universal value means cultural and/or natural significance which is so exceptional as to transcend national boundaries and to be of common importance for present and future generations of all humanity (WHC 2008: 13).

It is worth noting that even if WHL sites, natural as well as cultural, most frequently represent age and history, and thus indicate that 'universally outstanding value' is in some way historical or accumulated over time, the past is not really constitutive in this paragraph. Heritage is related to that which transcends the present, pointing to the future as well as to the past. Heritage is the sites, buildings and so on whose 'natural and/or cultural significance' is so great that it ought to be the heritage of future generations. From the outset, sites nominated as cultural heritage were assessed according to a list of six criteria, while another list of four applied to sites of natural heritage. The two lists were combined in 2005, making the system simpler and also enabling the category of 'mixed sites', representing both cultural and natural values.

Under the convention, states are entitled to nominate new sites for inscription on the list. They do so in the form of establishing 'tentative lists', which in practice work as national waiting lists. These lists are prepared according to instructions found in the 'Operational Guidelines'. The candidate sites themselves will have to correspond to the list of criteria, which is used to assess the proposals. When the inscription finally is gained, the relevant criteria are cited on the WHL website. The procedures imply that the WHL system, despite its relative lack of explicit and theoretically elaborated definitions, works as a very effective mill, turning places, buildings, monuments, landscapes, artwork and other traces of human activity into 'heritage' of the same kind, understandable through the same formula, all equally 'universal' and 'outstanding'. The impact of this process on an individual location, building or monument will without doubt vary, according to political, social, economic and other circumstances. Some general effects may still be addressed.

Norway's two earliest WHL sites, inscribed in 1979, are both rather traditional historical monuments. One of them is the stave church at Urnes, situated on the north bank of Sognefjorden in western Norway. It was also among the churches published by the painter J.C. Dahl in his work *Denkmale einer sehr ausgebildeten Holzbaukunst aus den frühesten Jahrhunderten in den innern Landschaften Norwegens* from 1836–37 (Chapter 5 in this volume). Since then, it has been a national monument. How has its meaning changed? And what is the impact of the WHL inscription? To Dahl, the church was a testimony of a highly developed art of construction, demonstrating that the plastic arts were cultivated by the ancient Norwegians. Dahl and his contemporaries understood the quality of the stave churches in rather international terms (cf. Chapter 5 in this volume). What made them valuable was not so much the national distinctiveness of the buildings as the fact that they made Norway appear on a par with other civilized countries, possessing an ancient culture of high quality as well as historical monuments to adorn its landscape. Only during the latter decades of the nineteenth century did the stave churches became monuments to national particularities and a distinctive national history.

Apart from the fact that it is now nearly two hundred years older, the building at Urnes has not changed much since Dahl visited it. Keeping it in good repair has had high priority with the Society for the Preservation of Norwegian Ancient Monuments, as well as with the national preservation authorities. On the WHL website, it is presented as follows:

> The wooden church of Urnes (the *stavkirke*) stands in the natural setting of Sogn og Fjordane. It was built in the 12th and 13th centuries and is an out-

standing example of traditional Scandinavian wooden architecture. It brings together traces of Celtic art, Viking traditions and Romanesque spatial structures (WHC 1979).

This statement is followed by a somewhat more detailed description. It starts by explaining that stave churches are 'one of the most elaborate types of wood construction which are typical of northern Europe from the Neolithic period to the Middle Ages' and goes on to inform the reader that thirty such buildings now remain in Norway. Among them, Urnes has been selected to represent 'this outstanding series of wood buildings'. The reasons for the choice are then given in a text that also functions as a presentation of the exceptional qualities of the church. Six arguments are given: antiquity; the exemplarity of the church's structure; the outstanding quality of the carved decorations; its wealth of mediaeval liturgical objects; its excellent conservation; and finally its location 'within the backdrop of a glacial valley on the north bank of Sognefjord'. A duality permeates the presentation and implies that the church is both unique (outstanding, exceptional) and in some way representative of a category. To gain inscription, a site has to be unique and possess outstanding qualities. The text is composed to show how such qualities are embodied by, in this case, Urnes. At the same time, the church is presented as an example. It is one of a specific kind of building. Names of other stave churches are mentioned, indicating that Urnes is one of a series. On a more general level, the WHL also presents the church as an example of world heritage. What constitutes the series here is not the shared qualities of a specific kind of old wooden building, but those defined by UNESCO as constitutive for world heritage. The website claims that among the criteria defined by the 'Operational Guidelines', those found pertinent in the case of Urnes are nos. 1, 2 and 3. The church has thus been judged to represent a 'masterpiece of human creative genius'; to 'exhibit an important interchange of human values, over a span of time or within a cultural area of the world, on developments in architecture or technology, monumental arts, town-planning or landscape design'; and finally to 'bear a unique or at least exceptional testimony to a cultural tradition or to a civilization which is living or which has disappeared' (WHC [n.d.]a). As world heritage, the church is an *example* of the qualities described by these criteria, an example of what is unique and outstanding. This ambiguity or tension between example and exemplarity is characteristic of the entire WHL rationality. With its insistence on a global dimension and universal values, and with its frequent use of the generic term 'human', UNESCO conceives world heritage in terms of the general and shared. Moreover, by being designated as world heritage, a site, building or landscape is defined – at least symbolically – as the common property and common responsibility of mankind. The unsolved paradox is that what gives these 'properties' their place on the list are their uniqueness and exceptional qualities, which means that the sites by implication must be specific, singular and local.

The WHL text about Urnes is closely mirrored on the website of the Society for the Preservation of Norwegian Ancient Monuments, which owns the building. Proudly referring to the inscription on the WHL, it adds that the northern church portal has carvings executed in 'what has been called the Urnes style', and that it is 'one of the real jewels in Norwegian history of art and architecture' (Society for the Preservation of Norwegian Ancient Monuments [n.d.]).[6] The Directorate for Cultural Heritage also repeats the WHL, but adds that even if the type of wooden buildings were found over a large area, the Norwegian examples have not merely been the most numerous, but also the ones with the best quality. The text goes on to mention that the church most probably originated as a private chapel built by a powerful local family (Directorate for Cultural Heritage [n.d.]). Despite their emphasis on national and local aspects, respectively, both these institutions seem to employ the WHL inscription as a certificate or guarantee. They both refer to the inscription of the church on the list and quote the WHL text more or less directly. The strong homogeneity of the presentations contributes very much to making the church (and its location) appear self-evidently as 'heritage', but it also produces a significant reification. The church is a building, an object and a locality, but as heritage it also becomes an item, a specimen, and, as ethnologist Owe Ronström underlines, a destination (Ronström 2007). As we saw (Chapter 5 in this volume), both Dahl and Faye were thinking of stave churches as tourist attractions as early as the 1830s. Nonetheless, as Ronström points out, the destinations created by the inclusion on the WHL are of a somewhat different kind. These destinations become increasingly more loosely connected to their actual, geographic locations, and ever more connected to the hyper reality of the global tourist industry (Ronström 2007: 94). The WHL system creates commodities. Commercial aspects aside, this refers to a rationality that transforms buildings, monuments and landscapes into the elements of a system, fashioning them as its easily inventoried items. The criteria and the terminology of the 'Operational Guidelines' supply the core of a global grammar that makes world heritage assessable, comparable, conceivable and coordinative and enables both classification and preservation (Ronström 2007: 103).

This systematic or 'grammatical' approach does in some ways resemble the methods of traditional antiquarianism, as it has been analysed by Momigliano and others (Momigliano 1990; Chapter 2 in this volume). Antiquarian study tended to interpret artefacts and sites as the items of systems of, for instance, law or (heathen) religion. Favouring system over chronology led to an understanding of the past as temporally 'flat': the objects and sites in question were 'ancient', but trying to relate them to specific, and different, historic epochs was not part of the interpretative work and ascribed little explanatory value. The system developed by the WHL is one of 'universally outstanding values' accompanied by a global responsibility to preserve these values and prevent their damage. Even in this case, chronology and history are subordinated to the overarching systematic project. The WHL is organized alphabetically according to states. The seven Norwegian sites are thus listed after the two Nigerian ones and before the four in Oman. The listing of sites for each state follows their year of inscription on the list, in correspondence with the internal chronology of the system rather than with its own historical epoch. On the web, the WHL is also presented as an interactive map, showing the geographical distribution of the sites while ignoring any historical dimension.

The systematic approach, the treatment of buildings, objects and sites as items and the corresponding 'flat' temporal dimension are important similarities between traditional antiquarianism and contemporary world heritage work. This comparison may also serve to emphasize some rather important differences. Antiquarianism aimed at understanding the past by finding the keys to its systems. The past was understood as remote, but thanks to the rationality of the system and to the universality of the phenomena in question – law, religion, warfare and so on – it was not really 'a foreign country'. It could be deciphered. The system created by world heritage and the WHL, on the other hand, is not about the past. It is rather conceived as a set of moral and political obligations that are highly active in the present. The past may be interesting as a supplier of attractive goods and commodities, even of threatened species. Nonetheless, heritage is a matter of the present and the future. It is being cut off from the period or historical context that has produced it and brought into the present in terms of property, owned by states, groups or even individuals who are encouraged to act according to the imperatives of the system.

NOTES

1. 'Tordenskiold heimatt til Noreg. Svar frá norske kvinner og menn'.
2. Jau, at me no tek til á flytja heim oska av dei gamle stormennerne váre er, etter mi kjensla, báde rett og vakkert. Sjølve yviføringi vert ei symbolsk gjerning diktert av vyrdsemd for eit stort historisk minne, og i det ligg von om aukande national styrke. Lat oss fá den gjæve trøndarhovdingen inn i Nidarosdomen, der han naturleg høyrer heime.
3. Finnes der en nordmann som, når han med blottet hode står foran Tordenskjolds sarkofag i det skumle Holmens kapell, synes at folkehelten er stedt til hvile på verdig måte? Danskerne har ikke villet gjøre det bedre. Vi vil.
4. Eg hev samhug med dei som vil flytta Tordenskjold heimatt. Han kunde brukast til á tukta svenskarne, dá dansken redd flaug undan. Men dei unte han ikkje ei skikkeleg grav, dá han var slokna. Han hev vore alt for lenge dernede. Lat oss taka han heim!

5. D'où peut-être cette expérience contemporaine d'un présent perpétuel, insaissable et quasiment immobile, cherchant malgré tout à produire pour lui-même son propre temps historique.

6. Den einestående nordportalen med skurd i det som er døypt 'urnesstil', er ein av dei verkelege 'kronjuvelane' i norsk arkitektur- og kunsthistorie.

9

Heritage and Presentism

The key to the success of the term heritage is the conceptualization of the past as property – personal, familial, national or other. As was pointed out in Chapter 8, an important implication of this is that what defines objects as valuable is not their age, as was the case with antiquities, nor their historical consequence, as for monuments, but rather the interest of some living subject who takes on the role as heir. In this way, heritage is basically anchored in the present of the inheritors, not in the past of the inherited objects. Furthermore, this also implies that in principle anything can become heritage, as long as somebody declares him- or herself its heir. Even if other factors also enter, the value of an object as heritage is fundamentally defined by somebody's willingness to inherit it, i.e., to enter into this special kind of relationship with the object in question. The argument here is not that what becomes heritage is completely arbitrary, left to the choice and taste of the individual, but that the valorization is produced in the present. It is fashioned by present values and issues and profoundly shaped by the present context.

The idea that 'anything' that is claimed to be significant to members of a modern democratic society may demand recognition as their heritage above all reflects the ideals of the equal rights of all citizens that such a society is built upon. Having a heritage becomes a civil right, as does the authority to define its contents. A broad concept of heritage thus is a consequence of liberal democracy. However, it is also deeply embedded in an experience of temporality that can justly be called presentist, allowing values of the present to invade and define the past not merely when it comes to selecting what is important, but also concerning the way this procedure is carried out. To a certain extent, even the idea of antiquities or of monuments had to be conceptualized from the perspective of the present. It is only from the perspective of a later period that an object is ancient or a monument has proven to be of historical consequence. Nonetheless, these terms still aimed at describing the objects themselves, while the notion of heritage above all addresses the relationship between the object and its present owner. Hence, there is good reason to explore the heritage discourse of our own time, regarding it not merely as a more or less arbitrary way of speaking about the historical monuments, sites and objects that started to attract attention some centuries ago, but as the expression of a distinctively contemporary way of understanding their significance and of experiencing their temporality.

This chapter will close the argument of the book by investigating some of the consequences of the shift in perspective and the broadening in approach that heritage implies. Does the rationality of the term lead to more and other objects from the past being collected, preserved and protected? Or does heritage rather represent new ways of giving legitimacy and authority to traditional monuments and antiquities? What kind of pasts does heritage produce, how is the past affected by the presentism embodied in the term? The case to be explored will be the activities of the Norwegian Heritage Year 2009 (hereafter NHY; see also the Introduction).

Heritage weaves together past and present in a complex pattern. Because its contents will be those elements from the past that somebody is willing or able to inherit, it is defined from the perspective of the present. On the other hand, this heir will acquire authority just because the heritage is rooted in the past. This is also part of the reason why heritage so often plays an important role in identity politics. Claiming a heritage means demanding recognition in the present, for heritage makes its heirs appear as social agents, provided with the resources of their exclusive property. In the same way as the elaboration of national history has been a successful strategy in nation building during the last two hundred years or so of Western history, emphasizing one's cultural heritage today is an effective and oft-used way of gaining social recognition for ethnic and religious groups or other kinds of minorities (Carman 2005; Walker 2009; Smith and Waterton 2009). The claim to possess a heritage will define the group as something more than a random accumulation of people. Being handed over from the past, heritage signals that the group is no mere whim of the present. As an imagined community, held together by a common heritage, it will include even past members of the group and thus appear larger. Furthermore, claiming a heritage indicates stronger and more obliging bonds between the living members than mere shared interest would do. Heritage thus confirms the social reality of the group both by reference to its age and by the distinctive character of the property that is passed on to it.

At the core of all this lies the fact that heritage is a very special kind of property. Inherited goods can only be acquired by being passed on from one generation to the next. Despite the values it may represent, and its potentiality to be transformed into regular commercial goods, heritage in itself is not commercial (Renfrew 2000; Cuno 2008). If it is bought or sold, it is no longer heritage. To remain so, it can only be transferred to the next inheritor. Hence, heritage is the exclusive property of the inheritor(s), a lawfully recognized privilege. In this way, it is a mark of distinction, representing symbolic capital as well as material resources. It marks the inheritor as a subject with a special kind of relation to the past as well as with exclusive access to the values in question. This relationship is fundamentally organic, depending on the life and death of successive generations of owners. Being an heir means being one link in a long chain, spanning time and creating bonds.

The notion of heritage also draws on another aspect of organic relationship. As heredity, heritage resembles that which is bred in the bone, that which exists in the blood. Even this may be a mark of distinction, but heredity in this sense of the word is also something one cannot escape, defining the individual beyond any personal choices and preferences. It cannot be discarded at will. While heritage as inherited property traditionally has been the privilege of the few, an exclusive source of wealth and pride, heredity is the obligation of all living species and a source of blessing as well as of trouble. Despite their difference, the biological and organic implications of the terms work together to naturalize heritage by placing it in a position above historical contingence as well as individual whims. By the same token it serves to situate any individual that can claim a heritage in a position of continuity and binding obligations, stretching from the past and into the future. In this way, claiming – or creating – heritage is a way of authorizing the self, individually or collectively, by gaining a position as an acknowledged proprietor of exclusive resources.

Regina Bendix has argued that the modern notion of heritage represents a kind of hybridity, emerging when goods and resources that used to be heredity – the inheritance of the few – are made the collective property of a nation or other kind of imagined community. What has happened is that: 'The term heredity connoting noble blood lines slowly expanded to refer to peoples and their cultures, as was typical of the nationalistic project sweeping across Europe. One might argue that transferring the idea of heredity from genetic to cultural "bodies" remains one of the most problematic legacies of the national project' (Bendix 2000: 40). By means of this process, what was formerly the inheritance of the elite, for instance castles, landed goods, artworks and other treasures, has become the heritage of the majority, despite our generally far more modest bloodlines. 'Our heredity remains that of footmen, soldiers, servants, and peasants. But what we claim is heritage. That final syllable "-age" in heritage, does away with the particulars of history and heredity, who governed and who was governed. Heritage puts everything into a collective pot of "culture" and "past"', Bendix argues (Bendix 2000: 42). The processes highlighted by Bendix can be said to represent democratization as well as valorization. What is named heritage today is still regarded as costly and is highly valued, but no longer remains as the exclusive property of the elite. Bendix's own perspective is nonetheless highly critical. She argues that 'heritage allows one to attract outsiders to come visit it for a suitable price', while at the same time it demands large resources for preservation and protection (Bendix 2000: 38).

Even more serious is the fact that heritage changes the past that it sets out to protect: 'The term heritage acts like a beautifying gloss, rendering the specificity of past political, economic, and social experiences into a far less complex whole than what a socio-historical scrutiny would reveal' (Bendix 2000: 38).

Bendix's criticism resembles to a high degree a more general argument accusing heritage of commodifying the past, turning it into sentimental kitsch and adapting it for the 'heritage industry' (see, e.g., Lowenthal 1985; Hewison 1987; Smith 2007). What is nonetheless distinctive about Bendix's analysis is her interest in the potentiality of the terms themselves. Her perspective implies that heritage is not merely 'bad history' – sentimental, uninformed and commodified – but that the terminology itself represents a transformative force. The great impact of terminology has been a basic assumption even in the present book. Without denying that the changes brought about by heritage may have the banalizing effects that Bendix and others suggest, it may also be argued that the changes are of a more complex nature. The transformative power of heritage should not be regarded in isolation, but as related to the presentism the term represents and the experience of temporality it is part of. In short, heritage and its ways of conceptualizing, even transforming the past is an integral part of the present historicity regime.

Cultural Heritage in the Age of Digitalization – Heritage Year 2009

The Norwegian Government designated 2009 as the 'Year of Cultural Heritage' in a White Paper from 2005. The main theme of the year was to be 'cultural heritage of everyday life'.[1] Two ministries and several government institutions were partners in the project, while the main responsibility for planning and organization was given to the Norwegian Cultural Heritage Association. This NGO is an umbrella organization, including about twenty societies and associations. Among them are the Society for the Preservation of Ancient Norwegian Monuments (cf. Chapter 5) and the highly academic Norwegian Historical Association, as well as more specialized and in some cases amateur groups like the Norwegian Society for the History of Lighthouses ('Norsk fyrhistorisk forening') and the Bus Historical Society of Norway ('Rutebilhistorisk forening'). Altogether, the Heritage Association has about 190,000 members. The sum of twenty million Norwegian *kroner* was granted to the NHY by the government. A secretariat was established with the responsibility for six main projects, three of them with an emphasis on digital media and planned to continue after 2009.[2]

When funding for local projects was announced, more than eight hundred applications were submitted from all over the country, and 357 projects received financial support. These initiatives, as well as the projects of the secretariat itself, involved close collaboration with a very large number of NGOs as well as with the Norwegian national broadcasting corporation, NRK. In this way, a very substantial number of people, organizations and institutions came to be involved in the Heritage Year, ranging from professionals working on a regular basis with the care and preservation of monuments and the administration of heritage, to amateur historians and other local enthusiasts. For a number of the professionals, the Heritage Year meant an intensification of their regular work, with some additional possibilities created by increased funding and the encouragement to launch new projects. For the amateurs, the Heritage Year was more of an exceptional event.

One of the declared goals of the NHY was to enhance cooperation between institutions and organizations in the heritage field, and by the end of the year great satisfaction concerning this was expressed. Attention was also given to collaboration between municipal and county administrative levels, as well as to establishing new contacts between history associations and other sectors, in particular the trekking and hiking societies. Establishing 'heritage trails' was one of the main activities during the Heritage Year. The trails were to be made locally, while their coordination was one of the six core projects administered by the NHY itself. Some of the trails that were made are short, simple and local, others long, ambitious and national in scope. The trails were constructed for use by school classes, families and hikers, and they were also intended as a starting point for activities organized by local trekking or historical associations. Promotion of tourism beyond the local level was only very rarely mentioned in relation to this activity.

The trails served to embed heritage in local landscape, making it accessible in very physical and direct ways. This was, however, merely one side of the project. The Heritage Trail (Kulturminneløypa), launched by the NHY project group, refers to a website, not to geographic locations. The site contains information about what a heritage trail is, how to make one and how to use it. It also presents a database containing all the trails that were made. What may come as a surprise is that all the instructions concern the use of digital tools involved for posting a description, mapping the trail and sharing photos and texts. A visit to the actual locations may have been a prerequisite for producing the descriptions and taking the pictures, but this is not directly mentioned, and making a trail appears to merely be a matter of digital editing. If you need 'more heritage' for the trail you are making, the site provides information about which databases or institutions to contact. Promoting the trails, the NHY argued that they 'can be experienced both digitally – and physically by way of walks and tours between heritage sites either on the net or out in the field'. Nonetheless, the digital aspect appears as the most important. The use of new technology is said to represent 'a lift for digital dissemination of heritage' and to mark a new era of heritage work (Om kulturminneløypa 2009),[3] while the actual experience of walking the trails – either to construct them or to visit a trail made by others – is given very little attention.

The strong emphasis on digital media, competence and experience corresponds well to the profile of the NHY on a more general level. Developing digital dissemination of heritage was one of its overarching goals:

> During the Year of Heritage 2009 it is our aim to lift our dissemination activities into the digital world. Heritage documentation and registration has long been ahead of the technological development. Now it is time to let the material come alive in social media. Now everybody can use the resources we publish, and they can publish pictures and stories themselves. The value of your chosen memories grows when you share them with other people (Mål og organisering 2009).[4]

The argument was later developed by one of the project workers on the NHY website: 'We think that digital media give room for more voices and make it possible for more people to speak about their heritage. This kind of communication opens the door to dialogue and reflections concerning the heritage of everyday life, and lifts the field' (Frøyseth 2009).[5] Quite a number of the projects that were launched consisted of developing new websites. Several of them shared the character of the Heritage Trails by being based on contributions from individuals and/or local organizations who wrote texts and published photos and sound files, rather than for instance on the databases of museums and archives or other kinds of preexisting material. The site *Dagligliv* (Everyday Life) invited people to post photos of their 'dearest heritage piece' and vote for the best contribution. While this was one of the six core projects, the site *Digitalt Fortalt* (Digitally Narrated) was constructed and maintained by ABM-U, the national directorate for archives, libraries and museums. This site is still growing and new narratives are being published.

The presentation of all these projects shares the same rhetoric. Digital dissemination is said to represent a 'lift' and to mark a 'new era'. Democratization is one element in the argument, another is the 'rich experience' that digital media repeatedly is said to offer. A glance at the various websites makes it nonetheless clear that their *content* very seldom reflects radically new ways of working with heritage, historical monuments and sites. Despite the modern technology and the work of the NHY secretariat, the sites and pages, with their numerous voices, often highly local horizon, somewhat random editorial work and at times poor proofreading, resemble very much, for instance, the unpretentious printed information leaflets that amateur historical associations traditionally have issued. The secretariats' own obvious enthusiasm for new technology may be one reason why they still insist on the rich and innovative character of what is being produced. Digitalization is ascribed value and innovative power in itself. This is nonetheless only one part of the picture. Building heritage websites based on user contributions shares the characteristics of new social media more generally, above all the possibility to share and publish material without representing an institution or an authority. In this lie both the intrinsically democratic nature of the new social media and the basic features of the cultural forms they produce. What is new, then, is above all the distribution of authority created by the new media. Closely following the democratization of possibilities to publish and edit comes the equally general distribution of the right to stage oneself as the holder of heritage.

The Heritage of Everyday Life

Another declared goal of the NHY was to 'broaden the notion of heritage'. This came to be the real *leitmotif* of the Heritage Year, as well as the cause of debate and criticism. On its websites and in its answer to the criticism the NHY administration had to elaborate and defend this primary aim of their undertaking. From these occasions it became clear that the desire to broaden the concept of heritage had a number of slightly different implications. In an initial statement of intent, the NHY presented this part of its work in the following words:

> The Heritage Year 2009 will broaden the concept of heritage with the aim to demonstrate that an active relationship with the past has great relevance to people today. Helberg underscores that heritage does not know national boundaries. Heritage and our understanding of it develop over time and due to meetings between cultures.
>
> During the Year of Heritage 2009 we will look into how heritage often is related to experiences with nature. We look at how heritage production can be related to artistic work. We establish that heritage may be your personal heritage. Therefore, the Year of Heritage 2009 will in many ways be the year of forgotten heritage. We will work to emphasize the small details in the great picture, and to let new voices be heard (Mål og organisering 2009).[6]

A number of motivations for widening the concept of heritage are mentioned here: bringing the past into the present; counteracting a nationalistic view of heritage; presenting heritage as something that can be 'experienced' in nature and/or expressed by artists; giving attention to small stories and new voices. The random character of this selection of arguments does not seem to have bothered the NHY secretariat. One reason may be that most of them in some way related to the overall theme, the *heritage of everyday life,* while others referred directly to specific projects that had already been initiated. Reading the different produced texts, it nonetheless soon becomes clear that this term was also not unequivocal. In some cases, like that of the heritage trails, it seems to have meant local heritage. In other contexts it referred to heritage from a very recent past and in yet others to the heritage of immigrants and other minority groups. Increasing the ambivalence even further, the leader of the NHY secretariat declared in an interview that 'everyday life is a completely new field for heritage work, at the same time as traditionally revered heritage helps to increase the quality of our everyday life' (Frøyseth 2009).[7] Here the cultural heritage of everyday life seems to mean both heritage produced by 'ordinary people' in their everyday lives today and the function of traditional historical sites and monuments in these lives.

It may be unfair to expect that the NHY secretariat, mainly comprising staff hired to coordinate activities, develop websites and administer the work, should also contribute to a theoretical and scholarly development of the concept of heritage. Moreover, the somewhat mishmash rendering of motivations and aims may stem from the fact that the ambition to broaden the concept of heritage, defined by the Government White Paper from 2005 as a main goal of NHY, already had a number of meanings and implications that stemmed from different and not always fully compatible rationalities and interests. A somewhat stricter presentation can be found in a text written by the leader of the Norwegian Cultural Heritage Association, J.S. Helberg at the start of the Heritage Year. He pointed out that the theme had been chosen to include all groups in society and was intended to concern both material and intangible heritage. He also emphasized the importance of including the recent past and private and family memory in the understanding of heritage. Furthermore, Helberg stressed the impact of globalization, migration and cultural encounters (Helberg 2009a). And not least important, he made it quite clear that the context for the NHY and what defined its approach were the explicit wishes of the Minister of the Environment[8] and the conclusions from the White Paper. His argument placed the project in its political context.

As it was described by Helberg, the NHY can be said to be presentist in its workings because it so directly answered to a number of issues and challenges in contemporary Norwegian society. The values and meanings that are articulated are very obviously found in contemporary society rather than in the objects designated as heritage. From this perspective, heritage and heritage work become a tool for addressing questions about the integration of minorities, about developing new possibilities for employment in communities where the traditional industry has been closed down and about increasing digital competence in the population. Moreover, the rationality of the NHY also seems to rely heavily on an idea of culture as a common good to be distributed by the welfare state to as many people as possible. In this perspective, heritage becomes a civil right to be possessed and enjoyed by every citizen. The wide range of issues is an important reason why 'the heritage of everyday life' may mean so many different things and be so difficult to present in a coherent way. The value and importance of the objects in their own time do not much enter into the picture and neither does the way they may have – or have not – influenced historical processes and events. Moreover, any rarity or exceptional qualities an object may possess are not what make it heritage. The focus on everyday life and every citizen or group rather works to the contrary and sees the most important heritage pieces in the most common and usual objects as the very best expressions of true democracy.

It is important to identify the contemporary concerns that influenced the NHY if we are to understand its design and workings, as well as the understandings of heritage that shaped the various projects it included. On a more theoretical level, looking for the experience of temporality that enabled these concerns to gain influence is also of some interest. Why is it unproblematic and politically correct to let contemporary political and social concerns define the understanding of the past and the values it is held to represent? Delving into the arguments that were presented can give an understanding of the rationality of presentism.

Doing Heritage

One common argument in the statements of the NHY organization was that the *work* with heritage must be as important as the heritage objects themselves (Helberg 2009a). Once again, this referred to the cooperation between institutions and to the dissemination of heritage by means of new digital media, but it also was presented as an independent value in a number of other contexts. The NHY expressed their intention to demonstrate that 'an active relationship with the past is of great relevance to people of today' (Mål og organisering 2009).[9] The numerous projects that were started locally reflect similar ideas. Among the purportedly innovative heritage projects reported by the organization leaders was for instance 'guerrilla embroidery', an action on Facebook started by some women who wanted to 'revitalize traditional embroidery' and invited everybody to share in, creating new and frequently highly untraditional works using traditional techniques (Frøyseth 2009; Facebook). While this project was national in its scope, the project that aimed at teaching the inhabitants of the northern Norwegian city of Tromsø how to row a boat had a considerably more local reach. What is characteristic of both, however, is that heritage is identified with doing something, with activity. In a number of projects, like the heritage trails, it was the task of the NHY secretariat to ensure the quality of what was produced. Nonetheless, activity, like the use of digital tools and the communication created by it, was most frequently promoted as a core heritage value.

The broad approach to heritage advocated by the NHY included both material and immaterial or intangible heritage. It also included individual and private heritage as well as that of the nation, the regions or the ethnic groups. This broad understanding of heritage was a key part of the NHY's claim to innovation. It was nonetheless contested by scholars and professionals who argued that a democratic and egalitarian understanding had been present in heritage work in Norway since the 1970s, implying that both intangible heritage and that of everyday life long had been included in professional collection and care programmes, for instance at the museums (Christensen 2011: 191). Other critics worried that the broad understanding now was being taken too far, defining mere trivialities as heritage and implying a levelling out that would finally undermine the economic basis for the care and preservation of historical buildings, sites and monuments (Sandberg 2008). In answer to this criticism, the NHY officials characterized their opponents as elitist, undemocratic, conservative and out of touch with general heritage trends (Helberg 2009b).

What gained far less attention in the debates, even if it probably was more radically new, was the emphasis on activity and the understanding of doing as a defining aspect of heritage. From this perspective heritage came to mean both documentation and (digital) publication of objects and traditions, the handling of physical objects (collecting, preserving) and the exercise of skills or activities that in themselves were understood as heritage, like embroidering or rowing a boat. It also implied juxtaposing heritage professionals, for instance the staff of the national heritage institutions, with the amateur enthusiasts or simply 'everybody', thus effacing professional difference, or even the difference between amateurs and professionals. They were all doing 'heritage work', even if their activities as well as their skills were of very different kinds. Moreover, this emphasis on activity, or practices, and their practitioners should not be discarded as a mere random whim of the Norwegians responsible. It corresponds very neatly to what has been argued in more theoretical contexts by influential scholars like Laurajane Smith (Smith 2006). In the introduction to her book *Uses of Heritage,* Smith is emphatic that '[w]hat makes these things valuable and meaningful – what makes them "heritage", or what makes the collection of rocks in a field "Stonehenge" – are the present-day cultural processes and activities that are undertaken at and around them, and of which the become a part' (Smith 2006: 3).

What is also intrinsic to this emphasis on practices is that heritage is something that takes place in the present. This represents a presentism that is far more fundamental than the political correctness governing the values and interests chosen to define the contents of heritage. It implies that the heritage objects – material or not – and the past that they represent unquestioningly are subordinated to the present and the practices of the heirs. Led by its own interests this present invades the past, not so much to investigate what is there, as to reclaim property. The past is a resource, but it becomes so through the use of its heirs, not through its own force. This understanding of past and present is also what makes it unproblematic to let contemporary concerns (political, social or cultural) quite openly shape heritage and its meanings. Doing so simply represents the best administration and use of one's own resources and property.

Valdimar Tr. Hafstein has argued that heritage is 'a culture of culture', a 'metacultural practice' (Hafstein 2009: 11f). As such, heritage creates a distance to the past, defining it as something fundamentally different from the present. It also singles out heritage as practices that are different from those of everyday life. He says that 'the self-conscious heir is alienated from her ancestors from whom she has inherited her heritage; the heir relates very differently to houses and sports, to handicrafts and foods that former generations took for granted'. The idea of heritage does not merely separate the past from the present, it also creates 'a distance between activities that are marked as heritage, on the one hand, and on the other everything else the same people do' (Hafstein 2009: 12). In this process, the past is changed because objects and practices acquire new meanings. What is original to Hafstein's line of argument and what separates his thoughts from the usual criticism against heritage turning history into kitsch is his insistence that heritage most of all transforms the present. Heritage practices refer to a social field: '[T]hey invoke a collective subjectivity such as family, community, ethnicity, or nation. Such heritage practices are performative: they bring about what they enact' (Hafstein 2009: 11). It is above all in this way that heritage is transformative: 'In spite of all the rhetoric of safeguarding, conservation, and continuity, heritage involves change. It is a change in relations. Heritage practices are a new way of relating to objects in one's surroundings and to one's own body. Heritage is innovative, in so far as it represents a new way of constituting social collectivity around representations of culture and pedigree' (Hafstein 2009: 16). This metacultural practice or relationship creates a discursive space in which social changes may be discussed, Hafstein maintains, as well as a language in which this change can be spoken of.

Seeing heritage as a metacultural practice makes sense of the emphasis on activity rather than on objects during the Heritage Year. It also helps explain why so many different activities – carried out by very different groups of agents representing different kinds of competence – all could be subsumed under the heading 'heritage'. Both professional conservation work and, for instance, posting one's 'favourite heritage piece' on a website, means treating the objects in question in ways that differ from a regular, everyday use of them. Both represent a metacultural level that gives the objects new meanings by lifting them out of their everyday life and 'squaring' them, as Hafstein names the effect of heritage activity.

The metacultural level of heritage implies reflexivity. Hafstein argues that the heritage relation is a dialogic process, one that creates a distance between the self-conscious heir and his or her heritage: the practice that is carried out, the object that is handled, the food that is eaten. This distance may set the stage for irony and inversion, he points out (Hafstein 2009: 19). Perhaps even more important is the general point that the reflexivity intrinsic to heritage, regarded as a metacultural practice, will produce quite a range of different attitudes, strategies and activities. Conservation work can be seen as one such strategy, an institutionalized way of relating to the metalevel represented by buildings, monuments and historic sites. The identity work of groups and individuals is another example, as is identity politics at large. Moreover, in this context even the commoditization pointed out by Ronström (cf. Chapter 8) and others as a main effect of turning the past into heritage, appears as little more than the exploitation of a potentiality that is integral to heritage. Commoditization and accompanying commercialization are not regrettable, but random side effects of letting history deteriorate into heritage, but materializations of the reflexivity that heritage invites. In this way, understanding heritage as a metacultural practice that creates a field for reflexivity, for performance of identities and for negotiation of social values and pressing political issues seems to provide a more fruitful perspective on contemporary heritage work and the present-ism it reflects. It also gives the key to explaining the force and vitality heritage so obviously has: it more than indicates that heritage is not first and foremost bad history, but represents attempts at dealing with cultural and political challenges of the modern world and in a contemporary context.

From Change to Choice – By Way of a Conclusion

This book has argued that the ways old objects have been spoken of from the eighteenth century till today reflect changing experiences of time and temporality. The terminological developments from the typical eighteenth-century term 'antiquities' to 'historical monuments', preferred by the nineteenth and early twentieth centuries, to the contemporary phrase 'cultural heritage' do not represent random linguistic variation, but are the expressions of different historicity regimes. Following the terminological changes and the shifts in temporal experience they are seen to reflect has been more important to this investigation than the study of the objects designated by the terms. It is nonetheless obvious that the range of objects named as heritage today is far larger than those once recognized as antiquities. New types of objects have been included all along the process, ending with the present potential all-inclusiveness of the term cultural heritage. Alongside this development, hardly any of the original types of objects have been excluded. Most of what was understood as antiquities in the eighteenth century is still termed heritage today. Barrows like the one opened by antiquaries like Vicar Bjerregaard in the eighteenth century as well the stave churches discovered by the romantic painter J.C. Dahl in the early nineteenth century are all recognized as heritage today. At the same time they are only small parts of the wide-ranging field embraced by the heritage discourse.

Accompanying this extension of objects is the increase in politicization. A number of studies have shown how antiquarian activities traditionally were used to support dynastic claims, for example. In a Scandinavian context, the Royal Resolution issued in Denmark in 1622, requesting civil servants to collect antiquities and inscriptions, as well as the appointment of Johan Bureus as a Royal Swedish antiquary in 1630, are good examples. In both cases the monarch's interest in antiquities and history was closely tied to his own claims to power (see, e.g., Svestad 1995; Hall 2000; Skovgaard-Petersen 2002). Similar trends are easily found in other European countries (cf. Schnapp 1996). These efforts were nonetheless largely restricted to an elite of princes and nobles seeking support for their claims to property, privileges and territories and were aided by the efforts of erudite scholars who likewise formed a learned elite. With the building of nation states from the late eighteenth century onwards, history and ancient objects became the tools to prove – or at least argue for – the age and political legitimacy of the national cultures of these states. Historical monuments were no longer mere witnesses to the history of a dynasty or noble family, but to the life of entire nations. Preservation and care of the monuments correspondingly became a matter of public administration, parts of the workings of civil society. Finally, with heritage, the political impact has increased further, embracing more and more fields and involving an increasing number of agents ranging from transnational organizations to private individuals. Cultural heritage is no longer a national matter. On the one hand, it has become a global issue, as in the work of UNESCO, on the other hand, it also concerns smaller groups, families or individuals. As a consequence, far more political issues are now argued and negotiated according to heritage. The discourse does not merely concern matters of dynastic claims and state power, but addresses a very wide range of contemporary political issues and challenges: Third World and postcolonial issues, immigration and integration, minority politics, the impact of armed conflict and even pollution and climatic change.

All the terms that have been investigated designate the objects in question as old, which implies that they share a retrospective view: the objects are seen and interpreted from the present of the spectator. In spite of this basic common feature, it has been the main argument of this book that the terms reflect different experiences of temporality, situating the present in different relations to both past and future. The age of the objects, and the temporal dimension in which both object and observer find themselves, are not conceptualized in identical ways. This is not due merely to the fact that the objects grow older and that the historical situations of the observers differ, but is also produced by variations in experience of temporality and hence in the understanding of the relationship between one's own present, the past that has been and the future that is to come.

The term antiquity in itself merely says that the object in question is old. Nonetheless, this was not an all-inclusive term. To the antiquaries of the eighteenth century, the past that the 'antiquities' referred to and represented was that of written, literary sources, mainly Norse and mediaeval literature, the Bible and Greek and Roman classical texts. The existence of past events and persons that were not mentioned in these texts were difficult to conceptualize. Objects that did not in some way relate to this textual universe were hardly regarded as interesting and normally ascribed little explanatory or other value. Moreover, antiquities were often treated in a systematic way, making their interpretation resemble the workings of a Linnaean system of nature. Both these principles, the literary approach and the systematic interpretations, contributed to flattening out the temporal distance between 'antiquity' and the present. Moreover, traces of the past were comparatively easy to find. They were 'here' – in the barrows and stones, in oral tradition, embedded in the landscape or embodied by the peasants. When the past seemed lost or enigmatic, it was not so much due to a feeling of any profound difference, but rather to the fact that antiquities were in fragments, subject to processes of physical and material decay. The pots were shattered, the swords broken, the metal corroded, the inscriptions effaced, and the oral tradition of peasants represented only a weak reflection of the ancient language and literature.

Only gradually did the past become 'a foreign country'. A common explanation of the historicist turn of the nineteenth century, and the interest in monuments that followed in its wake, is found to be the rapid, profound and numerous changes brought about by accelerating modernization. Landscapes, towns and cities changed their faces in dramatic ways during the nineteenth century. Old ways of life disappeared as urbanization and industrialization triumphed. The past became both different and remote, and a new anxiety to preserve some of its vestiges appeared. The creation of unintended monuments, as described by Riegl, provides a good example. Buildings and other constructions that had not originally been intended as such now were made into monuments because they were felt to reveal 'the passage of a considerable period of time' (Riegl 1903/1982: 24; Chapter 1, this volume). For such monuments to be established, the span of time between the origin of the artefacts and the present must in itself be experienced as important, according to Riegl.

The keyword for the nineteenth- and early-twentieth-century understanding of these processes was development, frequently articulated as progress. Progress came to be seen as a force inherent in the passing of time itself, bringing about continuous change (Koselleck 1985). On the one hand, the processes of development made the past remote and obsolete, with the monument speaking of this remoteness. However, development or progress, on the other hand, also created a form of continuity. Understood as a process, history was leading from the past to the present. The future came to be conceptualized as open and unknown, bringing new possibilities and even further development (Koselleck 1985), but the processual perspective did also imply that seen from the present, the past had a direction and a meaning. The passing of time and the change inherent in this movement was what produced 'us', 'here' and 'now'. This idea of continuity and coherence was not least important in the language of nation building and the use of historic monuments for such goals. Remnants from the past demonstrated national continuity and glory and could, for instance, be used by fresh nation-states to argue that history and past greatness supported their claim to recognition and respect in the present.

The notion of heritage shares some of the features of both these former conceptions, but it also differs from both. The idea that the past is disappearing due to dramatic changes and continuous development seems to persist. As several scholars have pointed out, scarcity or threat of disappearance is an intrinsic aspect of heritage – hence the more or less constant appeals for safeguarding and preservation (Klein 1997; Ronström 2007: 104). Ethnologists Barbro Klein and Owe Ronström also argue that this idea of decline and destruction has important ethical aspects because it creates a moral community of people engaged in stopping destruction, saving values and preserving objects and in this way defending the imagined community of the heirs (Klein 1997: 19; Ronström 2007: 88f).

The efforts to inventory heritage, be it through the workings of UNESCO's World Heritage List or on the websites of the Norwegian Heritage Year, may, on the other hand, resemble the principles of traditional antiquarianism. The work implies turning objects, buildings and sites into items that can be listed and set into prearranged systems. A consequence is that the rationality of the systems will eclipse the chronology of the objects and the processual aspects of development and historical change. This flattening out of the temporal dimension makes the rationality of heritage differ from that of historical monuments. The objects of heritage are 'old', and the past is 'different', but the way from then and there to here and now is no longer what attracts the most attention.

The moral and political dimensions of the appeals to save and preserve heritage nonetheless make it differ significantly from antiquarian ideas. For heritage, the key to understanding is not found in authoritative literary texts, but in its relevance to contemporary political, ethical and social issues. In this way, heritage also tends to conceptualize the difference of the past in terms of variety and choice, rather than as development and change. Like memory in contrast to history, heritage in opposition to monuments attempts to bridge ruptures and change rather than to explain them, hyphenating the present with the past to construct and enforce identities, address pressing social issues and negotiate cultural values. In this work, the past is not understood as the path to the present, but rather as a repository of available goods.

Despite its general inclusiveness, even heritage, like any other way of relating to the past, means discarding parts of it as unimportant or not relevant. When the past becomes a repository for the exclusive use of the present – the heirs – those parts of it that are without heirs will not gain much attention. While monuments are cherished for the historical persons, events or processes they commemorate or are made the representatives of, and antiquities gain their value through their connection to authoritative texts, it is the interest of the heirs that defines what is to be passed on as heritage. This will imply that objects or symbols in which nobody takes an interest in inheriting tend to be excluded: left to oblivion, damage or destruction.

NOTES

1. The Norwegian name was *Kulturminneåret,* and the theme *Hverdagens kulturminner.* The term *kulturminne* came into use during the 1970s and literally means cultural memory or cultural memories, while *kulturarv* is Norwegian for cultural heritage. Cultural heritage was nonetheless used in NHY's official English name and in its English texts. According to the NHY project leader Sidsel Hindal, the reason behind this was that heritage is now reckoned to be the accepted translation of the term *kulturminne* (email to the author 22/10/09). The terms will consequently be used in the same way here.
2. The website of the project group is the main source for the discussions in this chapter. See: http://www.kulturminneaaret2009.no/
3. Kulturminneløypa representerer et løft for digital formidling av kulturminner.
4. I Kulturminneåret 2009 skal vi løfte formidlingsvirksomheten vår inn i en interaktiv digital verden. Arbeid med dokumentasjon og registrering har allerede lenge vært i forkant av den teknologiske utviklingen. Nå er turen kommet til å levendegjøre dette materiale på sosiale nettsteder. Alle kan nå nyttiggjøre seg ressursene vi legger ut og legge inn bilder og fortellinger selv. -Verdien i det du velger å minnes blir større i det du deler det med mange.
5. Vi meiner at digitale medium gjev rom for fleire stemmer, og opnar for at fleire kan snakka om sine kulturminne. Denne typen formidling opnar døra for dialog og refleksjonar rundt dei kulturminna vi har rundt oss til dagleg. Dette er eit løft for feltet.
6. Kulturminneåret 2009 skal utvide begrepet kulturminne, for å vise at et aktivt forhold til fortiden har stor relevans for mennesker i dag. Helberg er opptatt av at kulturminner ikke kjenner landegrenser. Minnene og vår oppfatning av dem utvikler seg både over tid og i møte mellom kulturer.

   I Kulturminneåret 2009 gjennomgår vi hvordan kulturminner ofte er knyttet til naturopplevelser. Vi ser på hvordan kulturminneproduksjon kan knyttes opp til kunstnerisk virksomhet. Vi etablerer at kulturminner kan være dine personlige minner. Kulturminneåret 2009 er derfor på mange måter de glemte kulturminnenes år. Vi arbeider for å løfte frem det store i det lille og la nye stemmer slippe til.

7. Dagleglivet er eit heilt nytt felt å henta minne frå, samstundes som dei tradisjonelle høgverdige kulturminna er med på å auka trivselen i vårt kvardagslege daglegliv.

8. The Ministry of the Environment is responsible for the care and preservation of the built environment, monuments and sites in Norway. The NHY was a collaboration with the Ministry of Culture.

9. [E]t aktivt forhold til fortiden har stor relevans for mennesker i dag.

References

Aall, H. 1920. *Norsk folkemuseum 1894–1919. Trekk av dets historie.* Kristiania: Kirstes boktrykkeri.

———. 1925. *Arbeide og ordning i kulturhistoriske museer. Kort veiledning.* Oslo: Norske museers landsforbund.

Agulhon, M. 1988. *Histoire vagabonde 1. Ethnologie et politique dans la France contemporaine.* Paris: Gallimard.

Ågotnes, H.J. 2007. 'Lokalmuseet i det sosiale landskapet. Fortidsformidling i Hordaland gjennom hundre år', in T. Selberg and N. Gilje (eds), *Kulturelle landskap. Sted, fortelling og materiell kultur.* Bergen: Fagbokforlaget, pp. 45–67.

Andersen, H.W., et al. (eds). 2009. *Aemula Lauri. The Royal Norwegian Society of Sciences and Letters, 1760–2010.* Sagamore Beach, MA: Science History Publications.

Anker, P. 1997. *Stavkirkene. Deres egenart og historie.* Oslo: Cappelen.

Ashworth, W.B. 2003. 'Natural History and the Emblematic World View', in M. Hellyer (ed.), *The Scientific Revolution.* Malden, MA: Blackwell, pp. 132–56.

Assmann, A. 2011. *Cultural Memory and Western Civilization. Functions, Media, Archives.* Cambridge: Cambridge University Press.

Assmann, J. 1995. 'Collective Memory and Cultural Identity', *New German Critique* 65: 125–33.

Aubert, A. 1920. *Maleren Johan Christian Dahl. Et stykke av forrige aarhundredes kunst- og kulturhistorie.* Kristiania: Aschehoug.

Babelon, J.P. and A. Chastel. 1994. *La notion de patrimoine.* Paris: Liana Levi.

Bale, K. 2009. *Estetikk. En innføring.* Oslo: Pax.

Bang, M.L. 1987. *Johan Christian Dahl. Life and Works 1–3.* Oslo: Norwegian University Press.

Bauman, R. and C.L. Briggs. 2003. *Voices of Modernity. Language Ideologies and the Politics of Inequality.* Cambridge: Cambridge University Press.

Bendix, R. 2000. 'Heredity, Hybridity and Heritage from One *Fin de Siècle* to the Next', in P.J. Anttonen et al. (eds), *Folklore, Heritage Politics and Ethnic Diversity.* Botkyrka: Multicultural Centre, pp. 37–54.

Bendix, R. and V.T. Hafstein. 2009. 'Culture and Property. An Introduction', *Ethnologia Europaea. Journal of European Ethnology* 39(2): 5–10.

Bennett, T. 1995. *The Birth of the Museum. History, Theory, Politics.* London: Routledge.

Bonnet, J.C. 1998. *Naissance du Panthéon. Essai sur le culte des grands hommes.* Paris: Fayard.

Bo|rænius, M. 1724/2003. *Klostret i Vreta i Östergötland,* trans. K. Bergman. Linköping: Föreningen Klosterliv i Vreta.

Boym, S. 2001. *The Future of Nostalgia.* New York: Basic Books.

Braaten, I.G. 2003. 'Museet i byen', in I.G. Braaten (ed.), *Museet i byen. Aalesunds museum 1903–2003.* Ålesund: Aalesunds museum, pp. 9–104.

Bragr. 1925. 'Tordenskjold heimatt til Noreg. Svar frá norske kvinnor og menn'. Bjørgvin: Norrønafelaget Bragr.

Brøgger, A.W. 1914. '1844–1914. Et bidrag til Foreningens historie', *Foreningen til norske Fortidsminnesmærkers Historie Bevaring, Aarsberetning 1914*: 8–59.

Bukdahl, E.M. 1995. 'Diderot entre le "modèle idéal" et le "sublime"', in E.M. Bukdahl, M. Delon and A. Lorenceau (eds), *Diderot. Ruines et paysages, Salons de 1767.* Paris: Hermann, pp. 3–18.

Bukdahl, E.M., M. Delon and A. Lorenceau (eds). 1995. *Diderot. Ruines et paysages, Salons de 1767.* Paris: Hermann.

Cameron, J.W. 2009. *Heritage or Heresy. Archaeology and culture on the Maya Riviera.* Tuscaloosa: University of Alabama Press.

Carman, J. 2005. *Against Cultural Property. Archaeology, Heritage and Ownership.* London: Duckworth.

Choay, F. 1999. *L'allégorie du patrimoine,* rev. ed. Paris: Seuil.

Christensen, A.L. 2011. *Kunsten å bevare. Om kulturminnevern og fortidsinteresse i Norge.* Oslo: Pax.

Christiansen, R.T. 1958. *The Migratory Legends. A Proposed List of Types with a Systematic Catalogue of the Norwegian Variants.* Helsinki: Suomalainen tiedeakatemia.

Cnattingius, L.D. and N. Cnattingius. 2007. *Ruiner. Historia, öden och vård.* Stockholm: Carlsson.

Connerton, P. 2009. *How Modernity Forgets.* Cambridge: Cambridge University Press.

Cuno, J. 2008. *Who Owns Antiquity? Museums and the Battle over Our Ancient Heritage.* Princeton, NJ: Princeton University Press.

Daae, L. 1880. *Gerhard Schøning. En biographi.* Christiania: A.W. Brøgger.

Dahl, J.C. 1837. *Denkmale einer sehr ausgebildeten Holzbaukunst aus den frühesten Jahrhunderten in den innern Landschaften Norwegens.* Dresden: J.C.C. Dahl.

Dahlberg, E. 1716. *Suecia antiqua et hodierna.* Stockholm. Retrieved 26 November 2006 from http://www.kb.se/suecia.

Damsholt, T. 2000a. *Fædrelandskærlighed og borgerdyd. Patriotisk diskurs og militære reformer i Danmark i sidste del af 1700-tallet.* Copenhagen: Museum Tusculanum.

———. 2000b. 'Being moved', *Ethnologia Scandinavica. A Journal for Nordic Ethnology* 30: 24–48.

Daston, L. 2004. 'Attention and the Values of Nature in the Enlightenment', in L. Daston and F. Vidal (eds), *The Moral Authority of Nature.* Chicago: University of Chicago Press, pp. 100–126.

Daston, L. and P. Galison. 2007. *Objectivity.* New York: Zone Books.

Delacroix, C., F. Dosse and P. Garcia (eds). 2009. 'Sur la notion de régime d'historicité. Entretien avec François Hartog', in C. Delacroix, F. Dosse and P. Garcia (eds), *Historicités*. Paris: La Decouverte, pp. 133–49.

Diderot, D. 1767/1995. 'Le Salon de 1767 adressé à mon ami M. Grimm', in E.M. Bukdahl, M. Delon and A. Lorenceau (eds), *Diderot. Ruines et paysages, Salons de 1767*. Paris: Hermann, pp. 55–557.

Dietrichson, L. 1885. 'Middelalderens trækirker. Et indledningskapitel til de norske stavekirkers historie', *Nordisk tidskrift för Vetenskap, Konst och Industri* 2: 1–82.

———. 1888. 'Hov og Stavekirker i deres Forhold til de angelsachsiske Kirker', *Vidar*: 118–155.

———. 1892. *De norske stavkirker. Studier over deres system, oprindelse og historiske udvikling. Et bidrag til Norges middelalderske bygningskunsts historie*. Kristiania: Cammermeyer.

———. 1906. *Vore Fædres Verk. Norges Kunst i Middelalderen. En populær Fremstilling*. Kristiania: Gyldendal.

———. 2010. *Norges kunsts historie 1. Oldtid og middelalder*. Oslo: Messel.

Directorate for Cultural Heritage. [n.d.]. 'Urnes Stavkyrkje'. Retrieved 10 October 2011 from http://www.riksantikvaren.no/?module=Articles;action=Article.publicShow;ID=4425.

Djupedal, R. 1955–57. 'Den store innsamlinga av topografisk, historisk, og språkleg tilfang ved embetsmennene 1743 og "Det Kongerige Norge"', *Heimen* 10: 289–330; 337–62; 442–85.

Ekroll, Ø. 2004. 'Gerhard Schøning og domkirken i Trondheim', in G. Schøning, *Beskrivelse over Dom-kirken i Throndhjem*. Trondheim: Tapir, pp. i–xxxii.

Eriksen, A. 2001. 'Tordenskjold heimatt til Noreg. Om tilbakeføring av kulturarv', *Norveg. Tidsskrift for etnologi og folkloristikk* 44(1): 51–73.

———. 2007. *Topografenes verden. Fornminner og fortidsforståelse*. Oslo: Pax.

———. 2009. *Museum. En kulturhistorie*. Oslo: Pax.

Erll, A. 2011. *Memory in Culture*, trans. S.B. Young. Basingstoke: Palgrave Macmillan.

Erll, A. and A. Nünning (eds). 2010. *A Companion to Cultural Memory Studies*. Berlin: De Gruyter.

Faye, A. 1837. 'Gaara kirke i Bø i Telemark', *Skillings-magazin* 75: 177–80.

Fehrman, C. 1954. *Kyrkogårdsromantik. Studier i engelsk och svensk 1700-talsdiktning*. Lund: Gleerup.

———. 1956. *Ruinernas romantik. En litteraturhistorisk studie*. Stockholm: Bonnier.

Forero-Mendoza, S. 2002. *Le Temps des ruines. Le Goût des ruines et les Formes de la conscience historique à la Renaissance*. Seyssel: Champ Vallon.

Fritzsche, P. 2004. *Stranded in the Present. Modern Time and the Melancholy of History*. Cambridge, MA: Harvard University Press.

Frøyseth, H. 2009. 'Eit slag for kvardagsminna', *Kulturminneåret 2009*. Retrieved 15 December 2011 from http://www.kulturminneaaret2009.no/om_kulturminnearet_2009/eit-slag-for-kvardagsminna.

Gillman, D. 2010. *The Idea of Cultural Heritage*. Cambridge: Cambridge University Press.

Glambek, I. 2003. 'Kunstindustrimuseer. Opprettelse og opprinnelig formål', in A.B. Amundsen, B. Rogan and M.C. Stang (eds), *Museer i fortid og nåtid. Essays i museumskunnskap*. Oslo: Novus, pp. 228–44.

Grafton, A. 2005. 'The Identities of History in Early Modern Europe. Prelude to a Study of the *Artes Historicae*', in G. Pomata and N.G. Siraisi (eds), *Historia. Empiricism and Erudition in Early Modern Europe*. Cambridge, MA: MIT Press, pp. 41–74.

Grannes, E. 1992. *Minnestøtten på Dolstad i Vefsn. Minneskrift over våre falne*. Helgeland: E. Grannes.

Green, A. 2008. *Cultural History*. London: Palgrave Macmillan.

Grytten, H. 2003. 'Kæm é foresten du?', in I.G. Braaten (ed.), *Museet i byen. Aalesunds museum 1903–2003*. Ålesund: Aalesunds museum, pp. 147–63.

Hafstein, V.T. 2000. 'Biological Metaphors in Folklore Theory. An Essay in the History of Ideas', in U. Wolf-Knuts (ed.), *The Krohn Prize 1999*. Åbo: Nordic Network of Folklore, pp. 7–32.

———. 2009. 'Collectivity by Culture Squared. Cultural Heritage in Nordic Spaces', *Arv. Nordic Yearbook of Folklore* 65: 11–23.

Hall, P. 2000. *Den svenskaste historien. Nationalism i Sverige under sex sekler*. Stockholm: Carlsson.

Hamelmann, H. 1599. *Oldenburgisch Chronicon. Das ist Beschreibung Der Löblichen Uhralten Grafen zu Oldenburg und Delmenhorst [et]c. Von welchen die jetzige Könige zu Dennemarck und Hertzogen zu Holstein entsprossen. Sampt Ihres Stammens ersten Ankunfft, Thaten, Regierung, Leben Und Ende, mit künstlichen Brustbildern und Wapen gezie gezieret / auffs aller fleissigste zusammen getragen Durch Hermannum Hamelmannum*. Oldenburg: Berendt.

Hartog, F. 2003. *Régimes d'historicité. Présentisme et expériences du temps*. Paris: Seuil.

Harvey, D.C. 2001. 'Heritage Pasts and Heritage Presents. Temporality, Meaning and the Scope of Heritage Studies', *International Journal of Heritage Studies* 7(4): 319–38.

Helberg, J.S. 2009a. 'Dagliglivets kulturminner', *Kulturminneåret 2009*. Retrieved 15 December 2011 from http://www.kulturminneaaret2009.no/om_kulturminnearet_2009/kulturminnearet-2009-1.

———. 2009b. 'Johan Sigfred Helberg innlegg i klassekampen 17.09.09', *Kulturminneåret 2009*. Retrieved 15 December 2011 from http://www.kulturminneaaret2009.no/aktuelt/johan-sigfred-helberg-innlegg-i-klassekampen-17.09.09.

Herstad, J. 2003. 'De 43 spørsmål. En arkivnær introduksjon til politiske og administrative prosesser', in K.M. Røgeberg (ed.), *Norge i 1743. Innberetninger som svar på 43 spørsmål fra Danske Kanselli* 1. Oslo: Riksarkivet and Solum, pp. 9–40.

Hewison, R. 1987. *The Heritage Industry. Britain in a Climate of Decline*. London: Methuen.

Hillström, M. 2010. 'Contested Boundaries. Nation, People and Cultural History Museums in Sweden and Norway 1862–1909', *Culture Unbound. Journal of Current Cultural Research* 2: 583–607.

Hodne, Ø. 1995. *Fedreland og fritid. En mellomkrigsstudie i Noregs ungdomslag*. Oslo: Novus.

Hooper-Greenhill, E. 1992. *Museums and the Shaping of Knowledge*. London: Routledge.

Hunt, J.D. 2003. *The Picturesque Garden in Europe*. London: Thames and Hudson.

Hunt, L. 1989. 'Introduction', in L. Hunt (ed.), *The New Cultural History*. Berkeley: University of California Press, pp. 1–24.

Huyssen, A. 2003. *Present Pasts. Urban Palimpsests and the Politics of Memory.* Stanford, CA: Stanford University Press.

Jensen, B.E. 2003. *Historie. Livsverden og fag.* Copenhagen: Gyldendal.

———. 2005/2006. 'Harald Welzer som erindringsforsker. En viderefører af Halbwachs-Assmann-traditionen?', *Tidsskriftet antropologi* 52: 17–39.

———. 2008. *Kulturarv. Et identitetspolitisk konfliktfelt.* Copenhagen: Gad.

Jensen, J.M. (ed.). 2008. *Fynske antikvarer. Lærdom, fortid og fortolkninger 1550–1850.* Odense: Centre for Medieval Studies.

Klein, B. 1997. 'Tillhörighet och utanförskap. Om kulturarvspolitik och folklivsforskning i en multietnisk värld', *Rig* 80(1–2): 15–32.

Knutzen, K.O. 1922. *Dagbøger over Reiser i Norge i 1824 og 1828.* Kristiania: Norsk forening for bokkunst.

Koselleck, R. 1985. *Futures Past. On the Semantics of Historical Time,* trans. K. Tribe. Cambridge, MA: MIT Press.

Kverndokk, K. 2011. 'Krigens helter og ofre. Akershus festning som krigsminnelandskap', in S.A. Naguib and B. Rogan (eds), *Materiell kultur og kulturens materialitet.* Oslo: Novus, pp. 99–123.

Laqueur, T.W. 1994. 'Memory and Naming in the Great War', in J.R. Gillis (ed.), *Commemorations. The Politics of National Identity.* Princeton, NJ: Princeton University Press, pp. 150–67.

Lidén, H.E. 1991. *Fra antikvitet til kulturminne. Trekk av kulturminnevernets historie i Norge.* Oslo: Universitetsforlaget.

Livland, H. 1987. '"Fra loftsrom til herregård". Museumsutviklingen i Skien fra 1891–1910'. University of Oslo: Master's thesis in History.

Lowenthal, D. 1985. *The Past is a Foreign Country.* Cambridge: Cambridge University Press.

Löfgren, O. 1993. 'The Cultural Grammar of Nation-Building. The Nationalization of Nationalism', in P.J. Anttonen and R. Kvideland (eds), *Nordic Frontiers. Recent Issues in the Study of Modern Traditional Culture in the Nordic Countries.* Åbo: Nordic Institute of Folklore, pp. 217–35.

Lyons, J.D. 1989. *Exemplum. The Rhetoric of Example in Early Modern France and Italy.* Princeton, NJ: Princeton University Press.

Makarius, M. 2004. *Ruins.* Paris: Flammarion.

McClellan, A. 1994. *Inventing the Louvre. Art, Politics, and the Origins of the Modern Museum in Eighteenth-Century Paris.* Cambridge: Cambridge University Press.

Merryman, J.H. 1986. 'Two Ways of Thinking about Cultural Property', *The American Journal of International Law* 80(4): 831–53.

Molvær, E. 2003. 'Sunnmøre museum. Eit museum på trass?', in I.G. Braaten (ed.), *Museet i byen. Aalesunds museum 1903–2003.* Ålesund: Aalesunds museum, pp. 121–46.

Momigliano, A. 1990. *The Classical Foundations of Modern Historiography.* Berkeley: University of California Press.

Mordhorst, C. 2009. *Genstandsfortællinger. Fra Museum Wormianum til de moderne museer.* Copenhagen: Museum Tusculanum.

Mosse, G.L. 1990. *Fallen Soldiers. Reshaping the Memory of the World Wars*. Oxford: Oxford University Press.

Munch, A. 1856. *Billeder fra Nord og Syd*. Christiania: Johan Dahl.

'Mål og organisering'. 2009. *Kulturminneåret 2009*. Retrieved 15 December 2011 from http://kulturminneaaret2009.no/om_kulturminnearet_2009/mal_og_visjoner.

Niemi, E. 2009. 'Dagliglivets kulturminner. Hva slags status?', *Kulturminneåret 2009*. Retrieved 15 December 2011 from http://kulturminneaaret2009.no/om_kulturminnearet_2009/manedens-artikkel/dagliglivets-kulturminner-2013-hva-slags-status.

Nora, P. 1989. 'Between Memory and History. Les Lieux de Mémoire', *Representations* 26: 7–24.

'The Norwegian Year of Cultural Heritage 2009'. 2009. *Kulturminneåret 2009*. Retrieved 15 December 2011 from http://www.kulturminneaaret2009.no/english.

Olick, J.K., V. Vinitzky-Seroussi and D. Levy (eds). 2011. *The Collective Memory Reader*. New York: Oxford University Press.

'Om kulturminneløypa'. 2009. *Kulturminneåret 2009*. Retrieved 15 December 2011 from http://loype.kulturminneaaret2009.no/kulturminneloypa.

Passeron, J.C. and J. Revel. 2005. 'Penser par cas. Raisonner à partir de singularités', in J.C. Passeron and J. Revel (eds), *Penser par cas*. Paris: École des Hautes Études en Sciences Sociales, pp. 9–44.

Phillips, M.S. 1996. 'Reconsiderations on History and Antiquarianism. Arnaldo Momigliano and the Historiography of Eighteenth-Century Britain', *Journal of the History of Ideas* 57(2): 297–316.

———. 2000. *Society and Sentiment. Genres of Historical Writing in Britain, 1740–1820*. Princeton, NJ: Princeton University Press.

Piggott, S. 1989. *Ancient Britons and the Antiquarian Imagination. Ideas from the Renaissance to the Regency*. New York: Thames and Hudson.

Pomata, G. and N.G. Siraisi. 2005. *Historia. Empiricism and Erudition in Early Modern Europe*. Cambridge, MA: MIT Press.

Pommier, É. 1991. *L'art de la liberté. Doctrines et débats de la Révolution française*. Paris: Gallimard.

Renfrew, C. 2000. *Loot, Legitimacy and Ownership. The Ethical Crisis in Archaeology*. London: Duckworth.

Riegl, A. 1903/1982. 'The Modern Cult of Monuments. Its Character and its Origin', trans. K.W. Forster and D. Ghirardo, *Oppositions. A Journal for Ideas and Criticism in Architecture* 25: 21–51.

Ronström, O. 2007. *Kulturarvspolitik. Visby, från sliten småstad till medeltidsikon*. Stockholm: Carlsson.

Røgeberg, K.M. (ed.). 2003–05. *Norge i 1743. Innberetninger som svar på 43 spørsmål fra Danske Kanselli* 1–3. Oslo: Riksarkivet and Solum.

Sagen, L. 1842. 'Historisk Vandring i Bergen og dens nærmeste Omegn', *Urda. Et norsk antiqvarisk-historisk Tidsskrift* pp. 257–95.

Samuel, R. 1994. *Theatres of Memory 1. Past and Present in Contemporary Culture*. London: Verso.

Sandberg, L. 2008. 'Brennbart kulturminneår'. *Aftenposten,* 29 December.

Sandnes, J. 1970. 'Lokalhistorisk litteratur til omkring år 1900', in H. Bjørkvik et al. (eds), *Lokal historie i forskning og kulturarbeid gjennom 200 år.* Oslo: Universitetsforlaget, pp. 13–32.

Schnapp, A. 1996. *The Discovery of the Past. The Origins of Archaeology,* trans. I. Kinnes and G. Varndell. London: British Museum Press.

Schøning, G. 1762. *Beskrivelse over den forforn meget prægtige og vidtberømte Dom-Kirke i Trondhjem, egentligen kaldet Christ-Kirken.* Trondheim: J.C. Winding.

———. 1771–81. *Norges Riiges Historie* 1–3. Sorø: Mumme og Faber.

———. 1778. *Reise som giennem en Deel af Norge i de Aar 1773, 1774, 1775 paa Hans Majestets Kongens Bekostning er giort og beskreven af Gerhard Schøning.* Copenhagen: Gyldendal.

———. 1980. *Reise som giennem en Deel af Norge i de Aar 1773, 1774, 1775 paa Hans Majestets Konges Bekostning er giort og beskrven af Gerhard Schøning,* 3. *Gudbrandsdalen og Hedemarken.* Trondheim: Tapir.

Shetelig, H. 1944. *Norske museers historie.* Oslo: Cappelen.

Skovgaard-Petersen, K. 2002. *Historiography at the court of Christian IV (1588–1648). Studies in the Latin Histories of Denmark by Johannes Pontanus and Johannes Meursius.* Copenhagen: Museum Tusculanum.

Skrydstrup, M. 2009. 'Theorizing Repatriation', *Ethnologia Europaea. Journal of European Ethnology* 39(2): 54–66.

Sloan, K. 2003. '"Aimed at Universality and Belonging to the Nation". The Enlightenment and the British Museum', in K. Sloan (ed.), *Enlightenment. Discovering the World in the Eighteenth Century.* London: British Museum Press, pp. 12–25.

Smith, L. 2006. *Uses of Heritage.* London: Routledge.

———. 2007. *Heritage as an Industry.* London: Routledge.

——— and E. Waterton. 2009. *Heritage, Communities and Archaeology.* London: Duckworth.

Society for the Preservation of Norwegian Ancient Monuments. [n.d.]. 'Urnes Stavkirke'. Retrieved 10 October 2011 from http://old.fortidsminneforeningen.no/eiendommer/16/18.

Solheim, S. 1952. *Norsk sætertradisjon.* Oslo: Aschehoug.

St. Clair, W. 1998. *Lord Elgin and the Marbles. The Controversial History of the Parthenon Sculptures,* 3rd ed. Oxford: Oxford University Press.

Storsveen, O.A. 1997. *Norsk patriotisme før 1814.* Oslo: Norges forskningsråd.

Strøm, H. 1962–66. *Physisk og oeconomisk Beskrivelse over Fogderiet Søndmør, beliggende i Bergens Stift i Norge* 1–2. Sorø: J. Lindgren.

Sveen, D. 2004. *Fra folkekunst til nasjonalt kunsthåndverk. Norsk treskjæring 1847–1879.* Oslo: Pax.

Svestad, A. 1995. *Oldsakenes orden. Om tilkomsten av arkeologi.* Oslo: Universitetsforlaget.

Sweet, R. 2004. *Antiquaries. The Discovery of the Past in Eighteenth-Century Britain.* London: Hambledon and London.

Sørensen, E. 1990. '80-års tilbakeblikk på "pionertiden"', in *By og bygd i Buskerud.* Drammen: Drammens Museum.

Topographisk Journal for Norge. 1795. 12(3).

Tvedt, K.A. (ed.). 2010. *Oslo byleksikon,* 5th ed. Oslo: Kunnskapsforlaget.

Vergo, P. (ed.). 1989. *The New Museology.* London: Reaktion Books.

Warring, A. 1996. 'Kollektiv erindring. Et brugbart begreb?', in B.E. Jensen, C.T. Nielsen and T. Weinreich (eds), *Erindringens og glemslens politik.* Frederiksberg: Roskilde Universitetsforlag, pp. 205–34.

Welhaven, J.S. 1833/1991. 'Norske Musæer', in *Samlede Verker* 3. Oslo: Universitetsforlaget, pp. 181–92.

Wexelsen, E. 1973. 'J.C. Dahl. Forståelse og innsats for bevaring av norske fortidsminnesmerker. Et bidrag til Dahls biografi'. University of Bergen: Master's thesis in History.

Wiel, I. 1743/1970. *Beskrivelse over Ringerige og Hallingdahlens Fogderie. Hvor-udi findes anført dets Grændser, Situation, Størrelse, Vasdrag, Skoug, og Mark, Dyr, Fugle og Fiske, Mineralia, Naturalia og Antiqviteter med videre.* Oslo: [n.p.].

Wille, H.J. 1786. *Beskrivelse over Sillejords Præstegield i Øvre-Tellemarken i Norge.* Copenhagen: Gyldendal.

Woodward, C. 2001. *In ruins.* London: Chatto and Windus.

World Heritage Centre. [n.d.]a. 'The Criteria for Selection', *UNESCO.* Retrieved 10 October 2011 from http://whc.unesco.org/en/criteria.

———. [n.d.]b. 'The World Heritage Convention', *UNESCO.* Retrieved 10 October 2011 from http://whc.unesco.org/en/convention.

———. 1972. 'Convention Concerning the Protection of the World Cultural and Natural Heritage', *UNESCO.* Retrieved 10 October 2011 from http://whc.unesco.org/en/conventiontext.

———. 1979. 'Urnes Stave Church', *UNESCO.* Retrieved 10 October 2011 from http://whc.unesco.org/en/list/58.

———. 2008. 'Operational Guidelines for the Implementation of the World Heritage Convention', *UNESCO.* Retrieved 10 October 2011 from http://whc.unesco.org/archive/opguide08-en.pdf.

Young, J.E. 1993. *The Texture of Memory. Holocaust Memorials and Meaning.* New Haven, CT: Yale University Press.

Index

9 781785 332050